Brief Contents

Academic Language/Literacy Strategies for Adolescents

Fast-paced, practical, and innovative, this text for pre-service and in-service teachers features clear, easily accessible lessons and professional development activities to improve the delivery of academic language/literacy education across the content areas in junior/middle school and high school classrooms. Numerous hands-on tools and techniques demonstrate the effectiveness of content-area instruction for students in a wide variety of school settings, particularly English language learners, struggling readers, and other special populations of students.

Based on a strong professional development model the authors have been instrumental in designing, *Academic Language/Literacy Strategies for Adolescents* addresses:

- Motivation
- Attributes of Academic Language
- Vocabulary: Theory and Practice
- Reading Skills Development
- Grammar and Writing.

A wealth of charts, graphs, and lesson plans give clear examples of academic language/literacy strategies in action. The appendices—a key component of the practical applications developed in the text—include a glossary, exemplary lessons that address key content areas, and a Grammar Handbook.

In this era of increased accountability, coupled with rapid demographic change and challenges to traditional curricula and pedagogical methods, educators will find this book to be a great resource!

Debra L. Cook Hirai is Associate Professor, California State University, Bakersfield, where she teaches Masters courses in the Education and Bilingual Multicultural Programs.

Irene Borrego is Associate Professor and BCLAD Coordinator at California State University, Bakersfield, and a State of California School Assistance and Intervention Team member identified by the California State Department of Education.

Emilio Garza is Assistant Professor, School of Education, California State University, Bakersfield, where he teaches in the Advanced Educational Studies Department.

Carl T. Kloock is in the Department of Biology at California State University, Bakersfield, where he teaches courses for biology majors and integrated science for pre-professional teacher candidates.

Academic Language/Literacy Strategies for Adolescents
A "How To" Manual for Educators

Debra L. Cook Hirai
Irene Borrego
Emilio Garza
Carl T. Kloock
California State University, Bakersfield

With
Deborrah Wakelee
Vicki Murray
Grammar Specialists

Routledge
Taylor & Francis Group

NEW YORK AND LONDON

First published 2010
by Routledge
270 Madison Ave, New York, NY 10016

Simultaneously published in the UK
by Routledge
2 Park Square, Milton Park, Abingdon, Oxon OX14 4RN

Routledge is an imprint of the Taylor & Francis Group, an informa business

© 2010 Taylor & Francis

Typeset in by Minion by EvS Communication Networx, Inc.
Printed and bound in the United States of America on acid-free paper by Edwards Brothers, Inc.

Library of Congress Cataloging in Publication Data
Academic language/literacy strategies for adolescents : a "how to" manual for educators / Debra L. Cook Hirai ... [et al.] ; with Deborrah Wakelee and Vicki Murray, grammar specialists.
p. cm.
1. Language arts (Secondary)—Handbooks, manuals, etc. 2. Content area reading—Study and teaching (Secondary)—Handbooks, manuals, etc. I. Hirai, Debra L. Cook.
LB1632.A23 2010
428.0071'2—dc22
2009014702

ISBN10: 0-415-99965-0 (hbk)
ISBN10: 0-8058-6391-5 (pbk)
ISBN10: 0-203-85957-X (ebk)

ISBN13: 978-0-415-99965-6 (hbk)
ISBN13: 978-0-8058-6391-8 (pbk)
ISBN13: 978-0-203-85957-5 (ebk)

This textbook is dedicated to all educators who work tirelessly with students who are struggling to read—especially the teachers of the Delano Joint Union High School District in California. We also include the teacher candidates in our education courses. We thank our families for their support of our efforts in completing the text and are grateful for our "text" family and Debbie, Vicki, Merci, and Javier, our media guru and Mark—your book is finally written! We appreciate all of you for your contributing knowledge and expertise!

Contents

Foreword

Academic Language/Literacy Strategies for Adolescents: A "How To" Manual for Educators by Drs. Debra Cook Hirai, Irene Borrego, Emilio Garza, and Carl Kloock is a fast-paced, practical, and innovative textbook for preservice and in-service teachers. In this decade of increased accountability, coupled with rapid demographic change and challenges to traditional curricula and pedagogical methods, educators will find this book to be a great resource!

Reading in the content areas has been brought to the forefront most recently due to the fact that nationally 25% of our secondary students are reading at below basic levels. Content-area teachers face the challenge of teaching subject matter to students who struggle with comprehension and literacy skills. Yet, literacy programs for populations such as struggling readers and English learners have generally not taken into consideration the importance of teaching academic language in the content areas. The result has been low test scores in the content areas and high numbers of school dropouts. This textbook provides educators with resources and appropriate techniques to improve comprehension and English language literacy.

In this text, Professors Cook Hirai, Borrego, Garza, and Kloock have addressed a critical need for classroom practitioners and thus made a great contribution to the field of professional development and training as well as teacher preparation. The authors take simple concepts and infuse them with teaching strategies that use academic language. The chapters stimulate the "practical voice" for content-area teachers about key concepts in how to teach literacy in subject matter. The charts, graphs, and lesson plans give clear examples of how teachers can provide academic language in various settings including the use of "hands-on" ideas. The text includes an appendix of proven, exemplary lessons that address key content areas.

I know that my CSUB colleagues have not only put their hearts into this textbook about academic language use in the classroom, but all their ideas are based on their considerable experience with best practice research as well as their work with classroom teachers. I commend the authors for their hard work and dedication as they have accomplished their vision for supporting teachers in a meaningful way.

Dr. Sheryl L. Santos, Dean
College of Education
Texas Tech University
Lubbock, Texas

Preface

This book evolved out of the need to have easily accessible lessons and professional development activities to demonstrate the effectiveness of teaching literacy in the content areas at the upper elementary, junior high/middle school, high school, and college levels. This is, to our knowledge, one of the first texts available to specifically address strategies for academic language instruction in the content areas above the primary grades (K-3). The use of academic language instruction is relatively limited in intermediate and secondary schools. Most of the available material relates to English learners only and does not address all student populations. This book addresses academic language instruction across the content areas. We believe that the techniques it presents will aid instruction in the content area in a wide variety of school settings.

Academic Language/Literacy Strategies for Adolescents is intended for use in teacher education professional development training and credential coursework, college reading methodology, and literacy methodology classes integrating all aspects of the listening, speaking, reading, and writing curriculum, as well as staff development training. It will also be useful as a reference book, particularly the grammar section in appendix 7.

Our style of writing is friendly and comprehensible, yet academic in nature. We try not to lecture our audience, rather, we engage readers in the learning process. We offer valuable resources for instructional strategies using research-based theory presented in a user friendly format.

Overview

Chapter 1 provides a history of academic language and academic literacy and presents the arguments for why teachers need to address it in their content-area classroom.

Chapter 2 deals with the issue of student motivation, including data from student surveys. It presents not only information on what students themselves find motivating, but also specific strategies based on the survey information. This chapter also discusses lesson strategies to effectively engage students.

Chapter 3 breaks down the concept of academic language into observable teaching behaviors. Here we offer strategies to teach the receptive (R) and expressive (E) skills students would benefit from in understanding the language of their content areas. Chapter 3 also includes an observation checklist that can be helpful in peer coaching.

Chapter 4 addresses numerous effective strategies for vocabulary development, specifically highlighting the differences between acquisition and learning of vocabulary and the importance of developing both receptive and expressive language skills. In this chapter the reader will also find helpful the vocabulary lists, including signal words, root words, and affixes. These lists were developed by the authors, with the assistance of the English language development teaching staff at Delano Joint Union High School District in California.

Chapter 5 focuses on the receptive skill of reading and emphasizes the importance of reading in the content areas. Discussions of "Into," "Through," and "Beyond" reading strategies, as well as integrated reading strategies, include helpful examples.

Chapter 6 deals with the expressive skill of writing. It gives the rationale for teaching writing along with teaching and assessment strategies in the content areas. After a brief discussion of why grammar rules are important concepts for students to learn, this chapter also clarifies the pedagogy of teaching grammar. "The Grammar Handbook" (appendix 7) is a fairly comprehensive reference guide for both student and teacher use. This is included as an aid to teachers in the content areas who, based on our experience, are sometimes hesitant to engage in grammar instruction.

Chapter 7 offers a summary of what is covered in the preceding chapters and a short explanation of how to use the lessons for reviewing the elements of academic language.

The appendices form a major part of the practical applications developed in the book.

- Appendix 1 is a sample lesson plan outline which is used for all sample lessons found in the text.
- Appendix 2 includes three science and two math lessons, with the receptive and expressive skills for academic language identified in the lessons.
- Appendix 3 includes three math and two science lessons which do not have the receptive and expressive skills listed.

- Appendix 4 is a model rubric for writing assignments
- Appendix 5 is a list of Web sites which may be helpful for the math and science teachers.
- Appendix 6 is a list of social studies, math, and science Spanish cognates.
- Appendix 7 is the grammar handbook.

The intended overarching objective of this text is to share with readers the authors' wealth of experience in assisting teachers and schools to improve student academic achievement through the use of academic language instructional strategies in the content-area classroom.

This book evolved from two highly successful grant implementations and the experiences of the authors while designing effective staff development sessions and instructional strategies for these grants which were awarded to the teaching credential program at California State University, Bakersfield. The first grant, English Language Development Professional Institute (ELDPI), funded by the State of California, 2000–2003, produced many innovative instructional strategies for English learners, especially in the content areas. The latest grant, a 4-year grant from the California Post Secondary Commission (CPEC), which funnels No Child Left Behind funds through the State of California, called Cognitive Academic Language Literacy Instruction (CALLI), targets academic language instruction in the secondary math and science content areas (2005–2009). The intent of this grant was to create an effective professional development model through collaboration between faculty from the School of Education and the School of Natural Science and Mathematics at California State University, Bakersfield, and Bakersfield College and the Delano Joint Union High School District. The professional development model focuses on working with secondary math and science teachers to improve their delivery of academic language instruction embedded in their content-area classroom, and, through this process, increase the achievement of their students. The high school math and science teachers participating in this grant work in a low income, high English learner population district.

As we began to develop instructional strategies to provide professional development for the teachers participating in the grants, we realized that there were a limited number of resources currently available for instruction in academic language/literacy for content-area teachers of all students: not just English language learners. Thus, we began to develop our own materials and strategies, based on collaboration with content-area experts and the knowledge and expertise gained from teaching language acquisition methodologies courses for second language learners, literacy strategies across content areas, as well as other experiences such as grant presentations, conference presentations, and publications. The result is this book.

Acknowledgments

The authors wish to acknowledge subject matter contributors Dr. Janet Tarjan, math, Merci Del Rosario, math, Debbie Wakelee and Vicki Murray, grammar—thank you for your contributions! The California Post-Secondary Education Commission (CPEC), specifically, Improving Teacher Quality Grants under the administration of Karen Humphrey, is responsible for providing the impetus for this text and the dissemination of information regarding the effectiveness of teaching academic language in the content areas. Hisauro Garza (research director for Project CALLI) and Susana Mata of Sierra Research Associates were very helpful in analyzing student responses for the student motivation survey. Tawnya Conradi, administrative assistant for Project CALLI has been very helpful during every step of the writing process. We also would like to acknowledge the expertise and input from Katherine Richardson Bruna, Iowa State University, and Juliet Langman, University of Texas, San Antonio, whose reviews of our text were so helpful in clarifying our work and in revisiting the focus of our text.

CHAPTER **1**

Background

As we move forward in the age of curricular accountability in public schools, teachers find themselves "caught" between the demands for accountability from the No Child Left Behind Act of 2001 (NCLB) and the needs of their students. Data and standards based curriculum have become the norm as teachers are held more responsible for student achievement results on standardized testing. Academic language instruction is a tool which offers a solution for increasing student achievement in core subject areas. Students who are taught strategies to comprehend and effectively use academic language in core subject areas will score higher on achievement tests and will function better in school and college. All teachers, regardless of content area or the grade level they are teaching, should be aware of the research-based instructional strategies that will assist *all* students to more effectively comprehend content information.

In this chapter we will introduce the concept of academic language by including some history of the development of the major concepts included within the umbrella term *academic language* and provide the operational definition we will use throughout this book. We introduce the general instructional philosophy associated with a focus on academic language, but leave specific strategies for the individual chapters, especially chapters 4 to 6. We will also address the topic of why we feel teachers should use academic language strategies and introduce some of the current teaching context: both where our students are and teacher preparation for teaching language in the content areas. Finally, we offer a brief preview of the remaining chapters in the book.

A Short History of the Term *Academic Language*

We address the issue of the history of academic language so that the reader can understand not only the context of the term but also how it has evolved into a topic of major concern for educators today. Many educators consider the term *academic language* to mean the vocabulary of their discipline, when in reality it encompasses social and academic discourse, interpretation of content-area reading, and types of writing discourse. A brief history of the use of the term *academic language* will help to clarify this point. We will also introduce some of the terminology that we use throughout the text.

Hymes (1972) was one of the first researchers to introduce the concept of academic language, although he did not coin the term as such. He addressed "communicative competence" and the use of language functions in both formal and informal contexts within the classroom. Hymes (1972), who came from the field of linguistics, was one of the first to address the features, patterns, and appropriate use of language within the context of classroom content. Halliday (1975) followed up with the introduction of functional grammar. He described how a student could control the functions of language while performing numerous tasks within the classroom. This includes using language to express needs, gain knowledge, convey knowledge, command others, express feelings, and form relationships. This is not simply a question of using the students' "own words" or social discourse to communicate academic knowledge, but involves asking students to modify the language to accurately reflect what the content means. Halliday (1985b) further clarified the different language functions as a petition or request to satisfy needs (I want); control behavior (do as I say); for social interaction (getting along with others); as an expression of pride (here I come); to seek knowledge (why); to be imaginative (let's pretend); to communicate information (I've got something to tell you); and for diversion (jokes, riddles).

Canale (1983) further categorized communicative competence into four areas: grammatical; sociolinguistic (using specialized language use for different social contexts); discourse competence (conversation competence); and strategic competence (using language to communicate effectively—both verbal and nonverbal nuances). Stephen Krashen (1982) introduced the "input hypothesis," which discussed the use of students' prior knowledge to enable them to understand language in the classroom. This involved the teacher's use of gestures, context, pictures, and grammatical structures through "comprehensible input" to assist struggling students to understand the content knowledge.

The first researcher to label academic language as such was Jim Cummins (1980), who identified two different types of language proficiencies that English learners must acquire in order to acquire English. The first is basic interpersonal communication skills (BICS; which involves speaking and listening skills), and the second is cognitive academic language proficiency (CALP; which is related to reading and writing skills). Basic interpersonal communication skills are used for social conversational purposes and are much easier to master, whereas CALPs are used to convey academic learning and take much longer to acquire.

Definitions of Academic Language

Academic language is synonymous with academic English. The National Center for Research on Cultural Diversity and Second Language Learning defines academic English as language which includes

> semantic and syntactic features such as vocabulary items, sentence structure, transitions markers and cohesive ties, and language functions and tasks that are part of the social studies classroom routine, such as defining terms, explaining historical significance, reading expository text, and preparing research reports. (Short, 1993, p.1)

Academic language is sometimes defined as a multidimensional focus on the meaning and task (Cummins, 2000b; Krashen, 1982; MacSwan & Rolstad, 2003; Wong Fillmore, 2004). It is essential to understand how language is used in different areas in order to construe particular kinds of meaning as required by the content areas. Academic language is central to teaching any discipline content (see Figure 1.1).

As we focus on struggling readers, including English learners, academic language or academic proficiency (Krashen & Brown, 2007) can also be defined as cognitive academic language skills (CALPS) as opposed to basic interpersonal communication skills (BICS).

> As with all innovations, the BICS/CALPS distinction has been discussed in detail by many scholars. One of the more interesting comments is MacSwan and Rolstad's (2003) observation that non-academic language can be quite complicated and can take a long time to acquire. BICS, they suggest, is different, not less complex. Such criticisms are valuable in that they lead to deeper understandings of BICS and CALP, but they do not challenge the basic distinction." (Krashen, personal communication, July 8, 2008)

Mary Schleppegrell (2004) refers to academic language as the "*language of schooling.*" She considers it to involve the development of linguistic capacity which draws on meaning, thus using the resources of academic registers that enable students to demonstrate their knowledge through discourse.

ACADEMIC LANGUAGE

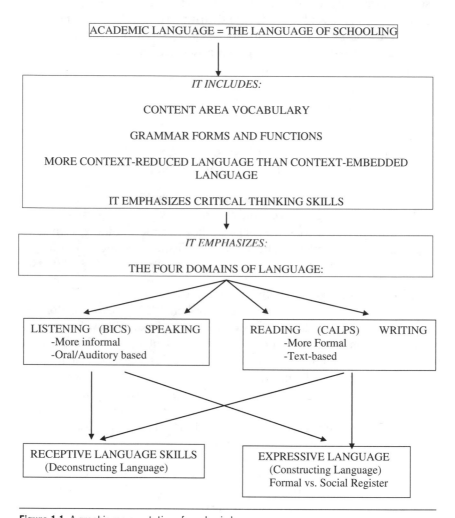

Figure 1.1 A graphic representation of academic language.

Anna Chamot and J. Michael O'Malley (1994) define academic language as: "the language that is used by teachers and students for the purpose of acquiring new knowledge and skills" (p. 40). They explain that it differs from social language and increases in difficulty as students progress through the grades. Chamot and O'Malley also point out that two factors affect comprehension: context (here and now—concrete information) and cognitive complexity (the abstract language of schooling that is decontextualized or without any concrete references for the learner).

According to Robin Scarcella (2003), academic language is: "a variety or a register of English used in professional books and characterized by the specific linguistics features associated with academic disciplines" (p. 19). She further explains that the "register" refers to many different forms of language used specifically for different contexts both in and outside of the classroom. This phenomenon occurs in all disciplines and includes a wide range of genres including biographies, lab reports, and journals, and involves listening, speaking, reading, and writing skills. Scarcella identifies five components of academic language: phonological (sounds, stress, patterns); lexical (word meanings including root words and affixes); grammatical (knowledge of syntax, grammatical forms, punctuation, and rules); sociolinguistic (appropriate production of sentences to match in school and out of school situations); and discourse (conversational language, both formal and informal).

Bailey, Butler, LaFramenta, and Ong (2001–2004) note that the term *academic language* is interpreted differently among researchers (see Cummins, 2000b, for a review). It also has a variety of meanings to teachers and among educators in general (Solomon & Rhodes, 1995). The definition of academic language used in this study is consistent with definitions used in previous National Center for Research on Evaluation, Standards, and Student Testing (CRESST) work (Bailey, 2000; Stevens, Butler, & Castellon-Wellington, 2000) that sought to characterize academic language at the lexical (vocabulary), syntactic (forms of grammar), and discourse (rhetorical) levels. This study also emphasizes that academic language is characterized by how it creates meaning within the context of the content area. They state that it is important to address the intersection of language and content without both basic language proficiency *and* content knowledge students will have difficulty understanding the academic language used on standardized tests. In this book, the authors seek to clarify the appropriate register of discourse used in the classroom as well as accurate usage and understanding of vocabulary, including the recognition of correct grammatical forms and functions (see Table 1.1).

Instruction from an Academic Language Perspective

What does academic language mean to our teachers? When we use academic language in math, science, and social studies, it means teaching the language as well as the content of the discipline. It involves teaching students the vocabulary, writing styles, and sophisticated grammatical forms associated with the content area. It includes a distinct differentiation between the social discourse used outside of school and the more formal academic discourse used in the classroom. It explicitly acknowledges the difference between reading and writing for pleasure and reading and writing to inform and convey

Table 1.1 A Brief Summary of the History and Development of Concepts Involved in Academic Language Literacy

Researcher	Phraseology	Brief details
Hymes (1972)	Communicative competence	Contextualization of language—especially regarding the difference between informal (i.e. social) and formal (i.e. classroom/academic) discourse
Halliday (1975, 1985)	Functional grammar	Focused on student language use to achieve specific goals. Emphasized the function and the expressive side (speaking/writing) of language
Cummins (1980)	Academic language	Characterized academic language into BICS (Basic Interpersonal Communication Skills) and CALP (Cognitive Academic Language Proficiency)
Krashen (1982)	Input hypothesis	Highlighted the importance of prior knowledge and context to language acquisition
Canale (1983)	Communicative competence	Divided language competence into 4 categories: Grammatical, Sociolinguistic, Discourse, and Strategic
Chamot and O'Malley (1994)	Academic language	Combines concept of register with abstract/concrete dichotomy
Scarcella (2003)	Academic language	5 components of Academic language: Phonological, Lexical, Grammatical, Sociolinguistic, and Discourse
Schleppegrell (2004)	The language of schooling	Emphasized grammatical and linguistic choices, especially in regards to registers of language
Stevens, Butler, & Castellon-Wellington (2000)	Academic language	Characterized academic language as lexical, syntactic, and discourse. Distinguishes between language proficiency and content knowledge

information. Academic language emphasizes critical thinking and inquiry, and is for the most part information dense. The term *information dense* is used to identify written passages that contain complex sentences and higher level vocabulary. Instruction using academic language emphasizes the use of concrete language (i.e., context embedded) instruction because students are often exposed to abstract and context-reduced instruction without the literacy support they require at the upper grade levels. For example, picture a person walking down the sidewalk who asks you the question, "How many?" Now picture that sidewalk located just outside a restaurant you selected to eat dinner. This exemplifies a context reduced versus context embedded situation: in the first setting the question is out of context, while in the second, there are clues from the context available to help figure out what is being referred to. A telephone conversation is the most context reduced form of oral language and the most difficult language task for a second language learner. Without the use of any comprehensible input, other schemata, or background knowledge to assist the learner, simple comprehension can be very difficult in this type of situation. For many of our students, reading in the content areas or listening to teachers' lectures can be compared to conducting a telephone conversation in a second language.

When teaching different disciplines (including math, science, and social studies), the use of academic language involves teaching some of the following skills—note how the skills increase in difficulty as they move up the hierarchy of Bloom's taxonomy (1956):

- reporting and describing information,
- presenting arguments,
- organizing and elaborating on information,
- interpreting and presenting data,
- comparing and classifying information, and
- providing solutions to hypothesized problems.

In other words, academic language begins at the comprehension phase of Bloom's taxonomy (excluding knowledge, or simple recall) and moves through application, analysis, synthesis, and evaluation. All students must master these skills in all their disciplines in order to be fully functioning and productive in their educational setting.

Academic language is a formal "register" of communication (Scarcella, 2003). People use different registers of communication in different social situations. For example, a different register of communication is used in the doctor's office from the one used on the playground or at home. It may also be argued that different households use different registers of language, which depend on their socioeconomic status. People in the service industry (restaurant servers, grocery checkout clerks, etc.) learn a specific register to use with customers. Imagine a receptionist in a doctor's office saying, "Hey! Go ahead and take your kid and sit down." Different registers of language are used in sports, the news, and with weather reporters. Have you ever noticed that newscasters across the nation speak, for the most part, with the same accent (dialect) but the weather reporters speak with the accent of the region they are located in? Academic language can also be construed as formal versus informal language, not simply social versus classroom language.

Why Should We Teach Academic Language?

When did math, science, and social studies teachers become language and literacy teachers? This became a necessity when there was a change in the diversity of the student population we serve in the public schools. As we educate increasing numbers of English learners and struggling readers, we recognize the need to differentiate our instruction in order to effectively deliver the content-area material. However, this change does not really necessitate that content teachers become literacy and language teachers, but it does require them to redirect their efforts and instructional strategies to ensure that the entire class comprehends the subject matter that is being taught.

The Context: Where Are Our Students?

We often hear teachers ask the question: Why can't we teach students the way we were taught? They are talking about traditional instruction: read the chapter, discuss it in class, take a quiz, have some more discussion, then take a unit test. In order to answer this question, educators must first look at student demographics and academic achievement. According to the National Center for Education Statistics (NCES), the number of young people in the total U.S. population aged 14 to 17 increased by .5% between 1960 and 2002 (totaling 108,000,000 students) with fluctuations in that percentage during that period (NCES indicator 1) across the United States. From this one can infer that schools are educating more students than ever before. Additionally, indicator 10 from NCES demonstrates that the ethnicity of our students has changed.

Table 1.2 (NCES indicator 10) indicates that the percentage of Whites enrolled in our schools has diminished, both in elementary and high school, the percentage of African Americans has diminished in elementary school, but has risen in high school, and the number of Hispanics has risen significantly in both school settings.

Table 1.2 Percentage of Students Enrolled in School, by Level of School Enrollment and Ethnicity

Year	Ethnicity	Elementary	High School
1975	White	76.9	80.5
2003	White	59.9	64.1
1975	African American	14.7	12.3
2003	African American	12.3	14.0
1975	Hispanic	6.7	5.4
2003	Hispanic	18.0	13.7

Source: U.S. Department of Education. Institute of Education Sciences, National Center for Education Statistics.

Table 1.3 Percentage of Persons Ages 16–24 Who Were Dropouts

Year	Ethnicity	% of Dropouts
1972	White	12.3
2003	White	6.3
1972	African American	21.3
2003	African American	10.9
1972	Hispanic	34.3
2003	Hispanic	23.5

Source: U.S. Department of Education. Institute of Education Sciences, National Center for Education Statistics.

Table 1.3 (NCES indicator 19) indicates that there is an almost 50% reduction in the dropout rates for Whites and African Americans and a 40% drop in the dropout rate for Hispanics.

Table 1.4 (NCES indicator 20), although somewhat limited in scope, demonstrates that a sample of the parents of our future students (25–26 year olds) are completing high school and degrees beyond high school. This is an additional indicator that more parents are receiving higher education. Given this factor, we would expect that our students should achieve more, not less.

As shown above, one can assume that although schools are educating more students, due to both an increase in numbers and the lower dropout rate, the shift in demographics points to many more Hispanics in school and concurrently parents with at least a high school education.

According to the Nation's Report Card (National Center for Education Statistics [NCES], 2005–2006), the trend for the mean scaled scores on the National Reading Assessment for 9, 13, and 17 year olds has not changed significantly from 1971 to 2004. However, in 2005, only 31% of the fifth and ninth grade students scored at or above proficiency level in reading, placing nearly 70% below proficiency.

With fewer students dropping out of school and more parents receiving higher education, why are students' reading levels still consistently low? Aranti (2006) states that it is difficult to identify one cause for the consistent decline in reading scores. He asserts that "Bad teaching, chaotic home lives, low expectations for some students, cultural bias, the fact that older students simply don't read enough—all have been faulted. And student attitude can be a factor." Other factors may include the fact that parents do not have time to emphasize the importance of education or assist their children with their education at home; poor school student attendance; the lack of school instruction tied to standards; and no emphasis on prior knowledge. The increase of video representation (games, DVD) in our lives, which gives students no reason to read, along with other factors may begin to explain

Table 1.4 Percentage of 25–26 Year Olds Who Completed High School and College

Year	Ethnicity	Less than HS	HS Complete*	HS Complete**	HS & Some College	BS	Higher than BS
1975	White	13.4	86.6	42.4	20.5	0	0
2004	White	6.7	93.3	28.6	30.2	28.0	6.5
1975	African American	28.9	71.1	43.6	17.1	0	0
2004	African American	11.3	88.7	36.8	34.8	14.1	3.0
1975	Hispanic	46.9	53.1	31.2	13.0	0	0
2004	Hispanic	37.6	62.4	30.1	21.4	9.2	1.6

*Indicates completion of High School and/or a GED
**Indicates completion of High School only
Source: U.S. Department of Education. Institute of Education Sciences, National Center for Education Statistics.

why students have difficulty reading, especially at the upper grade levels. In addition, there is a rising number of one-parent homes and parents are also spending more time on their own education rather than spending focused time with their children.

Cummins, in an interview with the *California Reader* (2001c), mentions the fourth grade slump and explains that the language of instruction and communication changes at the fourth grade level for most students.

> This slump refers to students who appear to have been making good progress in the early grades but who suddenly experience difficulty with the increasing language demands of the curriculum when the focus shifts from decoding written texts to understanding them and writing about them. (Cummins, 2001b, p. 1)

Students at this stage begin to encounter academic language, which consists of low frequency vocabulary, mostly derived from Latin and Greek roots, and is very different from the high frequency monosyllabic words readers are familiar with in the earlier stages of acquiring reading skills. In other words, as students progress from the early grades, classroom vocabulary and reading becomes more difficult as well as more abstract.

The authors have seen many students' cumulative files that depict standardized reading test scores at grade level up to fourth grade, but which dramatically drop by three to four grade levels below grade level by eighth grade.

Aranti (2006) quotes Timothy Shanahan, President of the International Reading Association (IRA) and a professor of urban education at the University of Illinois at Chicago, "Many school systems stop emphasizing formal reading instruction once children leave primary grades. It's not like a polio vaccine—a couple of shots when you're a little kid and then you're done." Reading skill development needs to continue throughout the students' educational career.

In reference to the "Reading Wars"—phonics (versus whole language instruction) was questioned as the most effective approach to reading instruction. The final conclusion was that literacy strategies actually need to be taught to students. Literacy strategies include teaching students to think metacognitively, to learn how to think about thinking, and thus, how to use these reading strategies more effectively on their own. In other words, students are instructed to construct their own meaning from the text (Farber, 1999). Likewise, it is critical that students are taught to monitor their own thinking while reading and to be able to use repair strategies when they do not understand what they have read.

We still need a balanced approach where continued comprehension strategies are taught to students. Students need to be taught metacognitively; they need to learn how to think about thinking and how to use these strategies. We are failing to instruct students how to construct meaning from the text (Farber, 1999). Students need to know how to monitor their own thinking when reading texts and to be able to use repair strategies when they do not understand the content. Using context clues and the students' knowledge of root words and affixes when they encounter a word they don't know, in order to ascertain the meaning of the unknown word, is a good example of a "repair strategy" (see chapter 4). Students often focus on words and their meaning and not on the comprehensive meaning of the paragraph or article they are reading. With this narrow focus, if they do not understand all the words in the selection they often stop reading to seek clarification of specific words or phrases instead of using repair strategies to assist them with the meaning. At this point students lose all interest or confidence in their ability to decipher the text.

Students learn reading strategies in stages. Jean Chall (1996) refers to the six stages of reading development when addressing how students learn to read. Learning to read doesn't just happen. It has to be taught through systematic, organized instruction. Reading skills are built through stages and they are an ongoing process. Learning to read also involves a core set of knowledge and skills.

If a stage of reading development has not been learned, students will flounder in their reading ability, which also affects their writing skills. Difficulties in reading and behavior problems seem to be related, particularly in older students (Chall, 1983). It is imperative that teachers support students throughout each stage of their reading development and ensure that they fully understand each stage of the reading and writing process as they move on to the next level.

It may not be necessary to identify the underlying causes of a student's reading problem in order to assist the student. Moreover, what is required of the teacher is an understanding of how reading develops and how a developmental approach to reading instruction can be applied to produce accelerated growth in this area.

We introduce Chall's strategies here to help explain where the typical high school student is on the reading development spectrum and what the teacher can expect in terms of relating students' language development to content knowledge. In other words, what stage are my students at and what will I have to pay particular attention to in order to enable them to fully understand and communicate ideas in my content area and grade level?

Stage 0/Prereading Stage   Readers in this first stage of development are able to "say back" materials that have been read to them repeatedly. Although they are not really reading yet—in the sense of identifying words on the page—they are able to engage in this "pretend reading" of books because they understand that books have meaning. They also know that groups of letters written on a page stand for words.

Stage 1/Decoding (grades 1–2; ages 6–7) This stage, when actual reading begins, is where many students begin to experience difficulties. Readers at this stage are beginning to associate sounds and spoken words with printed ones. They continue to sound out words in the process of acquiring skills, but stage 1 readers are able to read only a fraction of the words whose meanings they understand.

According to a study conducted by Chall (1983), approximately 10% of at-risk adolescents are at this stage of development. For many students the difficulty is compounded by a tendency to use phonics to "sound the word out" to determine meaning, instead of trying to decode an unknown word by guessing as well as looking at the word based on the context of what they are reading. Hence, teaching older adolescents at this stage of reading development usually involves two steps: first, direct instruction in letter-sound correspondences must be provided; and second, a great deal of encouragement must be provided along with multiple opportunities to apply the decoding skills once they have been acquired. The instructional materials used to teach adolescents at this stage of development also need to be carefully selected. Books and words need to be appropriate for their age level, so they can see immediate value in being able to read.

Stage 2/Confirmation (grades 2–3; ages 7–8) Readers at this stage are becoming fluent in dealing with print. Chall (1996) refers to this process as "ungluing" or becoming less and less dependent on having to sound out each word, which allows more attention to be focused on the meaning. The reading rate increases steadily for children who move though this stage without difficulty. In addition, by the end of stage 2, children are able to read and understand approximately 3,000 words, while another 9,000 words can be understood when heard.

About 13% of the students in Chall's study (1983) of at-risk adolescents were still functioning at this stage of reading development. The reading rate for these students is slow and the grade level of texts they are able to read *fluently* often lags several years behind the grade level at which they can read *accurately*. As a result, reading can become a task to avoid, one that brings very little pleasure or satisfaction to the student. For this reason, teachers of older students at this stage of reading development need to select reading materials that make the effort required on the part of the reader worthwhile.

Stage 3/Reading to Learn (grades 4–8; ages 9–13) This stage marks a transition from a focus on learning how to read to an emphasis on using reading as a tool for learning new information. Readers at this stage are able to decode in a more or less automatic way. As such, they may be able to read words but will not necessarily understand their meaning. Adolescents in this stage of reading development may also begin to encounter words that are not totally new to them but not totally known. Without a teacher's help, confusion and frustration can result, and interest and motivation can soon fade away.

Over 50% of teens who are struggling with reading are in this stage. Due to limitations in their knowledge bases, they lack familiarity with some words. They may recall seeing or hearing specific words, but they are unable to separate the meanings of the words from the contexts in which they have encountered them. This creates a type of vicious cycle: Their weak vocabularies cause their comprehension to suffer and, their difficulties in comprehension cause their vocabularies to remain weak. Breaking the cycle usually requires systematic, continuous, and direct vocabulary instruction.

Stage 4/Multiple Viewpoints (High School; ages 14–18)   Students in stage 4 are able to read and understand a broad range of materials. Still developing, however, is their ability to integrate the different viewpoints and perspectives they experience through their reading and in their own life experiences. Students in this stage are acquiring the ability to use a number of different sources of reading materials as a way to answer questions and to solve problems.

Based on current educational practice, stage 4 reading usually develops during high school. Consequently, all of the students whom teachers work with at the secondary level will benefit from some assistance in learning how to use the study skills and strategies necessary to organize and assess the multiple challenges required by reading at stage 4.

Stage 5/Construction and Reconstruction (College; ages 18 & up)   Stage 5 readers are able to use reading for their personal and professional needs in such a way that their prior knowledge becomes synthesized and analyzed by what they read. Few adolescents have reached stage 5 reading. According to Chall (1983), reaching this stage may be the most difficult transition of all because it depends on broad knowledge of the content being read, a high degree of efficiency in reading it, and the courage and confidence to form an opinion.

The stages are the milestones of reading development. They are built upon and achieved as students grow in their literacy development. At times, students may get stuck in one of the stages. It is our job, as teachers of adolescents, to help students to move on to the next stage and beyond, by empowering them to become enthusiastic readers and writers.

Context: The State of Teacher Training

Students may have learned to decode words, but still may not be able to comprehend the meaning of the words while they are reading. Secondary education teacher candidates at California State University, Bakersfield go out into the classrooms to assess secondary students' decoding, comprehension, and writing skills. They often come back horrified at the lack of language abilities of public school students. After this exposure they are ready to embrace the strategies for teaching literacy across the content areas. One comment echoed by several teacher candidates over a four-year period is that the students can read the words out loud, but they don't know what they mean.

Lack of teacher training in the reading process poses another problem for students and teachers. Much is currently being done at the federal and state levels to increase the effectiveness of teacher education programs. Michael Allen (2003), in his summary of "Eight Questions on Teacher Preparation; What Does the Research Say?" states that

> Field placement in an urban school, training in multicultural awareness, and effective recruitment and screening of teacher candidates are the only three strategies with any real support in the research—and of these three, field placement is the most commonly mentioned. (p. 5)

Field placement is crucial for teacher candidates if they are to understand the type of student that they will be teaching and begin to develop strategies for working with at-risk children. He also states that teacher education preparation programs need to be more responsive to the academic needs of the students in the classroom today. This should, of course, include more emphasis on language instruction in the content areas.

Peggy Farber (1999) cites that 37 states mandate a course in teaching reading in the teacher education preparation programs; however, very few teachers actually use the strategies they have learned once they acquire a teaching position. These courses, if designed properly, present reading methodology in the context of the content-area classroom. They teach teachers how to incorporate reading strategies into the science, math, social studies, and other classrooms. The Single Subject Reading Task Force for the California State University Office of the Chancellor (Brynelson et al., 2004) has published a monograph that lists the principles all secondary teachers need to know before they enter the classroom, including the reading process, comprehension and content learning, adolescent literacy assessment, differentiation of instruction and planning and integration—again, more emphasis on academic language instruction.

Michael Pressley (2006) discussed the extremely high reading and writing achievement rates at Bennett Woods Elementary School near East Lansing,

Michigan. He cited strong teacher collaboration (including the regular use of thematic units across the content areas) and professional development for teachers as contributing to the high quality reading and writing instruction and student achievement.

Traditionally, English learners have been the targeted students for direct reading strategy instruction, who, because they lack CALPS (Cummins, 1980) and thus lack academic language proficiency, have difficulty demonstrating content-area knowledge. Most often they may be able to comprehend the curriculum (with strategized assistance); however, they do not perform well on assessments. All school populations need and will benefit from the integration of academic language instruction.

How This Book Can Help

Academic language instruction in the content areas can assist English language learners and struggling readers by increasing their receptive and expressive skills, as well as enhancing the highly critical content-area vocabulary and reading comprehension skills necessary to successfully navigate context-reduced academic text. It also can improve content-area skills and achievement.

The big question now is: How do math, science, and social studies teachers teach academic language skills in their classes without taking critical time away from content-area skill instruction? This text proposes to answer that question by embedding the instruction of language into content-area education.

First, chapter 2 addresses the all-important topic of motivation. Chapter 3 introduces two important concepts from academic language: receptive and expressive language use. Chapters 4 to 6 provide specific methods in the areas of vocabulary, reading comprehension, and writing. Chapter 4 addresses academic language strategies for strengthening vocabulary; chapter 5 focuses on student reading; chapter 6 takes on the topic of writing.

CHAPTER 2

Motivation

Before we begin looking specifically at academic language literacy and applications of the research base to classroom practice, we want to spend some time on the topic of student motivation. During the course of the Cognitive Academic Language Literacy Instruction (CALLI) project that inspired this book (see preface), one of the major issues that arose was resistance to the ideas we were presenting that was based, in large part, on the general teacher complaint that their students didn't want to learn. Teachers said that if the student doesn't want to learn, applying the best techniques and practices to the student gets you nowhere. We found ourselves in the position of not only needing to address the topic of student motivation, but we also realized that we needed to motivate the teachers participating in the project to learn the academic language techniques we were advocating.

An entire book could be written on the subject of student motivation, but it is not our intent here to offer a full treatment of this critical subject. Instead, we just want to provide a brief discussion of motivation and present a few simple strategies that are particularly useful in the specific context of developing academic language skills.

Most teachers have their own anecdotal evidence of the powerful influence of motivation on students, and we introduce a few of our own anecdotes just to set the stage. Then we will present a brief analysis of some of the literature on motivation and compare this to our own data on students' perceptions of what motivates them to learn. We also offer some specific strategies and advice for devising motivating activities for your students, focusing on three general strategies for motivation: anticipatory sets, hands-on activities, and modeling and guided practice.

The Importance of Motivation

Activities that are fun, engaging, interesting, and those which we can be successful at, usually motivate us to learn. Students who are actively involved in our lessons will also be actively involved in learning the academic language of the content. Motivating students/teachers to learn is the first step, enabling them to use the skills taught is harder to accomplish. As teachers, what is our "charge"? Is our job merely to teach students, or are we also obligated to entertain them? As educators our job is to teach our students, and entertainment can be a powerful tool to accomplish this as long as we ensure that the entertainment is purposeful, meaningful, and applicable. Below are some examples of how motivation can effect student participation.

A new fifth grade teacher in a very low income, rural middle school extols the virtues of finishing school and going on to college. After all, she did; she grew up in the small town of Weedpatch (true name, but that is another story), and she made it. She is now their teacher. During her first year the principal allows a very talented new teacher to use the fifth grade teacher's class to teach a lesson to be observed for university credit. The new teacher is inspired and energetic as she takes the students on a virtual field trip to the Los Angeles Museum of Art. During the trip the students view slides of artwork, experience the bumpiness of traveling in a school bus through Los Angles traffic, eat lunch, and then get ready to come home. They are all tired and ready to board the bus for home, she explains to the students, and most of them will probably sleep on the trip. She prepares them mentally for the trip home when two of the students exclaim, "But I don't want to go home yet! I'm having too much fun!" The fifth grade teacher then asked the principal, "Do you have to be that animated to be a good teacher?"

It is not just what information you present, but also how you present it. The key is to engage students first. Forty trainers (teachers, consultants, university faculty, etc.) received 3 days of intensive instruction in how to prepare teachers to use the Hampton Brown *High Point* textbook series for secondary English learners and struggling readers. The training was intense, pedantic, and simulated the training we were to give secondary teachers across the state of California. Everyone was to be "lock-step" during the week-long training sessions we were to give. Although very thankful for the huge binders of training materials, we were not happy with the prospect of conducting this training with junior and senior high school teachers. Nevertheless, happily ensconced in the Hyatt Regency Hotel in Los Angeles, 40 of us proceeded to lead approximately 2,000 Los Angeles Unified School District (LAUSD) teachers through the training. The results were surprising. Trainer presentation styles and personalities proved to be a key factor in the effectiveness of the delivery of the training, as evidenced by participant response. What we don't know is whether or not the participants used the training in their classrooms. It is possible that the participants were well entertained during the training but did not find the material presented very useful. However, Jeannie Chall (1996) stated, when asked in an interview, if she would rather have a bad teacher with a good method or a good teacher with a bad method, she responded, "That's easy, I'd rather have a good teacher with a bad method because it wouldn't be a bad method anymore!" (Turner, 1993). The point is that we need to present new skills in an engaging manner. If new knowledge and skills are presented in a way that is relevant to real world application, consumers will more readily apply the skills.

Research on Student Motivation

Motivated students achieve more than students who are not motivated. Student motivation was one of six key factors for increased student achievement at Bennett Woods Elementary School (Pressley, 2006). Brewster and Fager (2000) provide five techniques for motivating students to spend more time on task:

1. Ensure course materials relate to students' lives and highlight ways learning can be applied in real-life situations;
2. Allow students to have some degree of control over their learning;
3. Assign challenging but achievable tasks for all students, including at-risk, remedial, and learning disabled students;
4. Arouse students' curiosity about the topic being studied;
5. Design projects that allow students to share new knowledge with others. (p. 7)

Student motivation increases when learning is linked to background knowledge. If students can relate learning to prior knowledge, they will be more inclined to engage in the learning process. Students learn when they are able to make sense of their environment and when they are engaged (Lumsden, 1994). Building student motivation requires commitment on the part of the teacher to implement highly structured, multimodal lessons. When identifying the best strategies to implement academic language in the content areas, building on prior knowledge, using strong anticipatory sets which relate to the students' real world, using projects, creating "big questions" for students to answer, and scaffolding information are key instructional strategies. They also motivate students.

Motivating students includes inspiring them to attend school. As mentioned previously (chapter 1), with a high divorce rate, single parent homes, and homes where both parents work, it is easy for students to simply stay at home and play video games or watch television. If students actively engage in the learning process, attendance in school should increase (Brewster & Fager, 2000).

Deborah Stipek (2002) shows that students ask themselves three questions before completing a task:

1. Why am I doing this task?
2. Can I succeed at this task?
3. Do I want to do this task?

Teachers who want to successfully motivate their students must be able to answer these questions. Better yet, they should design lessons and activities that allow the *students* to answer them appropriately.

John Dewey, as early as 1944, reasoned that education focuses on what is expected, not what is relevant. Teachers spend too much time preparing students for college and not enough time relating to how the content is practical for them. John Dewey and his wife spent time in a chemistry class teaching chemistry by cooking breakfast. Many elementary teachers use cooking and following a recipe to teach math concepts. Unfortunately not all of our instruction is reality based, or relevant to the students. Our general education preparation in high school is geared toward the college entrance student. Some schools do have a vocational track and the vocational track (teaching relevant skills) is becoming more popular, but college prep classes are still the norm. College prep classes typically teach material which intends only to give students a "well-rounded" background to prepare them for liberal arts classes in college. Many colleges overemphasize the need to have a well-rounded background and we find students mired in the maze of general education to the point that when a major is finally selected, the college student does not have enough background when they graduate to get a job in the chosen major field. The development of high school curriculum has paralleled this trend.

With this emphasis on college prep classes comes the idea that the teacher must get through the material in order to cover all of it, which leaves little time for innovative teaching that would engage students. Also emphasized is the common notion of "habitus" which is still prevalent in education today: The way things are is the way they have to be. In other words, we have to prepare you for college, so you have to learn all of this (Smith & Wilhelm, 2002). It doesn't matter if you can use the information in real life, but you must learn it to be prepared for college. Yes, we can teach skills which will prepare students for college in an engaging fashion. To motivate students, educators should modify instruction and include academic language strategies in order to motivate and challenge all students.

Students' Perception of What Motivates Them

The authors have recently been involved with a federal grant funded through the California Postsecondary Education Commission. The 4-year grant purports to improve academic language instruction in math and science classrooms in a semirural high school district in the San Joaquin Valley. This cognitive academic language literacy instruction (CALLI) grant project was awarded in November 2005. During the second professional development project session with the teachers, many of them expressed a need to know what would motivate their students to do their best in their classes. A survey of 2,131 students in math classes revealed some very interesting, but not surprising results.

This survey on student motivation was conducted in a semirural high school district in the San Joaquin Valley with a high poverty index, high English learner population, low performance on state standardized tests, and a total enrollment of 4,325 students (81.4 % Latino and 13.2% Filipino). The results of this survey are presented in Tables 2.1 through 2.5, which detail the responses of students in math and science classes to questions regarding the elements that the students themselves feel to be effective motivators.

In terms of homework (Table 2.1), it appears that the greatest motivating factor teachers have available is immediate applicability (i.e., it relates to what was done in class) or projects. Novelty of the information does not rank high as a motivating factor, coming in slightly below the one factor that every teacher wishes they could control: my parents make me do it.

When students were asked to describe how a specific, effective teacher motivates them to do their best (Table 2.2), student responses had to do primarily with teacher emphasis on the future (including the idea of a better future paycheck), again emphasis was on the idea of applicability. Teacher enthusiasm also ranks high. Other factors which influence students to do their

Table 2.1 Response of All Students in Math and Science to the Prompt: I Do My Work When ...

I do my homework when:	Percent of Responses
It talks about what we did in class	32.4
When it is a project	17.8
When my parents make me do it	15.4
When it introduces new information that I have not learned	14.9
Other:	9.8

Total number of students =2,365. Because some students were present in both a math and a science class where the survey was taken, the total number of responses was 3,804. Responses grouped in other were each ≤5%.

Table 2.2 Answers of 914 Students Who Responded to the Following Prompt: Describe, in One Word, Why You Think a Certain Teacher Motivates You to Do Your Best

Word Chosen	Percent of Respondents
Future	59
Enthusiastic	15
Paycheck	12
Cares	5
Understandable	4
Grades	4

best were what they will do with their future (college, good job, etc., Table 2.3.) and making their parents proud, or responding to parental pressure.

In specific classrooms, motivating factors identified by students include projects, making learning fun, more group work, and when the teachers are having fun (Tables 2.4 and 2.5 note that on these questions students were allowed to respond to as many categories as they felt applied, so the total number of responses is much larger than the total number of students). Although there were some differences between the two disciplines, general trends are apparent. Good anticipatory sets (having fun), hands-on activities, group work, social discourse, and a clear understanding of the task motivate these students. Stand-alone vocabulary work and simple reading of the text aloud without interaction ranked very low among the motivating strategies regardless of discipline, and the important motivation supplied by a teacher who enjoys him- or herself should not be overlooked. In order to motivate

Table 2.3 Responses of 1,356 Students to the Prompt: What Other Things Really Motivate You to Do Your Best in School?

Motivator	Percent of Responses
Parents	28
Future	17
Graduation	9
Friends	9
Teacher	7
Grades	7
College	6
Money	6
Sports	5
Reward	3
Myself	3
Competition	1
Reputation	0
Son	0

Table 2.4 Total Number of Responses and Percentages of Students Selecting Each Response to the Prompt: I Learn More in Math When . . .

Strategy	# of Responses	Percent of Students
We work in groups	1238	52%
I understand what the teacher wants me to do	1219	52%
When I'm having fun with the class work	1184	50%
We do "hands-on" activities in class	918	39%
I get a good grade	866	37%
I get to discuss the class work with another student in my class	837	35%
My parents expect me to get good grades	730	31%
When the teacher is having fun	696	29%
When the teacher expects me to do well	557	24%
We try to answer questions which relate to real life	521	22%
I understand the vocabulary used in the classroom	478	20%
We draw pictures or write lists to organize the notes in class	459	19%
The teacher lets me do the work on my own	443	19%
I'm given a list of vocabulary words to do on my own	204	9%
The teacher reads the text to me or uses the CD from the text	175	7%

Remember that students could select multiple responses to the prompt, so the percentages sum to more than 100%. The total number of surveys completed was 2,365.

your students, you will sometimes be called upon to display extraordinary acting skills, acting as if something very basic, that you've taught many times is really new, exciting, and revelatory, as it can be to students encountering it for the first time.

Taken together, these data provide information on a variety of strategies to motivate students. In order to motivate students, successful teachers reframe teaching as inquiry and focus more on the *how* than the *what*. Students must see in school what they see in real life. Education should focus on experience relating to what students can do and what they see in real life. If the content is not real for them, they are less motivated to learn. Active participation in the learning process is critical, as well as sharing new knowledge, the ability to feel successful with their assigned tasks, and the inclusion of multiple modalities of instruction because some students are visual learners and others are auditory learners. Daggett and Blais (2006) explain that project based learning addresses the different interests of students as well as the different

Table 2.5 Total Number of Responses and Percentage of Students Selecting Each Response to the Prompt: I Learn More in Science When...

Strategy	Number of Responses	Percent of Students
We work in groups	1232	52%
We do "hands-on" activities in class	1087	46%
When I'm having fun with the class work	1042	44%
I understand what the teacher wants me to do	989	42%
I get a good grade	706	30%
I get to discuss the class work with another student in my class	699	30%
When the teacher is having fun	630	27%
My parents expect me to get good grades	620	26%
I understand the vocabulary used in the classroom	590	25%
We try to answer questions which relate to real life	563	24%
We draw pictures or write lists to organize the notes in class	535	23%
When the teacher expects me to do well	486	21%
The teacher lets me do the work on my own	360	16%
I'm given a list of vocabulary words to do on my own	379	15%
The teacher reads the text to me or uses the CD from the text	233	10%

Remember that students could select multiple responses to the prompt, so the percentages sum to more than 100%. The total number of surveys completed was 2,365.

learning styles and therefore is effective in increasing student motivation and engagement. Expect that our students will be most engaged when they are involved in the learning process, as are teachers when they attend teacher training classes or professional development workshops.

Setting a Purpose for Learning: The Anticipatory Set

A common caricature of high school teachers has them saying, "Today, class, we are going to learn...." This statement may truly relate and be meaningful to the students, however, what exactly are we saying? First, this communicates to students that formal language in the classroom is not important and second, it tells them very little of importance about the purpose of the lesson for that day. Clearly, setting a well-understood purpose for learning the skill being taught is critical to student motivation and involvement. It is arguably more important to tell students why they will learn something than to tell them what they will learn—after all, if the lesson is good, they should be able to figure out what they learned without being told.

An anticipatory set is simply an introductory portion of a lesson designed specifically to get students interested in the topic of the lesson and present a clear purpose for learning; it sets up the academic language which will be used throughout the lesson. Imagine beginning a lesson by telling high school students: "Today we are going to learn about plate tectonics and earth structure. Turn to page 113 in your book. Sam, will you read the first paragraph?" and so on. How does this ignite interest in plate tectonics? Instead, imagine beginning the lesson: "Today we are going to learn about plate tectonics and earth structure, but, first, I want you to build a structure that can survive a simulated earthquake. Take the marshmallows, Jell-O, and toothpicks in front of you, and using *all* the materials in front of you, create a structure that will not fall down when I shake the plate" (see Figure 2.1 for instructions for this activity). After much discussion and concentrated effort, one group succeeds and you discuss why it succeeded and others failed. This metacognitive thinking and use of materials the students can identify with leads naturally to questions about how different materials respond to shaking and to why the shaking happens in the first place. This example demonstrates how the teacher forms a big picture and puts the student into a hands-on situation where they can solve a simple problem for themselves and explore the question: Why are some structures more likely to withstand an earthquake than others? From this point, and with student interest and participation, the teacher can begin asking a deeper question: what causes the earthquake in the first place? This leads naturally into a lesson about the earth's structure and the movement of tectonic plates. This could be the lead lesson of a unit on plate tectonics, where you first explore how we react to an earthquake and then explore what actually causes the earthquake. Through the use of meaningful engagement, teachers have hooked the students and piqued their desire to learn more.

JELL-O LESSON INSTRUCTIONS:

1. You have 10 marshmallows, 10 toothpicks, a square of gelatin (3"×3") and a paper plate.

2. The gelatin is your base. Construct a guiding using the toothpicks and marshmallows.

3. Do not pick up the gelatin.

4. Shake your plate from side to side. If your building does not collapse, you are successful!

Figure 2.1 Instructions of the lesson in the text on building and "earthquake" resistant structure.

Another example that would work for math and science would be to go to YouTube and access videos for the 2004 tsunami. Show the videos (which can be quite graphic) and then begin a discussion of what type of wave action could create such a disaster. This could lead into a discussion of wave action and velocity in relation to distance and the amount of destruction. For a math lesson, visit the *Washington Post* Web site (http://www.washingtonpost.com/wp-srv/world/daily/graphics/tsunami_122804.html) and bring up the tsunami in South Asia. There is an excellent map of the wave force, the location of the epicenter for the tsunami, and the number of deaths and the distances from the epicenter at which they took place. This can be used to teach graphing (bar graphs, chart graphs, stem and leaf plots, etc.) or to generate equations that relate wave force and destruction. Both of these examples focus on first developing the issue of why the knowledge is important or relevant before going on to worry about just what knowledge is being taught.

Schleppegrell (2005) discusses how students can learn what happened (observe), how it happened (analyze and interpret), and make a judgment of why it happened (evaluate). As an example in social studies (overheard while observing teachers at Delano High School in Delano, California), a teacher showed a series of videos on the Holocaust. However, the "big question" students had to answer was: "Prepare a list of charges that the Allied Forces would file against the Germans." If this question was followed up by a brief trial, it would be an excellent review lesson, engaging all learners and scaffolding information through the use of relevant visual aids. It also targets one of the main goals of a history class, which is to enable students to write tasks specific to content (see sample lesson in chapter 6 for a full development of this idea).

These anticipatory sets demonstrate a clear purpose for learning, access prior knowledge, use visuals and realia, and encourage student engagement and discussion. Often students are "caught up" with the challenge of the anticipatory set or project and forget that they are actually learning new skills or knowledge.

If the students' purpose for learning is merely to pass the next test, they will likely "memorize and dump" the information, if they bother learning it at all (and haven't we all been tempted to answer the question "Why should I know this?" with "Because you'll be tested on it!"). With a clear purpose for learning developed by a strong anticipatory set, teachers go beyond creating just another lesson to be learned and likely forgotten by the students after (or even worse, before) the test. Teachers need to develop their own anticipatory sets that they are comfortable with and work with their audience. Some basic strategies for developing anticipatory sets and brief examples are provided in Table 2.6.

This situation also demonstrates the effectiveness of giving students the big picture first, breaking it down into smaller pieces, then returning to the

Table 2.6 Strategies for Developing Anticipatory Sets*

Strategy	Details and/or Brief Examples
Link to real life	Start with video of an actual Earthquake to introduce the topic. How many lives could be saved if we could predict them, and what do we need to do for that? Talk about the classic mouse in a Bell-jar experiment to introduce photosynthesis. Films or guest speaker from Vietnam as an introduction to Vietnam conflict.
Link to prior knowledge	Ask some questions that students already know (you think) the answer to, then build the lesson off of what they know. Asking "why" is generally a good strategy. See sample lesson 3.3 in appendix 3.
Gross 'em out	For a lesson on enzyme action, have them collect saliva as a source of amylase. See word-root lesson, chapter 4; Also see "Geek humor", below Bring in "delicacies" from other cultures when studying languages/geography (e.g. serve snails when studying France);
Discrepant events	Demonstrate (or have them do it) things they don't think are possible before lesson. Boil water in a paper cup; follow with a lesson on heat transfer and changes in state. Blow across a piece of paper and watch it move toward the moving air, then a lesson on airplane flight/the Bernouli effect
Challenge activity	Give students materials and challenge them to build a structure that can survive an earthquake/hurricane/tornado/flood/fire: introduce history/impact of disasters. To introduce leverage, challenge the students to figure out a way to lift a heavy mass using only the force of a small mass and a few simple materials. Give them a code-breaking exercise (for example, type a sentence in Wingding font) to introduce translation or military history (i.e. "windtalkers").
Challenge misconceptions	Make a statement out of a common misconception (e.g. "Heavier masses fall faster"). Have students agree or disagree, then discuss.
Humor	Even, maybe even especially, horrible jokes, including "Geek-humor". Work=Force*distance (W=Fd). And force=mass*acceleration. (F=ma) Thus by substitution, W=mad. This explains why work makes you mad. Remember Taxonomy: Dumb Kids Playing Catch On Freeways Get Squashed. (Domain, Kingdom, Phylum, Class, Order, Family, Genus, Species)

(continued)

Table 2.6 Continued

Strategy	Details and/or Brief Examples
Play a game	The game Clue™ is a good intro to the scientific method. A Dradle can be used to introduce *The Diary of Anne Frank*.
Encourage creativity	Have students build a model, write a rap/poem/story, draw a picture, create a puzzle (crossword/word search etc.) relevant to the topic without extensive directions. Make a prop skull to introduce Hamlet. Build simple DNA models from shiny beads as holiday decorations.

*Anticipatory sets should perform one of two main functions (preferably both):
1) Answer or introduce the basic student question "Why should we learn this?" and/or
2) Attempt to capture the student's attention.

big picture (whole to part instruction, chapter 5). For example, in the social studies lesson, the use of certain videos (those which give us an overview of the Holocaust) would provide an opportunity to present the big picture. This stimulus would bring up questions as to why and how the war occurred, which could then be brought back to the big picture, and, in review, a discussion could be developed as to how these events/mistakes could be avoided.

Anticipatory sets can include or inspire critical thinking questions along the lines of Bloom's taxonomy (Bloom & Rathswohl, 1956) which ask: How would you design, develop, generate, explain, document, and interpret? Consider a teacher preparation program. Which classes or training do we learn most from: Lectures and testing or classes/training where we have hands-on activities and relevant projects?

Active Learning and Hands-On Activities

Hands-on activities and active learning are critical for learning to take place (Smith & Wilhelm, 2002). They can also motivate students (see Tables 2.4, 2.5), as well as encourage academic literacy and language use. In the social studies lesson mentioned previously, students would have to look further than the videos to determine all the charges the Allied Forces would have to file against the Germans. This involves guided reading and research by the teacher and students, along with group discussion as to what the students perceived from the video and any reading they have completed. A teacher can only lecture briefly unless they are star comediennes or entertainers who are able to hold the interest of students without asking them to practice what they are learning. Almost all effective learning occurs when participants are actively involved in the learning process.

Modeling and Guided Practice

A powerful method of instruction, after the anticipatory set in a lesson, is for the teacher to model what she or he wants the students to do, guide them through one or more practice sessions, then ask them to work in groups, pairs, or alone to assess their knowledge ("I do it. We do it. You do it"). Again, appropriate use of academic language and guided interpretation of language must occur in order for students to build content knowledge and develop their ability to discuss and write about it. A student, in front of the class, practicing the procedure for solving linear equations states, "You times this by 3 and you plus 4." At this point the teacher interjects and asks, "Is there another way you can say that?" Whereupon the student responds with *multiply* and *add*, using academic language.

Prediction plays a key role in anticipatory sets, hands-on activities, and in modeling and guided practice. Asking students to predict what will happen next is an excellent way to monitor student acquisition of knowledge and their use of academic language. According to Echevarria, Vogt, and Short (2004), prediction also involves clarifying issues and leads to more questions regarding the issues and increased application of academic discourse in the classroom.

We all agree that it takes multiple exposures to learn something. What have we all been taught to do that we have been able to perform perfectly the first time—kissing, cooking, driving a car, riding a bike? Our students need multiple sessions of modeling and guided practice before teachers should assess whether they have learned effectively. The attention span for younger students is probably about 6 to 8 minutes and about 15 minutes for older students. Even as adults, we do not care to sit though hours of lecture, nor does it help our acquisition of knowledge. Thus, the lesson plan should include an anticipatory set to introduce the topic, a short lecture with appropriate vocabulary introduction (next section), multiple modeling and guided practice sessions (preferably with some hands-on component), followed by a pair/group or individual practice for assessment. Of course, for some topics this set of activities needs to be stretched out over several days to effectively cover the entire topic

Summary: What Motivates Students?

As can be seen in the data from our student surveys (Tables 2.1–2.5) students perceive themselves as being motivated by a wide variety of factors, some of which are not under the control of their teachers. However, some broad patterns emerge from these data and the research presented in this chapter that are relevant to what we can do as teachers to motivate students. If we are to motivate students, we need to link lessons to real life, and avoid the sometimes sterile ivory tower mentality of knowledge for knowledge's sake. Strong anticipatory sets can accomplish this well. Whenever possible, connect your lessons to something that students can use in "real-life" not just on the next test. Incorporating hands-on activities in your instruction and giving students a challenge to solve a problem can both make connections to the real world and give students an immediate application for the knowledge and skills you are teaching them. A teacher that is perceived as taking pleasure from the class and material is also a strong motivator for students. A major goal for all teachers should be to provide students with a role model for the enjoyment of learning—think about the teachers who influenced you—were they the miserable, "mean" teachers or the ones who seemed to enjoy themselves in the classroom?

In order for students to succeed at these types of tasks, they need to see someone perform similar, but not identical tasks (if they are just copy you, they lose many of the benefits of hands-on exploration). This is modeling and guided practice, but it must go beyond simple monkey-see, monkey-do modeling and repetition. If you model adding 5 + 5, then ask the student to add 5 and 5, the student is not really applying knowledge, just mimicking. Instead, model how to add, using multiple examples, then have the student practice adding other numbers with feedback before assessing their ability to add (i.e., modeling followed by guided practice before assessment).

Ideally, these strategies work together, and motivation builds. A student who comes to expect interesting and useful activities in class will be more likely to show up regularly and come prepared to be an active participant in your classroom. A well-motivated class tends to have fewer discipline problems, and is more efficient despite the extra time it takes to perform these motivating activities. Finally, and not inconsequentially, the student who is used to getting these types of reinforcement from a teacher will tend to be more forgiving on those occasions—and they happen to everyone—when this doesn't happen.

Additionally, telling students they have to learn a new skill because they need the knowledge in order to perform well in college is not a motivating reason to learn. But if the skill is linked to prior knowledge, real life, and a problem they have to solve, this is engaging, and, as a result, it motivates students. For example, instead of teaching the concept of *area* in math because it is tested on the state standardized test or because students need to know it to get into college, having the students design a 1,000 square foot house or a kennel for their dog which is twice as long as it is wide could be a valid reason (in the student's mind) to learn the skill. Motivated, engaged students are more likely to use the academic language of their content area in their oral discourse and writing and are more likely to acquire a skill which they will then use repeatedly instead of memorizing information for one particular assessment, then never applying it again.

CHAPTER 3

Attributes of Academic Language

This chapter presents a number of strategies or guidelines, which are intended to assist the teacher to emphasize the use of academic language in the classroom. When the use of academic language is facilitated in the classroom it also enhances the acquisition of content-area skills. Here we break down the concept of academic language into actual teaching behaviors, and we finish the chapter by providing an observational checklist for the behaviors which can be a very useful tool in teacher peer coaching. For a view of teachers demonstrating the strategies/behaviors presented in this chapter, please visit the Project CALLI Web site (http://www.csub.edu/calli/).

A major concept within the idea of academic language is the ability to use the appropriate academic *register*. Students use different registers for different types of communication. The spoken academic register for the classroom is more formal than the playground register. Giving a sermon in a church is a more formal register than classroom talk. Text messaging on cell phones or in chat rooms on the Internet is very different from writing a note to a friend, and that in turn is very different from writing a paper in a class. Students need to be able to distinguish the difference between formal and informal registers and use them appropriately both in and out of the classroom. The behaviors identified in this chapter are intended to assist the teacher to develop the student's academic language register.

Receptive and Expressive Language

Academic language literacy can be divided into two categories—receptive language and expressive language. Receptive language can also be classified as deconstructing language, and expressive language as constructing language. When one receives language (receptive language), one listens and reads for understanding: here the process of "breaking the language down" for meaning takes place. On the other hand, when language is expressed, one speaks and writes language to construct and to demonstrate knowledge with that information.

Academic language literacy includes the four domains within receptive and expressive language: listening, speaking, reading, and writing (Figure 3.1). Simply stated, literacy is communication and understanding, both formal and informal. Our job, as teachers, is to use instructional strategies in the classroom that help students to understand and to communicate using the more complex language of schooling: in other words, to develop literacy with academic language. Academic language includes not only written language (e.g., textbooks), but also the language that teachers use to instruct and that students use to communicate with one another in the content area (gossip about each other doesn't count!). Both oral and written language have important roles in communication from teachers to students, from students to teachers, and between students. To encourage the receptive and expressive use of academic language literacy in all content areas, teachers should explicitly use both oral and written language when teaching vocabulary (chapter 4), reading (chapter 5), and writing (chapter 6) within the content area. When we receive language, we are, of course, listening and reading. During this phase we deconstruct language in order to comprehend it. When we express

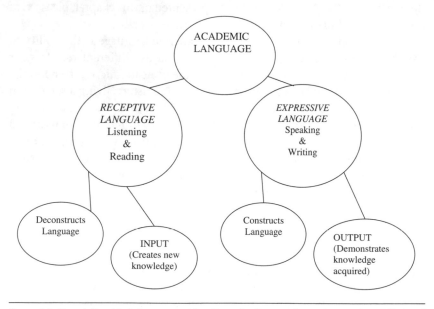

Figure 3.1 The relationship between—and functions of—the receptive and expressive attributes of Academic language including the four domains of language.

language, we are speaking and writing; we have to construct language in order to convey our thoughts and feelings.

When teaching students, we need to be keenly aware of our academic social discourse so as to set the appropriate tone for learning. We are creating new knowledge through teacher discourse and the writing our students read. Our classroom discourse and readings should be sophisticated enough to approximate the demands for understanding in a content area, yet not so difficult that the student does not understand us or the reading. The same holds true for our students' speech and writing. We need to address the instructional level of most of our students, and still challenge them to move out of their comfort zone, or zone of proximal development (Vygotsky, 1978), without reaching their frustration level.

Decades of research have resulted in significant implications about best receptive (listening and reading) and expressive (speaking and writing) vocabulary instructional methods used to support students' literacy development (Echevarria, Vogt, & Short, 2004; Halliday, 1985a; Scarcella, 2003; Scheleppegrel, 2005; Stahl, 1999).

Application of Receptive and Expressive Strategies

For the purpose of developing methodology to transfer the pedagogy of academic language, the authors analyzed this research to determine what teacher and student behaviors would be beneficial to enhance academic language development for all students. From this analysis they also developed a list of traits or attributes which would enable teachers to identify effective instructional strategies in their classrooms. This list delineates specific student and teacher behaviors and instructional strategies to assist students to build their level of academic language in any core-content class. This list of receptive (R) and expressive (E) academic language strategies was initially designed to facilitate implementation of a California Post-Secondary Education Commission (CPEC) grant—project Cognitive Academic Language Literacy Instruction (CALLI). The grant funded a 3-year professional development training program designed to strengthen the academic language skills of math and science students at the high school level. Before implementation of the grant began, the basic components of academic language instructional strategies and classroom behaviors were isolated by the authors in order to compile the receptive and expressive academic language list (Table 3.1). The authors determined, after much research and based on their experience in the field and two successful professional development grant implementations, that if a teacher were to implement these strategies and behaviors in their classroom, they would be successful in delivering academic language as well as content-area skills to their students.

Table 3.1 Academic Literacy in the Content Areas: (CALL Project—Funded by CPEC)

Academic language: a variety or a register of English used in professional books and characterized by the specific linguistic features associated with academic disciplines. (Scarcella, 2003)

- It is the language used by teachers and students for the purpose of acquiring new knowledge and skills.
- It assists in imparting new information, describing abstract ideas, and developing students' conceptual understanding (Chamot and O'Malley, 1994)
- It focuses on understanding, using, and reflecting on written material to develop new knowledge and potential—read to learn and build conceptual knowledge.
- Academic literacy is the use of metacognitive strategies—"thinking about thinking"—using thinking skills to acquire new knowledge.

RECEPTIVE ACADEMIC LANGUAGE	VS.	EXPRESSIVE ACADEMIC LANGUAGE
DECONSTRUCTING LANGUAGE (Analysis of how listening and reading is used to create knowledge for the student)		CONSTRUCTING LANGUAGE (Using speaking and writing to demonstrate knowledge)
R1. Teacher identifies similarities and differences: students and teachers read passages to analyze and organize information		E1. Students identify similarities and differences by discussing comparisons and writing them down on graphic organizers to later expound on information
R2. Teacher guides students through appropriate note-taking and summarization of information (graphic organizers)		E2. Students summarize information using notes and graphic organizers they created
R3. Teacher conducts 'whole to part to whole' instruction: big picture first, then parts, then reassemble		E3. Students experience 'whole to part to whole' instruction and are able to perform appropriate assessments
R4. Teacher uses prior knowledge to create anticipatory sets which capture students' attention		E4. Students create "big questions" or problems to answer regarding the anticipatory set

R5. Teacher models and students (through guided practice) conduct intensive vocabulary development: using affixes, cognates, root words, and context clues to understand text

R6. Teachers ensure that students have multiple exposures to new vocabulary

R7. Teachers conduct text analyses: reviewing subtitles, graphics, titles, predicting and identifying difficult vocabulary

R8. Teachers and students personalize new vocabulary by building the new vocabulary into their background information

E5. Students operationally define words by relating them to steps in a sequence or by using them appropriately in writing

E6. Teachers and Students speak using the appropriate register

E7. Journal writing

E8. Students generate and test hypotheses/math word problems

E9. Students and teachers interact formally and informally to express knowledge

E10. Teachers use higher order questioning strategies to conduct ongoing assessment and students use the appropriate register to answer

E11. Teachers scaffold information to build on prior knowledge

E12. Teachers model corrective feedback for speech and writing

E13. Projects, portfolios, and other assessments are differentiated to match student ability levels

- Teacher has high expectations and gives positive feedback to students when appropriate

The behaviors identified by the authors on this list include listening, speaking, reading, and writing skills with an emphasis on building anticipatory sets, scaffolding and building on prior knowledge, higher order questioning, and thorough vocabulary development. The receptive and expressive instructional strategies apply what we know about how students can deconstruct what they hear and read to create new knowledge, as well as how they can construct new academic language to demonstrate what new knowledge they have acquired. These receptive and expressive strategies were identified by the authors as primary concepts to infuse academic language into content-area instruction.

These strategies include asking the teacher to identify similarities and differences in what they are telling students as well as what they are asking students to read. While teachers and students read passages from texts or other content-area material together, the teacher can assist the students to identify similarities and differences between what they are reading, what their prior experience is, and what they have previously read, in order to analyze and organize information and concepts (Table 3.1; R1), including modeling the development of graphic organizers (R2). After identifying the similarities and differences in the material they have read, it is helpful to not only discuss these comparisons, but also to write them down, either in journals (E7), notebooks, or student-generated graphic organizers (E1). They can then refer back to these organizers to synthesize and summarize information in their writing (E2).

Other effective instructional practices include the following: when introducing a new concept or skill, the teacher identifies the big picture (R3, E3). The instruction begins with the big picture where students generate questions and predict answers and then the teacher continues to review the parts, followed by a summary of the big picture. We call this instruction "whole to part to whole," and this concept informs several of the strategies (R3, R4, E3, E4, and E8). Think of introducing a group of young children to the concept of any food product produced from a recipe. If you give young children flour, salt, butter, sugar, milk, and cubed bitter chocolate and ask them if they like the product, they will probably tell you "no," especially if they try to taste the chocolate. However, if you give them a brownie to eat, then show them the ingredients and the procedure for baking the brownie, they will, more than likely, be more eager to participate in the baking process This is an example of using an anticipatory set (R4, see chapter 2) and whole to part to whole instruction. Asking students to create big questions (E4), such as guessing at the quantities involved in the brownie recipe and what the procedures for baking brownies would be (E8), is also extremely beneficial in building their academic language. Students should respond by using precise language in the appropriate classroom register. "A little bit of butter and a lot of chocolate" will not produce an edible brownie. This is an appropriate lesson for both the math and science content areas as students learn the quantities of the ingredients and the effects of mixing the ingredients and adding heat to them. The teacher could also tap into the students' prior knowledge by asking them to describe the taste of chocolate and then perhaps by asking several students to taste the baking chocolate (horribly bitter!). Building captivating anticipatory sets for lessons not only motivates students to participate, but also keeps them engaged throughout the lesson, accesses their prior knowledge, scaffolds information (E11), builds their academic language, and facilitates acquisition of new knowledge. Negotiation of how to make the brownies constitutes oral discussion among students which, if monitored properly by the teacher, also increases oral academic language (E9). Asking one group of students to explain the steps or procedure in a science experiment, using newly acquired academic vocabulary, and then requesting that they write the instructions down for another group to use certainly would constitute reinforcement of academic language in the content-area classroom (E5).

Another set of strategies for building academic language is involved in intensive vocabulary development (R5, R6, R8, and E5). Here the teacher ensures that students are able to recognize root words, affixes, and cognates of words (R5), in addition to being able to use that knowledge to ascertain the meaning of unknown words when presented in written context. To assist in the acquisition of academic vocabulary (see chapter 4), students also experience multiple exposures to new words (R6); they learn to personalize new vocabulary by building the new vocabulary into their background information (R8), and they learn to operationalize new vocabulary by using the new words appropriately in speaking and writing (E5).

Ensuring that students use the appropriate classroom register in their speaking (E6) necessitates thoughtful modeling and guided practice through interaction between teacher and student using the appropriate register (E9). When observing students in a math classroom to ascertain the level of academic language used, one of the students was standing in front of the class, explaining the procedure for a math problem. The second time the student said, "And you times this number…," the teachers responded with: "Can you give me a more accurate word instead of 'times'?" To which the student responded, "And then you multiply…"—a good example of monitoring the use of academic language in the classroom with appropriate modeling of corrective feedback (E12). We have also heard teachers (and ourselves) say, "Today we are going to learn all this *stuff*…."—not exactly appropriate modeling of the correct academic language register in the classroom. We certainly wouldn't use the word *stuff* in a formal speech (E6).

When we take the time to preview a chapter before reading it, we also assist students in acquiring academic language. During the review process, a text analysis, where teachers review such elements as the subtitles, graphics, and bold face text would be an excellent chapter preview and text analysis (R7). During the text analysis, the teacher calls attention to those organizational pieces of a chapter which are highlighted (bold or italicized text, subheadings, chapter titles, pictures, etc.) and asks the students to either turn a phrase into a question or ask a question about a picture. These questions then become the big questions (R3 & E4) as students pair/share sections of the text (students each read a different section of the text and then discuss what they have read) to find the answers. Predicting answers to the questions, or predicting what occurs next in the text, builds student engagement along with the development of academic language. This practice also assists the teacher in discovering what vocabulary the students are having difficulty with, whether brick or mortar words (academic vocabulary or frequent use signal words; see chapter 6). At the same time teachers are then building their awareness of what big questions can lead the theme for a possible portfolio or project which will be conducted at the end of the unit to reinforce newly acquired knowledge (E13). This practice can serve as a useful guide for determining student ability level and thus help the teacher decide what type of project her or his students are capable of, and what modifications will need to be made to accommodate the struggling learners in the class, in addition to reinforcing the use of academic language.

Inherent in the process of teaching content skills is the ability of the teacher to use higher order questioning strategies for comprehension monitoring, while monitoring student responses for the appropriate academic register (E10). The authors have found that it is not easy, even in the college classroom to avoid the inevitable "Does everyone understand?" or "Do you have any questions?" Even asking students to list attributes or recall facts does not really inform us as to whether they haves actually acquired the concept or not. As we move higher up on Bloom's taxonomy in our level of questioning, we also increase our students' use of academic language (Bloom & Rathswohl, 1956). Asking students to rephrase a concept is above the knowledge level (comprehension level) but still not at the analysis level. By simply asking a student to explain why it is not possible for something to occur we have moved up to the analysis stage of Bloom's taxonomy, and we have determined at what level they have been able to comprehend the concept we have just taught—all by increasing their receptive and expressive academic language skills.

Of course, you cannot expect to use all 21 of the strategies outlined in Table 3.1 in every lesson. Each lesson should focus on some of these, while a few strategies (e.g., E6, E9) we would hope to see most of the time. Ideally, over the course of a unit, students would experience all of the strategies multiple times, as appropriate for the content being studied.

Professional Input and Feedback for Academic Language Literacy Instruction

During the implementation of Project CALLI the authors also developed a classroom observation protocol to determine if the participating teachers were actually displaying behaviors in their classrooms which would assist in the development of academic language. The grant required a research component to examine the effectiveness of the professional development training conducted by grant personnel. This observation feedback form was one method we used (see Table 3.2).

This form is divided into four parts: vocabulary, listening and speaking, integrated reading and writing, and basic instructional strategies. It includes all the behaviors on the Es and Rs list, with some additional behaviors/strategies which we felt would support academic language acquisition. Included are behaviors such as the percent of teacher/student talk, noting the occurrence of student/student interaction, giving clear directions, and ongoing checking for understanding. The integrated reading/writing discusses preformatted essays and short sentences, as well as math word problems and science lab reports. If many of the behaviors identified on the Rs and Es list are observed, then we should also expect to find cooperative grouping, differentiated assessment, and assessment that informs curriculum (basic instructional strategies) present in the classroom.

Cook Hirai and Garza used the feedback form to observe math and science teachers in a semirural high school district in California (this was our collaborating Local Education Agency for the Project CALLI grant) for three consecutive years (2006–2008). We were able to make some preliminary conclusions *based on anecdotal data only*.

The first year we observed teachers (before any substantial professional development had begun) we noticed that the teachers probably modeled less than half of the behaviors listed on the feedback form. There appeared to be very little vocabulary development except for the typical list of new words which students were to look up and memorize. Listening and speaking were evident, but the percentage of teacher/student talk was mostly 90% teacher and 10% student, with students answering mostly knowledge-level questions. The students were performing some writing exercises, but they were mostly just to fill in practice sheets. Notes were taken, as dictated by the teacher or copied from the overhead projector. There was little to no cooperative grouping or pair/share, and we observed mostly paper and pencil assessments which were not differentiated to meet the needs of struggling students.

Over the next 3 years we observed the targeted behaviors begin to increase most notably within the areas of intensive vocabulary development as we witnessed teachers carefully explain root words, cognates, and affixes. We

Table 3.1 Professional Input and Feedback for Academic Literacy Instructions

DATE_____   SUBJECT/GRADE_____

☑	STRATEGY	EVIDENCE	☑	STRATEGY	EVIDENCE
///	**VOCABULARY:**	/////////////////////	☑	**INTEGRATED READING /WRITING:**	/////////////////////////
	Intensive Vocabulary Development (Roots, Cognates, affixes etc.)		//	Pre-Write Short Sentences, Paragraphs then essays or fill in Preformatted Essays/ Paragraphs (for ELLs)	
	Multiple Exposures to New Vocabulary			Use of Graphic Organizers	
	Pre-Reading for Vocabulary Development			Expository Writing: Outlining Summarizing, Comparing, Etc.	
	Personalizing New Vocabulary (Background information)			Writing Math Word Problems, Science Lab Reports	
	Operationally Defining New Vocabulary (Hands-on experience with the words)			Text Analysis Including Syntax Analysis and Vocabulary: Deconstructing Academic Language (Clause Level)	
	Academic Word List			Listening & Note-Taking	
	Appropriate Register			Journal Writing	

///	LISTENING & SPEAKING:	/////////////////////	//	BASIC INSTRUCTIONAL STRATEGIES:	/////////////////////
	Listening, Reading and Writing Sources of Academic Language Material Readily Available to Students in the Classroom			Appropriate Modeling & Student Guided Practice Students model appropriate academic language (vs. social) register	
	Questioning Strategies: Higher Order LSRW			Accessing Prior Knowledge/ Scaffolding	
	Students Appropriately Explain, Persuade, Respond Orally (Formal & Informal) (Expressive Language & Constructing Language)			Teacher uses prior knowledge to create motivating anticipatory sets which link content to real life experiences	
	Presenting, Classifying, Demonstrating, Giving Clear Directions (Teacher/Student)			Cooperative Grouping Used to Practice Academic Lang.	
	Percent of teacher/student talk			Students predict and summarize	
	Student to Student Interaction			Differentiated Instruction, including alternative assessments (projects, portfolios, etc.)	
	Ongoing checking for understanding			Teacher models corrective feedback for speech and writing	

√+ (Observed & Effective), √ (Observed), √- (Not Observed, but could be inserted in the lesson), N (Not observed, but could be evident in another lesson)

©Dr. D. L. Cook Hirai, California State University, Bakersfield, 2009 also observed most teachers offering multiple exposures to the vocabulary in the way of games and work sheets. Students were observed personalizing and operationalizing the academic vocabulary (chapter 4) in formal presentations and in class discussions. We still did not observe formal academic word lists, but we did observe teachers and students using a more formal register, especially in the science classes.

Although some content reading material (other than the textbook) was a bit more evident in the science classrooms by year 3, the lack of material led us to reconsider the importance of exhibiting this behavior due to the economic restrictions in many classrooms today. There appeared to be a more even distribution of teacher/student talk, perhaps weighted more on the student side, with more student/student interaction because teachers were very careful not only to give very clear directions themselves, but also to monitor student discussions to ensure that the students were also using the appropriate academic register in content classes. The academic level of questions increased markedly as most teachers appeared to request more explanations and less knowledge-level questions.

We observed fairly extensive use of graphic organizers, preformatted essays and notebooks for lab reports, journals and class notes in the science classes, but still little to no text analysis, although this could have occurred on occasions when we were not in the classrooms. Expository writing, in general, was increased.

In the category of basic instructional strategies we observed a marked increase in cooperative grouping, the use of engaging anticipatory sets and differentiated assessment, particularly in the science classrooms. Science and math teachers seemed to be more aware of modeling for students, along with guided practice (in lieu of only using direct instruction) with science teachers appearing to be more cognizant of accessing prior knowledge for students. During the first observation we observed that all teachers consciously used scaffolding when presenting their lessons and that they also had high expectations for their students.

Each succeeding year that we observed, we saw more of the behaviors modeled, with science teachers appearing to model more of the behaviors than math teachers. We also observed another interesting trend (Garza & Mata, 2008)—achievement scores for science students increased on the California state standardized test over the 3-year period of the grant. This increase in achievement, along with our observations, is indicative that the types of behaviors isolated and emphasized in the Rs and Es list and on the professional input feedback form were, indeed, behaviors that could possibly be those that (1) represent effective use of academic language in the content-area classroom, and (2) represent effective instruction in that they contribute to an increase in student achievement.

The correlation between use of the strategies (science teachers used them more than math teachers) and increases in student achievement (student scores in science improved more than scores in math) strongly supports this conclusion.

Summary

That is not to say that it will take 3 years for teachers to acquire and display these behaviors and strategies. We cite the aforementioned information from our grant to demonstrate the link between teachers emphasizing the use of the Es and Rs strategies and increased student achievement. We developed the list and the professional input form as a guide to drive our professional development training in the quest of our grant objective: Increase the use of academic language strategies in math and science classrooms in order to increase student achievement. As the grant progressed, however, we realized that the Es and Rs list and the corresponding professional input form were fairly accurate descriptors of what academic language should look like in the form of instructional strategies in the classroom. Teachers given the opportunity to acquire these strategies and behaviors (note that we say "acquire," not "learn" as in the Krashen definition of acquisition vs. learning; 1993), and the time to collaborate with other teachers in their field will most likely see an increase in student achievement in their classrooms. The Es and Rs professional input feedback form can be used as a self-checklist or as a rubric to guide peer coaching to monitor your teaching of academic language and that of your peers.

Schleppegrell (2004, p. 74), refers to the expressive features of academic language literacy in the classroom: simply displaying knowledge requires less sophisticated knowledge of grammar than to "be authoritative" (in interpersonal conversation, summarizing or explaining) or "to structure text in expected ways" (see Figure 3.2).

Using the appropriate register for expressive and receptive language in the content area is challenging, but its use is in the students' best interest for the sake of appropriate academic and social communication. The challenge we face is making language comprehensible and accessible to the student, yet difficult enough to move students on to a higher level of thinking. We want to challenge students; we don't want to frustrate them. When teachers accomplish this and differentiate their teaching methods and assessments to meet different levels of language and student learning, teachers will ensure active student engagement in the learning process.

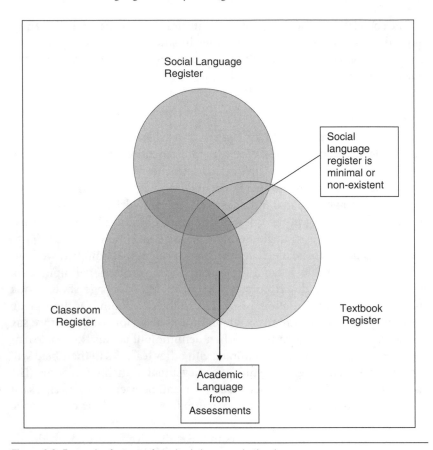

Figure 3.2 Expressive features of academic language in the classroom.

CHAPTER 4

Vocabulary
Theory and Practice

Vocabulary is the basis for the development of language. Very simply put, without knowing the vocabulary of a language, higher level language use (grammar, syntax, expository writing) is difficult, if not impossible. Each academic discipline has its own register and its own vocabulary, so developing the vocabulary of your students within their discipline is a key part of their education within the discipline. In this chapter we will explore ideas behind the development of vocabulary, and look at the research on effective strategies of vocabulary instruction. We will provide a brief inventory of sample strategies for vocabulary instruction, and finally present a model lesson plan, using it to demonstrate some of these strategies, and explain how the vocabulary instruction suggested in this chapter can help students achieve academic language literacy.

Developing Vocabulary

Children are avid developers of vocabulary. Within the first few years of life, children develop impressive vocabularies without the need for direct instruction (Table 4.1, Krashen, 1982), and evidence shows that adults can also perform remarkable feats of language development without the need for explicit instruction (Krashen, 2004).

Why Teach Vocabulary?

Some evidence even indicates that direct vocabulary instruction is less effective than implicit instruction (Krashen & Terrell, 1983). Krashen (1993, p. 22), when referring to free and voluntary reading, states: "...Reading is a powerful means of developing literacy, of developing reading, comprehension ability, writing style, vocabulary, grammar and spelling. Direct instruction is not." According to Greenwood (2002, p. 258), "Looking up words in a dictionary or committing definitions to memory leads to at best a superficial understanding and rapid forgetting of words [Mckeown, 1993]. Yet this activity (look it up, define it, use it in an original sentence) is a daily occurrence in thousands of classrooms." On the other hand, current best practices advocated by Marzano, Pickering, and Pollock (2001) on academic achievement and literacy show that explicit instruction is important. Incidental or other types of nonteacher directed instruction are not the most effective strategy for teaching *academic* literacy. Explicit and direct instruction is extremely important for student success in understanding key vocabulary and concepts. How do we explain this apparent contradiction?

The first thing we must realize is that these studies are comparing apples and oranges. The studies showing large language increases with implicit methods (usually free and voluntary reading) commonly focus on general language skills: the development of basic fluency in either young children or second-language learners. Studies that show the importance of explicit instruction tend to focus on the development of more technical uses of languages. In other words, implicit instruction works well for developing important basic language skills, a more informal register of language, while as the register becomes more formal (i.e., more academic), explicit vocabulary instruction becomes more important.

Vocabulary is a vital factor in the total comprehension process for reading. The National Reading Panel found, from analyzing the results of several hundred studies, that vocabulary was one of five key elements to becoming

---

- The English language has approximately 5 million words.
- The average child enters school knowing approximately, 5,000 to 6,000 words.
- Children learn 2,500–5,200 new words per year. Some learn 8–10 words per day; other 1–2, depending on variables such socioeconomic status
- Over 12 years of school, children learn another 36,000 words.
- It takes 10 exposures to a word to learn it.
- There are 110,000 words in printed school materials.
- Vocabulary is the most important influence on reading comprehension, which relates to academic achievement; the more words a child knows—the better the achievement.

Figure 4.1 Vocabulary fast facts.

a good reader (Dougherty-Stahl, 2005): The other four key elements are phonological awareness, phonics, fluency, and comprehension.

Vocabulary development is a major area of concentration for most academic language researchers and theorists. Chamot and O'Malley (1994), Schleppegrell (2005), and Echevarria, Vogt, and Short (2004) all emphasize vocabulary as a key area of academic language. Biemiller and Slonim (2001) cite evidence that the lack of vocabulary is a major indicator for school failure of disadvantaged students. As teachers work to close this achievement gap, they must remember that vocabulary is a major component of academic achievement across the content areas.

Most teachers have not placed enough emphasis on appropriate vocabulary development in their instruction. They assume that students have a much higher level of understanding and comprehension than they actually do. The 10 to 20 vocabulary words assigned each week to be memorized for a quiz at the end of the week do not meet the needs of struggling readers (Beck & McKeown, 1993). Teachers have relied largely on teaching vocabulary through sustained silent reading and other independent reading (Krashen, 1993; Cunningham, & Stanovich, 1998). This has not proven to be the most effective strategy for all children (Baker, Simmons, & Kame'enui, 1995), especially content-area specific vocabulary.

A flurry of vocabulary research has been conducted since Becker's (1977) observations regarding the relationship between vocabulary knowledge and academic achievement with the following results:

- First, due to the fact that vocabulary and reading are closely related, the highly publicized concern about declining literacy levels has affected the way we teach vocabulary (implicit vs. direct or explicit instruction). Rote memorization has been emphasized in an attempt to focus on skills-based instruction, but the research supports a move away from rote memorization and toward context-based vocabulary acquisition (Adams, 1990).
- Second, as Beck and McKeown (1991) observed, "the shift to an information-processing orientation in psychology...provided rich theory from which to draw in conceiving the relationship between words and ideas" (p. 790). Research in vocabulary and literacy demonstrates that building knowledge requires more than accumulating facts about specific elements, such as word definitions. Most struggling reader strategies have involved this method and often these students have failed to become better readers.
- Third, according to Beck and McKeown's (1991) comments about building knowledge, the shift in education from emphasizing basic skills— such as defining vocabulary words—to emphasizing problem-solving

and higher-order thinking skills has resulted in additional research directed toward understanding language and vocabulary acquisition within the context of prior knowledge and constructivist viewpoints. Lessons should stress a constructivist approach that links student's prior knowledge with new information and creates opportunities for applying this new learning.

Knowing a word for any content area requires that the student can recognize it and use it in novel contexts. Constructing meaning for a text requires knowledge of the word in combination with other types of knowledge. It is important to understand that knowing a word means knowing how to do things with it, not just how to write its definition (Nagy & Scott, 2000).

For example, in the realms of science and social studies, the word *expose* will have entirely different meanings. "The body was exposed to the burning sun and other elements for so long, it was unrecognizable." Or, "This historian was exposed to school for 12 years, yet he could not read or write in an understandable fashion, even though he could quote history, fact for fact" (see Table 4.1 for interesting facts regarding vocabulary acquisition).

In summary, the research for vocabulary development and academic literacy demonstrates that there are strategies both in the decoding and understanding of words/concepts which help with overall student achievement (Beck & McKeown, 1991; Becker, 1977).

Learning and Acquisition: The Importance of Multiple Exposures

Dougherty-Stahl (2005) emphasizes that, after explicit direct instruction on vocabulary, students need multiple exposures to a word if they are to acquire its meaning. This raises the distinction between learning and acquiring vocabulary.

Language learning is formal and explicit; language acquisition is informal, involves communication, and is implicit (Krashen, 1982, p. 26). Acquisition is unconscious learning and thereby requires multiple exposures (Table 4.1). The more often students are exposed to vocabulary the more rapidly they will acquire the meaning and use the word when communicating in the content-area classroom. When we look at the dichotomy from the previous section in this light, we can see that frequency of encounter with vocabulary is a crucial difference between the implicit acquisition of the "common" register skills by children and second-language learners and the more specialized vocabulary needed to be fluent in the academic register.

High frequency words (from *a*, *an*, *the*, to *substances*, *arrived*, and *located*, etc.) are acquired easily due to the number of times a student is exposed to them, unlike low frequency academic words. Frank May (May & Rizzardi, 2002) states that we have over half of a million words to work with and half

Table 4.1 Learning vs. Acquisition

Learning	Acquisition
Conscious	Subconscious
Explicit, direct instruction	Implicit, multiple exposures
Uses formal grammar rules	Uses language acquisition device (LAD)
Depends on aptitude	Depends on affective filter, attitude
Faster to learn & forget	Longer to learn, longer lasting

of what we read and write uses just 0.02% of those words: roughly the 100 most frequently used words. Manzo, Manzo, and Albee (2004) stipulate that students need more instruction in how to decipher low frequency words. Part of the rationale for this, like it or not, is that standardized tests contain more low frequency words than most of the material a student would find in the typical classroom, and certainly more than they encounter in their everyday lives. However, a more important rationale is that understanding of our academic disciplines really requires the acquisition of those low frequency words that are important within the discipline.

Low frequency words are, by the very fact that they are low frequency, more difficult for students to acquire. Although teaching vocabulary is perceived as a relatively easy task, it is relegated in many classes to the presentation of a list of vocabulary words assigned to be memorized for a quiz at the end of the week. This addresses only the learning phase, not the acquisition phase. Acquisition of a word means knowing how to do things with it, not just memorizing a definition temporarily. As Nagy and Scott (2000) stated, "A person who knows a word can recognize it, and use it, in novel contexts, and uses knowledge of the word, in combination with other types of knowledge, to construct meaning for a text" (p. 273).

Guided and independent practice builds background knowledge, provides multiple exposures, and helps students develop specific strategies for contextual and structural analysis. Together, these improve students' abilities to infer meanings from words. These strategies also help students develop independence in solving word problems, thus increasing their potential for incidentally learning the huge number of new words they encounter in school texts (Baumann et al., 2002). The ability to effectively apply words academically depends on metalinguistic sophistication which can be fostered by teachers who assist students by thinking aloud, modeling, and guiding until effective learning strategies become automatic. The root-word sample activity presented at the end of this chapter explicitly uses thinking aloud, modeling, and guided practice with a strategy for constructing meaning from new words. Repetition in different contexts provides the opportunity for the skill of constructing meaning from novel combinations to develop into a more automatic process. Students need explicit instruction to understand what strong readers do when they encounter unknown words; this metacognitive strategy (thinking about thinking) will enable them to decipher the meaning of unknown words. They will then realize that they too are capable of using appropriate strategies as they read material with which they are not completely familiar.

According to Griswold (1987), students who knew more word meanings prior to studying unknown words learned the meanings of more new words after studying and using metacognitive strategies. The authors suggested that "prior knowledge contributes more to vocabulary learning than memorization strategies as they are typically defined" (p. 625). The results of this study have implications for the timing of vocabulary interventions, and the importance of explicitly highlighting the semantic associations between words, as one method to help students build background knowledge.

On a related theme, Chomsky (1959) introduced the concept of the language acquisition device (LAD), which he describes as a processor in our minds that enables us to unconsciously acquire correct usage of grammar. Through multiple uses of grammatical forms and functions, one learns how to speak and write correctly. This is also a major component in acquiring or losing a local dialect or accent (the way words are pronounced in different parts of the country).

The first settlers who eventually established the 13 colonies, settling along the eastern side of the country, all migrated from different parts of Europe, thus, they all had different accents or ways of pronouncing the English language. Today, if one travels 60 miles in any direction throughout the Eastern states, one can find a completely different accent or dialect. As our people moved West, accents and people began to merge, and we begin to see a pattern of larger regional dialects, such as the Midwestern "twang" and the Texas "drawl," instead of localized accents. When settlers finally reached the West coast, the population was so mixed that the distinction between some of the different accents was lost. If our LAD is strong and we like the way someone speaks, either the context of what they say or the way they pronounce the word, they may influence us subconsciously to speak with the same pattern. One interesting pattern that has developed as a result of this process is that while newscasters across the country use the standard "West Coast" accent, weather announcers usually speak with the local accent.

Notice again the importance of repeated exposures: without repeated exposure to others using a particular accent, people tend to lose an accent over time, acquiring the local accent—although a return "home" or a visit from someone still speaking the accent (renewed exposure) can often result in a rapid return to the previous accent. If you consider the academic register of language to be just another accent or dialect, the relationship becomes clear between the LAD and the idea of multiple exposures necessary to acquire language. Thus, while implicit instruction is sufficient for everyday fluency due to the abundant opportunities for repeated exposure in different contexts, academic language literacy requires more explicit instruction to provide similar opportunities for repeated exposure to the low frequency words, phrases, and structures associated with academic discourse and our measures of academic competency. Our job as teachers is to provide our students with multiple exposures to this language to help them develop academic language literacy. Later in this chapter we will provide strategies for doing this.

Cognates, Root Words, and Affixes

In English, as in many other languages, complex words are often built by combining simpler, more commonly used words. The meanings of the more complex words are then constructed from the meanings of the simpler words. Some words, called root words, generally form the main part of these more complex words, while other words, the affixes, are usually associated with either the beginning of a complex word (prefixes) or the end of the word (suffixes). Of course, we must also acknowledge the "sloppiness" of English in this area, as root words are sometimes used as prefixes and suffixes, and some have multiple meanings which require context to determine, but the general concept remains, and can be a powerful tool to use in extracting meaning from language. Table 4.3 provides a simple strategy for extracting meaning from words using roots and affixes.

As a simple example, the root word *tract* means to pull or drag. When combined with the prefix *ex-* which means "out," we get the meaning of the word *extract*, to pull out, as in the phrase "...extract meaning from language" above. Combined with the prefix *con*, meaning "with," we get to pull with, or come together; of course contract is a word that depends on context: in law, a contract is a document used for two parties to "come together" in agreement, while in science, if something contracts, it is "coming together" by getting smaller. The root word *tract* can be combined with many prefixes and suffixes to develop a variety of meanings, each of which you can extract using knowledge of the meanings of the specific affixes used. We present a small sample of root words and affixes in Tables 4.3 and 4.4 which can provide the knowledge necessary to extract meaning from a large number of words frequently used in content areas.

It is estimated that over two-thirds of our content-area vocabulary (academic language) comes from Latin and Greek roots (Goulden, Nation, & Reed, 1990). Think about how much easier it would be if students could, at the very least, approximate the meaning of the word simply by knowing what the root of the word meant (Table 4.2). Knowledge of common roots

Table 4.2 Strategies for Understanding Academic Language with Affixes

1. Refer to tables 4.3 & 4.4 on Greek and Latin roots and affixes.
2. Remove affixes—whether prefix or suffix.
3. Check to see if a word that makes sense remains.
4. Think about the meaning of the root word and the affixes
5. Combine meaning of root word with affixes and see if you can infer the meaning of the word.
6. Try out the meaning of the unknown word in a sentence and see if makes sense. If it does, keep reading; if not use another strategy to decipher the word

and affixes can assist the student with deconstructing words to determine their meaning.

The four prefixes *un* (not), *re* (again), *in* (in), and *dis* (not) are very common and can help students figure out the meaning of over 1,500 words. When teaching morphemes to help students build meanings for words, it is

Table 4.3 Sample Root Words

Word	Meaning	Example	Word	Meaning	Example
Act	Do	Actor	Logos	Speech, Science	Logotype
Acro	Air	Airplane	Mar	Sea	Seaside
Agr	Field	Agrarian	Mania	Madness	Manic
Ann	Year	Annual	Miss, mit	Send	Transmit, mission
Aqua	Water	Aquatic	Micro	Small	Microscope
Aud	Hear	Audience	Migr	Change, Move	Migrate
Bene	Well	Beneficial	Mob, Mot, Mov	Move	Movie
Bi	Two	Biannual	Mono	One	Monosyllabic
Biblio	Book	Bibliography	Mortis	Death	Mortal
Bio	Life	Biography	Not	Note, Mark	Note
Card, Cord	Heart	Cardiovascular	Octa	Eight	Octagon
Cede, Ceed	Go, yield	Recede	Opt	Visible	Optical
Cept	Take	Accept	Ora	Speech	Orator
Chron	Time	Chronology`	Ortho	Straight, Correct	Orthodontist
Circum	Around, about	Circumference	Ped	Foot	Pedestrian

Word	Meaning	Example	Word	Meaning	Example
Cogn	Know	Cognitive	Phob	Fear	Claustrophobia
Credo	To believe	Credible	Phone	Sound, Voice	Microphone
Cycle	Circle	Recycle	Photo	Light	Photograph
Div	Separate	Divide	Polis	City	Metropolis
Dem	People	Democracy	Poly	Much	Polyglot
Dent	Tooth	Dentist	Pon, Pos, Posit	Place, Put	Deposit, Position
Derm	Skin	Dermatologist	Porto	Carry	Portable
Dict	Tell, Say	Predict	Primus	First	Primary
Doc	Teach	Document	Psych	Mind, Spirit	Psychic
Duc	Lead	Conduct	Quest	Ask, seek	Question
Equi	Equal	Equilateral	Rupt	To Break	Interrupt
Fer	Carry	Transfer, Ferry	Schola	School	Scholar
Flect, Flex	Bend	Genuflect	Scrib, Script	Write	Prescribe
Flu	Flow	Fluctuate	Scopoe	See	Telescope
Form	Shape	Formula	Sens, Sent	Feel	Sensitive
Fract, Frag	Break	Interrupt	Sophos	Wise, Clever	Sophisticated
Funct	Perform	Function	Spec, Spect	Lok	Spectator
Gen	Birth	Generation	Tain, Ten, Tent	Hold	Contain, Attention
Geo	Earth	Geologist	Tele	Far, Distant	Telephone
Grad	Step, Stage	Graduate, Gradual	Theo	God	Theology
Gram	Letter, Written	Grammar	Therm	Heat	Thermometer
Graph	To Write	Paragraph	Turb	Confusion	Disturb
Homo, Hom	Man	Homogeneous	Utilis	Useful	Utility
Heteros	Other	Heterogeneous	Var	Different	Variety, Vary
Hydro	Water	Hydroplane	Ven, Vent	Come	Convention
Ignis	Fire	Igneous	Video	See	Videotape
Loc	Place	Location	Voc	Voice, Call	vocabulary
Log	Reason, Study	Biology			

probably best to begin with these four prefixes because students have probably already encountered them frequently. Once students are comfortable with these four, you can teach some of the less common prefixes. See table on "Understanding Academic Language with Affixes" (Table 4.2).

In addition, because these roots are so common, they are also frequently encountered, and so they are relatively easy to learn if the student is aware of them and the different forms they can take. Similarly, word cognates from other languages (see appendix 6) can serve as a key bridge when dealing with English learners, especially those speaking a language derived from Latin.

Table 4.4 Common Prefixes

Prefix	Meaning	Examples	Prefix	Meaning	Examples
A	From	Absent	Kilo	Thousand	Kilometer
After	After	Afternoon	Micro	Small, Short	Microphone
Ante	Before	Antecedent	Mon, Mono	One	Monorail
Auto	Against	Antiwar	Multi	Much, Many	Multicolored
Bi, Bin	Two	Bicycle	On	On	Ongoing
Cent	Hundred	Century	Over	Too Much	Overactive
Circu	Around	Circumference	Pent	Five	Pentagon
Co	Together	Cooperate	Poly	Many	Polygon
Con	With	Confer	Post	After	Postpone
De	Away From	Deduct	Pre	Before	Prefix
Dec	Ten	Decade	Pro	Forward	Progress
Deci	Ten	Decimal	Quadr	Four	Quarter
Dis	Opposite	Disagree	Quint	Five	Quintuplet
Du	Two	Duet	Semi	Half	Semicircle
E	Out of	Exit	Sex	Six	Sextet
En	In, At	Enter	Tele	Distant	Telephone
Extra	Outside	Extraordinary	Tetra	Four	Tetrahedron
Hemi	Hale	Hemisphere	Trans	Across	Transfer
Hept	Seven	Heptagon	Tri	Three	Tricycle
Hex	Six	Hexagon	Un	Opposite	Undo
Inter	Among, Between	Interrupt	Under	Below	Underneath
Intro	Beginning	Introduce	Uni	One	Unite
Ir	Not	Irregular			

We can address the language needs of the rising number of English learners in our classrooms by indicating which vocabulary words are cognates. In fact, many affixes and root words are Latin based, and often share meanings important in Spanish, French, Italian, and English—especially academic English. For example, in Spanish the prepositions *a* (to), *de* (from), *en* (in), and *con* (with) are common prefixes in English and have synonymous meanings in both languages. Many content vocabulary words with Latin or Greek roots are cognates in these and other languages (Fry, Kress, & Fountoukidis, 2000). This is particularly true in the sciences, where a knowledge of Greek and Latin roots is crucial for academic language literacy for all students, not just English learners.

Another important skill which students can use to acquire academic language is to look at context clues in sentences and paragraphs. Context clues (Table 4.5) include transition words (*first, second, third,* etc.), signal words and conjunctions (e.g., *this way, these, like, such, or, for, but, since, although, because,* etc.) adjectives, adverbs, and clauses which relate to the unfamiliar word in the context (*whose, whom, which means,* etc.), repetition of words, compare and contrast references, synonyms, antonyms, and inferences which tap into students' prior knowledge (Richardson, Morgan, & Fleener, 2006). When students are taking formal assessments, dictionaries or glossaries are typically not available to them. If they have acquired the knowledge of root words, cognates, affixes, and context clues, they will be better equipped to attempt to understand prompts, especially on standardized tests, rather than "hit the wall" and give up. These skills are also of tremendous value to build academic language literacy.

Learning new vocabulary by analyzing the cognates, root words, and affixes reduces the need to tell students to "Look it up in the dictionary." Research indicates that looking up word meanings in a dictionary has minimal impact on learning academic language (McKeown, 1993). Yet this activity ("Look it up, define it, use it in a sentence") is a daily occurrence in thousands of classrooms. There are two problems with definitions—a context-reduced activity—as a way to learn new words: (1) definitions do not necessarily contain enough information (especially context) to allow for complete understanding and ease of use; and (2) often a person must know a word to understand the definition. Miller and Gildea (1987) concluded that looking up words in the dictionary and then writing them in sentences was "pedagogically useless." Although studies indicate that some intervention is better than none, rote memorization of words and definitions is a minimally effective instructional method, resulting in little long-term effects on learning (Baker, Simmons, & Kame'enui, 1995; Kame'enui, Dixon, & Carine, 1987).

Knowledge of a word involves more than lifting its meaning from context or reading its meaning in a dictionary. True word knowledge involves a

Table 4.5 Signal Words for Context Clues

WORDS WHICH SIGNAL LOCATION:

above	around	between	inside	outside
across	behind	by	into	over
against	below	down	near	throughout
along	beneath	in back of	off	to the right
among	beside	in front of	under	on top of

WORDS WHICH SIGNAL COMPARE/CONTRAST:

after all	also	although	as	at the same time
beside	but	different	even though	instead of
however	in the same way		like	likewise
on the contrary	on the other hand		otherwise	nevertheless
rather than	similarly		such as	though
whereas	yet	still		

WORDS WHICH SIGNAL TIME:

about	after	afterward	at	after a few days
as soon as	before	during	finally	first
in the meantime	later	meanwhile	next	second
soon	then	third	today	tomorrow
until	when			

WORDS WHICH EMPHASIZE OR SUMMARIZE:

accordingly	again	above	along with	and
another	also	as a result	as well	because
besides	consequently	due	equally	finally
for example	for instance	for this reason	further	furthermore
hence	important	in addition	in conclusion	in fact
in other words	in short	in summary	just as	lastly
moreover	most important	next	so	so that
therefore	thus	unfortunately		

WORDS WHICH SIGNAL SEQUENCE:

additionally	after	afterward	always	another
as soon as	at once	at last	at the same time	before
beforehand	during	earlier	(a) few	finally
first	further	furthermore	immediately	in addition
in the first place	last	later	more	next
now	second	since	subsequently	then
thereafter	third	until	when	

complex process of integrating new words with ideas that exist in the reader's schema. Picture students trying to learn new vocabulary in a content area: They come across a word they do not know and we tell them to look it up in the dictionary. They look up the word and find anywhere from two to seven definitions for it. Confused, they try to find the word in the middle of the paragraph. They finally find the word and then go back to the dictionary. Imagine instead students who have been prepared to analyze words by breaking them down into their roots and affixes. These students, just by having this information, can approximate the meaning of the word without having to resort to another source, so they can use the content and context of the word where they encounter it to help them refine the meaning of the word in that context. It is clear which students are more likely to finish their reading and grasp the concepts being discussed.

Understanding and using root words is also a self-reinforcing activity. Many roots are used in a variety of words across disciplines. As we saw above, more common words are acquired more easily. Thus, the more students use roots, the better they acquire them, and the more useful they become to students. However, if we replace the drill-and-kill approach to vocabulary with the same approach to root words, we will not achieve much. In order to teach the skill of using root words to figure out meanings of novel words, we still need to keep in mind the principle of multiple exposures and multiple contexts. At the end of this chapter we will present a root-word activity and modifications to it that replace the drill-and-kill mentality with an active approach to introducing students to the concept of constructing their own meaning from words by using root words.

Contextualizing Vocabulary

Learning new words also depends on the context they occur in, and context can be in terms of either the learner's mind or the situation. For example, previous and existing word knowledge provides a helpful context for learning new words: learning the meaning of the word *cool* is easier if you already know the words *cold*, *hot*, and *warm*. Similarly, the meaning of a specific word may depend on the current context. Cool has a very different meaning in the context of "it's a cool day" than it has in the context of "he's a cool guy". To learn the meaning in the second context, it would also be valuable to know the meanings of "stylish" or "nerdy". Finally, one has to consider contextual differences when students encounter a new word. Hearing a new word in oral language brings another advantage of context—one can use tone, speaker gestures, the speaker's rephrasing, and even ask questions about the meaning. Unfortunately, the existence of different words that sound the same adds difficulty as well (i.e., whole vs. hole) and may require more contextual clues for a listener to discern meaning.

To understand the meaning of context dependent words requires not only prior knowledge and scaffolding, but also the context in which it is used. *Miss* is another word which is context dependent. Are we referring to the salutation, Miss Garcia, the *Miss* which students call their teacher in the classroom ("Miss, can you help me with this sentence?") *or* are we referring to the verb *miss*? "Oh, Adam, I *missed* you!" (Is that because he was gone a long time, or was it this meaning? "As she raised the pistol and fired it one more time she *missed*?")

Nagy and Anderson (1995) described the problems that arise when attempting to arrive at a standard meaning of the verb *give*. According to Webster's *New Third International Dictionary* (1976), the first standard meaning of *give* is "to confer ownership of something without receiving a return." As Nagy and Anderson (1991) pointed out, this definition works fine in the context of "John gave Mary a present," but in the context of "John gave Mary a kiss," or "Mary gave an excellent performance," the standard meaning of "conferred ownership" is crude at best. Knowing definitions of words is not sufficient to reach literacy with the word.

Robin Scarcella defines contextualization as: "An instructional technique in which grammar rules and vocabulary are couched in a meaningful context, such as a hands-on, theme based activity" (2003, p. 175). Contextualized language is usually spoken and uses schemata (background information) to assist the student in understanding the communication. Similarly, (Echevarria & Graves, 2003) states: "It is through contextual practice that students acquire the depth of knowledge of words that allows them to understand and use those words in meaningful ways" (p. 20).

In terms of teaching vocabulary, the importance of context to word meaning and use makes it clear that in order to provide students an opportunity to develop academic language literacy, it is crucial that they encounter words not only multiple times, but in multiple contexts. Thus when we use the term *multiple exposures*, we do not mean mindless repetition. Obviously, reading a definition 20 times is not the same type of multiple exposure as encountering a word (or word root) in a series of different contexts. Ideally, words that we want to students to learn need to be encountered in a series of different contexts—starting with a definition is fine, but students should also encounter the word multiple times in each of the domains of language, and its use in a variety of ways.

It is necessary to teach the direct and explicit understanding of words through both free association and intensive vocabulary instruction. Piaget (1959) defines free association as the ability to make connections between new vocabulary terms and prior background knowledge and schemata.

When students encounter unfamiliar vocabulary, they need to feel comfortable enough with their command of the language to be able to associate root words, affixes, cognates, and context clues in order to derive meaning from the text. Only when this fails will most readers resort to a dictionary (and, frequently, not even then). The skill of constructing meaning from text, along with basic receptive and expressive language skills, will add to acquiring and learning academic language for reading success.

Personalizing and Operationalizing Vocabulary

Another important skill in vocabulary development involves learning to personalize and operationalize new words. When we personalize new vocabulary by learning meaning through the application of root words, affixes, cognates, and context clues, we acquire new vocabulary by developing ownership of it. Personalizing vocabulary means that students connect a vocabulary word with specific background experience. In other words, we learn meaning through scaffolding information and by accessing prior knowledge. Adding multiple exposures to the new vocabulary enhances and accelerates acquisition of new word meaning. Learning vocabulary includes memorizing it for a short period of time, but acquiring new vocabulary means internalizing it or personalizing it and that you have gone beyond memorization—you can now use the word in novel situations, and manipulate it effectively in novel contexts.

Students operationalize words by placing them into categories and using relevant examples of the words: in other words, by using the new words in context. Conceptual axioms in mathematics such as distributive and associative properties will be better understood with examples and relevant attributes. The student understands by operationalizing the concept. The same is true in language. For example, if students learn to categorize with relevant attributes, a specific hierarchical concept like the shared traits of reptiles, can develop (i.e., reptiles are animals that have vertebrae, breathe air, have scales, lay eggs, lack feathers or hair, are ectotherms). The student operationalizes the hierarchical concept by applying examples to it (Does this lizard have the characteristics of a reptile? Does this frog?) and can then acquire the concept in a useful fashion. The role of the teacher is to provide concrete examples of vocabulary use so that students can better understand and operationalize vocabulary in the academic field. In other words, students can acquire vocabulary more readily by practicing it in appropriate contexts than through rote memorization. When students operationalize new vocabulary, they express it appropriately in the classroom, and in the proper context. For example, students should be able to articulate whether a given animal is a reptile or not by referring to the shared traits given above, using appropriate vocabulary.

Operationalizing vocabulary is part of the metacognitive process. When students have acquired vocabulary and are able to speak and write it with the appropriate academic register they have mastered new academic language!

Academic language is precise and accurate. It is also dense or heavy with information. In order to understand and produce the academic language produced in our content-area classrooms, students need skills to facilitate their comprehension. Those skills rest heavily in the realm of vocabulary development. According to Stahl (1999), understanding words does not necessarily guarantee comprehension of a reading selection. "Word meanings are not just unrelated bits of information, but are part of larger knowledge structures" (Stahl, 1999, p. 5). Thus, we need to teach not only the meaning of words, but also how language is used, or the metacognitive strategies for comprehending new words. This requires the basic elements we have just finished discussing: learning and acquiring vocabulary; understanding the structure behind words, especially in terms of root words and construct-ing meaning; providing multiple contextual opportunities for interacting with the language; and allowing students to personalize and operationalize their experiences with the language. As we have seen, the idea of multiple exposures to vocabulary recurs throughout this discussion as a key element in any successful instruction. Students need to see words repeatedly and in different contexts to facilitate acquisition of new knowledge (Beck, McKeown, & Kucan, 2002). In the next section of this chapter, we present a series of strategies for providing your students with rich, multiple exposures to the academic language of your content area.

Strategies for Teaching Vocabulary

Marzano, Pickering, and Pollock (2001) show that explicit instruction is extremely important for student success in understanding key vocabulary and concepts. Thus, currently accepted best practices need to reflect the basic principles of effective explicit instruction, which includes: the use of a word's context and definition; opportunities for "deep processing" (e.g., finding a synonym or antonym, making up a original sentence with the word, classifying the word with other words, relating the definition to one's own experience, reading and using the word in an appropriate context); and multiple exposures to the new word (Dougherty-Stahl, 2005). Finally, vocabulary should be taught through *productive* approaches that optimize word learning (Snow, 2002). Thus, rather than focusing on a set of targeted words, instruction might focus on one word with multiple semantic con-nections to other words (Stahl, 1999). For example, the word *product* means the number obtained by multiplying two or more numbers, the substance resulting from a chemical change, a work of art or literature, or a result of a manufacturing process. Thus, the word *product* can have different meanings in different content areas; that is, different contexts. Word families (to be introduced in chapter 6 on grammar and writing), would lead us to related word forms such as *produce* (both the verb *to create* something, and the noun *vegetables* in a market); *product, production* (the process of creating something), *producer* (one who creates something), *productive* (creative); and *productivity* (the act of being creative).

General Approaches

According to Pressley (2006) direct vocabulary instruction for academic literacy can improve reading comprehension if students are taught many specific words thoroughly and in depth, over time. When instruction targets and teaches definitions and synonyms effectively, the number of words students learned exceeds the number they learn incidentally from reading. Direct instruction and explicit learning can also speed up vocabulary acquisition. In order for students to acquire new vocabulary, we need to explicitly teach new definitions as well as teach the students strategies to connect prior knowledge with unfamiliar words.

One of the major difficulties in any approach to teaching strategies is to balance the desire for instructional continuity; that is, to use techniques multiple times so that students can learn what to expect and how to succeed in a specific type of activity, and instructional novelty; that is, keeping things different enough so that students do not get bored with a specific technique (the "Oh, this again" response). Below, we present a series of activities, ranging from fairly simple memorization–reinforcement activities to more in-depth, "deep-processing" type activities. Given your specific students, circumstances, and content, some subset of these will likely prove useful. We recommend using a small subset of these activities, and using them repeatedly. By using different activities, you introduce instructional variety, but by cycling through the same small set, you can still provide your students the opportunity to become familiar with the activities.

Specific Activities/Techniques

Listening and Speaking Strategies

Strategies which encourage verbalization of vocabulary are often overlooked by content teachers. It is not that they aren't happening, just that there may not be a focus on them. Content teachers sometimes see them as rather trivial parts of overall instruction. A small investment in explicitly including these simple strategies can have big payoffs simply as a result of providing more exposures and more contexts. Most of these strategies are simple and self-explanatory, so we will confine ourselves to a quick list without much explanation:

- Say the word orally to students phonetically.
- Read the word in context.
- Paraphrase the word as to its meaning in the lesson.
- Have the students repeat the word.
- Write the word on the board and say the word.
- Verbally deconstruct the word as to its root and any affixes.
- Have students do a "pair-share" and talk about the word.
- Write and read aloud (and/or have students read it aloud) a sentence with the word in context.

The "Slap" Game

The "slap" game involves having students write the new words on index cards. The students are then grouped together (three or four to a group) and the teacher reads the definition of the word while the students "slap" the correct card. The student with the most cards at the end wins the game. This primarily reinforces memorization of definitions, but adds the verbal component of language as well as being a bit more motivating than reading or copying definitions.

Vocabulary Cards

Students can work in groups to produce vocabulary cards for the introduction of new vocabulary using index cards and the pattern shown in Figure 4.2.

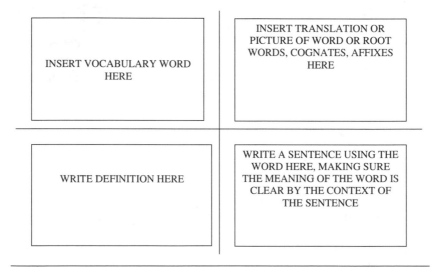

INSERT VOCABULARY WORD HERE	INSERT TRANSLATION OR PICTURE OF WORD OR ROOT WORDS, COGNATES, AFFIXES HERE
WRITE DEFINITION HERE	WRITE A SENTENCE USING THE WORD HERE, MAKING SURE THE MEANING OF THE WORD IS CLEAR BY THE CONTEXT OF THE SENTENCE

Figure 4.2 Sample vocabulary card format.

The teachers can then collect these cards and type up a list of sentences the students write. Five to ten sentences from this list, with the new vocabulary word left out, can be posted on the board as an opening daily activity. The vocabulary card explicitly includes activities for using the word in context. By requiring that the sentence or picture be related in some way to current content, the vocabulary card not only helps with vocabulary, but can reinforce conceptual material from the unit as well.

Cloze Activities

In cloze activities, the teacher has students fill in the blanks in sentences or paragraphs with the new vocabulary. The teacher can pull a paragraph out of the content-area text, write one up using the new vocabulary words, or omit the new vocabulary, putting blanks for the students to fill in. One may start with displaying the words on the bottom of the page. In later exercises, remove the words, and later still ask students to write their own sentences including the new vocabulary. The teacher can use the student generated sentences (see vocabulary cards, Figure 4.2, for another method of obtaining student generated sentences) as an opener for the daily lesson. Finally, students can write a paragraph using the new vocabulary. This staging of difficulty level helps push the students further as they become comfortable with the technique, and the reading within context allows them to get another exposure to the conceptual portion of the content at the same time as they work on vocabulary.

Explicit Strategies Instruction

In explicit strategies instruction (Marzano, Pickering, & Pollock, 2001) teachers show students how to apply prior knowledge as they also use context clues and break down word structures to figure out meanings. For example, if the unfamiliar word is *podium*, in a story about an athlete who wins an Olympic gold medal, the teacher may ask students to visualize the ceremony and analyze text around the word that describes how athletes step up to receive the medals. Similarly, students may be prompted to analyze the word's structure into its smallest meaningful parts, the morphemes *pod-* and *-ium*. Questions such as "What's a tripod?" (a stand with three legs and a podium is a stand with legs). "What is a *stadium* or a *coliseum*?" (both are places to exhibit events) may be used to trigger prior knowledge that anchors new understandings of a podium as the place where someone steps up to or stands at in a large room. When referencing the root word *podos* or foot, we are also reminded of context dependent vocabulary. These are words which depend on the context for meaning. When taken out of context, the words mean something entirely different. If the passage (in a science text) is about sea stars, then a *podium* is a specific body part, also called a "tube" foot. In this case we would generally see the plural form of the word, because sea stars have hundreds of *podia*.

Quick Game Sets

Quick game sets expose students to vocabulary in a variety of settings. Quick game sets can be used as an opener for a class period, a closure activity, a quick transition, or a "pick-me-up" activity. Word association games provide an excellent example. The teacher puts pictures or words on the overhead projector (e.g., in a unit on presidential history, you could use pictures of different presidents), asks students to pair up and asks one student to look at the board, while the other sits with his or her back to the board. The first student calls out word associations (e.g., *civil war, emancipation, assassinated*) until the partner is able to guess the name of the president or whatever concept is displayed. For those of you who remember, this is a type of "Pyramid" game shown on TV.

There are many games and game shows (*Jeopardy, Password*) on TV currently and in the past, which can be adapted for classroom use, including the once famous *Pictionary*, which can be excellent for use in most content areas. These strategies have the advantage of typically being highly motivating for the students.

Cooperative Grouping

Students work cooperatively to analyze a piece of writing, focusing on the vocabulary, in context. For example, if your social studies class is studying the Declaration of Independence, you might break the class up into groups of three (a reader, recorder, reporter) and have them read their section to each other. After completing the reading, they identify unfamiliar vocabulary terms. They then replace those words with familiar words or synonyms.

This group activity serves the purpose of lowering the affective filter of working with unfamiliar vocabulary and allows students to tap each other's knowledge base. Additionally, students can rely heavily on context clues to comprehend the text. The students participate at an appropriate instructional level, yet will still be challenged academically. The additional benefit of this activity is having the students, not the teacher, identify difficult vocabulary. This is a student-centered activity which will yield high student engagement. It is also another method to deconstruct language.

Graphic Organizers

Graphic organizers include a wide variety of devices for allowing students to visualize information, and for putting it into a form that is more readily comprehensible. Using graphic organizers at the beginning of a unit is an excellent method for introducing a concept and also for assessment to demonstrate acquired knowledge at the end of a unit. Graphic organizers also help build on prior knowledge and bring the academic language into context for students.

A common graphic organizer is the Venn diagram, useful for comparing similarities and differences. The basic Venn diagram involves writing two words (or concepts) in a set of overlapping circles (see Figure 4.3 for an example). Elements that the words share are then written in the region of overlap, while elements that are unique to each word are written outside the area of overlap. For more complexity, more circles can be added. Many variations on this basic structure exist, and we will not go into all of them, but this is an excellent way to get students to understand the relationships between words.

Graphic organizers can display large amounts of information in small places; the Periodic table of the elements is good example of an incredibly information dense graphic organizer, showing visually a number of relationships between the elements. Although we don't typically think of these types

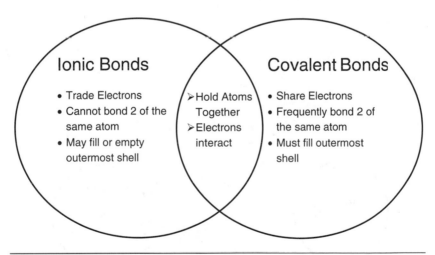

Figure 4.3 A simple example of a Venn Diagram relating Ionic and Covalent bonds to one another. Statements in each circle apply only to the bond in that circle, while statements in the region of overlap apply to both types of bonds. See sample lesson 2.3 in the appendices for a lesson that this diagram could apply to.

of graphic organizers in the context of vocabulary, they can be very helpful in providing students with multiple exposures in context, especially if you have students build the organizer themselves (see sample lesson 2.3, which provides students instructions for building a portion of the periodic table using three simple rules). Semantic maps, spider maps (Figure 4.4), and concept maps are all good examples of organizers which can assist students to visually interpret the meanings of academic vocabulary.

To help demonstrate the ideas presented here, we will refer to the root-word lesson below. This lesson focuses on teaching vocabulary skills using root words, and is written as a stand-alone lesson that could potentially be run "out of the box." However, we want to stress that the lesson plans we provide in the appendices are not intended as "perfect" lessons—we do not believe that such a thing is possible. Instead, all of the lessons we provide should be seen as applications of specific strategies that can and should be modified as needed to provide students with the best possible instruction given the teacher's specific content and situation. It is for this reason that, as well as using a specific lesson as a model, we also include several suggestions for potential modifications.

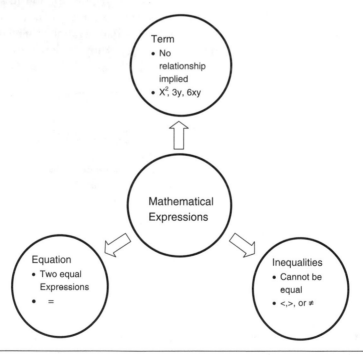

Figure 4.4 Radial diagram (a.k.a. "spider") showing relationships between three types of mathematical expressions. See sample lesson 2.2 in the appendices for a lesson where this graphic organizer could be useful.

The basic activity in the lesson is very simple. Index cards are made and randomly passed out to the class, each student receiving only a subset of the cards. Each card has a root word or affix on one side and its meaning (or meanings) on the reverse. Students will use the cards to find the roots of various words (vocabulary words from the current unit, for example). In activity one, teachers put a new word on the board and say the word to model proper pronunciation. Students then look at the roots and affixes on their cards until all relevant cards are found. Once the appropriate roots are discovered, the cards are flipped over and the meanings read aloud to the class. The students are then asked to construct the meaning of the word based on the meanings of its parts. Activity 2 reverses this process: Teachers provide meanings and students find meanings on their cards, then they construct the word from the word parts associated with the meanings. Note that although the lesson was developed by a science teacher and it is embedded in a science context, the basic idea can be applied to any content area.

A Sample Lesson

Unit: Variable
Position within unit: Variable: Should be introduced early in year, becoming a vocabulary preview/review activity as the year progresses and students build familiarity with more words.

Expressive and Receptive Language

This lesson uses all four domains of language, including the receptive skills (listening and reading) and the expressive skills (speaking and writing). Students listen to the teacher pronounce the word, and read it, both on the board and on their card. They also read the definitions and, in the whole-class version, have to say the word, both in parts and as a whole. In small groups (see reflection portion of lesson plan) they will still practice this skill,

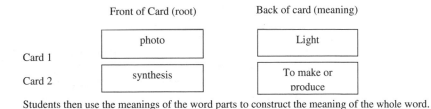

Students then use the meanings of the word parts to construct the meaning of the whole word.

Figure 4.5. An example of the functioning of the vocabulary card activity for the word "photosynthesis". Cards are distributed around the room and students are asked to identify themselves if they find part of the word on one of their cards.

Table 4.5.1 Root Words in Science

OBJECTIVE(S) PURPOSE	To help students master science vocabulary by teaching them to break down and build up words using root words and affixes.
CA STANDARDS	Depends upon vocabulary being taught. Can be modified to fit specific units, or used on a larger scale as review.
MATERIALS	Cards with various word roots and affixes, Each card has a Latin root or affix on one side, and the English translation on the other (see figure 4.4). Cards can be laminated for permanence if desired. Tables 4.3-4.5 serve as mini-references.
ACTIVITIES **Anticipatory Set** (5 minutes)	Ask the students if they can figure out, just from the name, what the spider *Ornithoscatoides decipiens* looks like (unfortunately, the name of this spider has recently been changed to *Phrynarachne decipiens*, but *Ornithoscatoides* is better for our purposes). Next show them how to break down the latinized name: Ask the students if they know what *Ornitho-* might refer to (Bird). What about *scat*? (scat is another word for feces), *-oides* (like, or similar). So Ornithoscatoides literally means "like a bird dropping" What about the word *decipiens*? Does it sound like any words you know? (deception, deceit, etc.). Then show a picture of the spider which can be found on the web—does it look like a "fake bird dropping"? There are actually a lot of words that are built up from other words or parts of words, and they are used frequently in science; "Today's lesson will work on your ability to break down and build up words using Greek and Latin roots."
Activity 1 (Timing varies) R3, R5, R6, R8 E6,E12 Modeling & Guided practice	Pass out cards to students in lab groups. The teacher then provides a word on the board or overhead, saying the word out loud and pronouncing it correctly as they do so. Each group needs to run through their cards to see if they have part of the word, then find who has the other part(s); this may be within the same group or a different group, but once they find the parts of the word, they can flip over the card to figure out the definition of the word. To begin, lead them through the process by asking who has the first part, who has the 2nd, then get them together to show the meaning, as well as repeating the proper pronunciation. After they get the idea, you can put several words up at once so that students aren't sitting around waiting for others. You can give each lab group a complete set to split up among the group so that more students are working simultaneously. This activity gives the students practice in decoding scientific words, which should help them in their reading of textbooks,

etc. It will also help them in basic reading skills, since there are plenty of non-science words that knowing roots can help with.

Activity 2 (Timing varies) R3, R5, R6, R8 E6,E12	The teacher provides a definition, and students build up the word using their card set. This requires constructive language skills. Sometimes, different word forms or endings need to be added to the basic word on the card to get these to the correct word form. Students can also use the cards to make "new" words. In one of our workshops, a participant coined the term "dermagraph"—literally skin writing—as a "scientific" alternative to tattoo.
As an Ongoing Activity:	After students have gotten the idea, either of these activities can be used as a vocabulary introduction for a new unit, or review. Use cards with vocabulary from the unit to reinforce the unit's vocabulary.
ASSESSMENT	An easy assessment can be done by creating a worksheet with either the words (activity 1), definitions (activity 2), or both already on it, and then pick students to come up with the corresponding definition or word by using the root-word cards.
REFLECTION & EXTENSIONS	This activity can be used as a closer for the last few minutes of a class, especially after students have been introduced to it in a longer class session, so they'll know how to do it and what to expect.

This basic idea can also be used for more specific vocabulary instruction. Two examples include naming rules for organic compounds (-ane, -ene, -yne etc.) and metric system naming conventions (kilo- centi- milli- etc.). See table 4.7 for a simple demonstration of this activity using the metric system

Deeper vocabulary instruction can be added by having students use the cards to help with an assigned reading containing vocabulary (with a card set focused on that vocabulary). This has the advantage of providing the students with an additional opportunity to interact with the vocabulary in context.

Another simple extension would have the students use the cards to "create" words that are synonyms or antonyms to specific vocabulary words. This would be a particularly useful exercise to help students get experience with words that either do not have easy Latin roots, or have Latin roots that are less logical. For this type of activity, deriving the correct term would be less of a focus than proper and logical use of root words. This allows students to engage in wordplay, which can lead to amusing (for example, see "dermagraph", mentioned above) results and serve as a motivation technique.

Table 4.6 Sample Card Set for a Unit on the Metric System. Note That Not All Words Can Be Combined Meaningfully (i.e. femtopico?).

Root or Affix	Meaning	Root or Affix	Meaning
femto-	10^{-15} one quadrillionth	kilo-	10^3 Thousand
pico-	10^{-12} one trillionth	mega-	10^6 Million
nano-	10^{-9} one billionth	giga-	10^9 Billion
micro-	10^{-6} one millionth	tera-	10^{12} Trillion
milli-	10^{-3} one-thousandth	peta-	10^{15} Quadrillion
centi-	10^{-2} one-hundredth	meter	Standard unit of distance
deci-	10^{-1} one-tenth	liter	Standard unit of volume
deca-	10^1 ten	second	Standard unit of time
hecto-	10^2 hundred	gram	Standard unit of mass

but in their groups. Writing can be added as the teacher collects works for later assessment.

Constructing and Deconstructing Meanings

In activity 1, students deconstruct the word, breaking it into its component parts. They must also then construct the meaning of the word from the meanings obtained by the deconstruction process. In activity 2, students must deconstruct the definition provided, breaking it into pieces. Next, students find the parts of the definitions in their cards. They then construct the new vocabulary word based on the prior deconstruction. Thus we see that deconstructing and reconstructing language is the main focus of the lesson.

We frequently hear students complain about the complexity of the vocabulary in the content areas. A focus on deconstructing the language can help to both simplify the language and provide an explanation for why and how the "complex" vocabulary is used. A major goal of this lesson is to teach students that when they encounter a word that they haven't seen before, they actually have a powerful tool—their existing vocabulary—to help them figure out the meaning of the word. Thus it draws on prior knowledge. Instead of the drill-and-kill memorization approach to vocabulary that is frequently used and often thought of by the student as the only way to learn vocabulary, this lesson has a "figure it out" approach that is inherently more motivating and engaging (see chapter 2).

A side note regarding motivation: Notice that the anticipatory set in the lesson follows one of the basic rules for a good anticipatory set—it's a little gross. This example also tends to encourage students to be creative with the language in order to try to find ways to say inappropriate things, in acceptable (maybe) language. For example, you probably shouldn't say bird— in class, but *Ornithoscatoides* is perfectly acceptable. You can channel this creativity by having students create their own words using the cards, though you may need to censor them somewhat.

Multiple Exposures

As written, the lesson does not have multiple exposures to specific words as an explicit element. This is because repeated exposures in the same context are minimally effective: we don't want to drill and kill. However, multiple exposures are still a significant part of this lesson.

Students are not exposed to specific words repeatedly, but they will be exposed to word parts repeatedly, and in slightly different contexts. To give a simple example, they would, over the course of this activity, be exposed to kilometer, kiloliter, and kilogram, giving them multiple exposures to the word part *kilo-*, and reinforcing the idea that it means one thousand—thus if they are later exposed to terms like *kilocycle* or *kilobyte*, they will know that these refer to 1,000 cycles or 1,000 bytes.

Remember that this is a technique that could be used multiple times; for example, you could use this during units on cell biology and on ecology, both of which include numerous examples of words based on Greek and Latin roots. This technique could also be used in math, social studies, language arts, or any other content area. This way, students gain multiple exposures to the activity, and will get multiple exposures to the word roots in different contexts.

Contextualization

This lesson is a relatively decontextualized exposure to the words involved. However, some simple modifications can help put the words in context and provide more contextualization. Students could be given a short reading passage (from their text or another reading source) and asked to use their cards to help them deconstruct any words they don't know and construct the meaning. The lesson plan we have included here is intended as an introduction to the technique, and we recommend that it be done in its simpler form, without this modification, when it is first introduced to the students because they will need some instruction on how to use the cards before they will be capable of the more integrated use in the modification.

Another way to contextualize the activity is to include a hands-on component in situations where it is appropriate. Table 4.7 presents a sample card set for this lesson using metric system vocabulary as an example. Consequently, as the term *kilogram* is introduced and defined, students could then be asked to measure 1 kilogram of sand. Or, they could measure 1 milliliter of sand when the term *milliliter* is introduced, then find its mass when the term *milligram* is introduced to help them understand the distinction between mass and volume. This way, you could combine learning the terminology of the metric system with learning the skills involved in measuring the different quantities.

Personalizing and Operationalizing

In this lesson, students are given vocabulary words from their current unit, and asked to determine their meaning by using the root-word cards supplied by the teacher. With this information, they can now construct new meaning for themselves. Full understanding of a word requires more context-specific elaboration and detail, but the root-word meaning provides a scaffold upon which this information can be placed and retrieved. Practice with this skill will prove useful later in the class, and in other contexts as well, because the root words and root-word analysis are useful in nearly any task that involves reading. Students will encounter problems that this skill can help them solve in their everyday life (reading newspapers, magazines etc.), which will lead to personalization.

Several of the modification ideas already discussed also serve these goals; for example, combining the lesson with a hands-on activity provides both context and personalization. Allowing students to use the cards to form their own words is a personalization technique as well as a motivator. Using the cards to decipher readings other than the text (*National Geographic* magazine, for example) can help them see that it is a useful skill outside of the classroom. Finally, we want to reinforce the idea that this is a skill that will be useful in a wide variety of contexts, both in and out of school, and that it is really the usefulness of the skill that will lead the student to use it and personalize it.

Other Modifications

As presented, the lesson is given as whole-class instruction. In a small class this will probably work fine, and the lesson should be introduced this way regardless, but in a large class, keeping students engaged when they do not have cards relevant to the current word will likely be difficult. One possible modification would be to provide complete card sets to small groups, and then have the groups work independently to construct the meanings of the words. This will help get more students actively engaged at the same time. A competition to see which group can find the cards and get the word right the fastest could be instituted to increase motivation to participate. Asking students to write down and to turn in the definitions may also help keep them on task. Remember, in the end, nobody knows their class as well as the teacher, so modify as you see best to fit your particular situation.

Summary

Vocabulary instruction includes etymology, context clues, syntax, and grammar. It also includes explicit instruction of specific context dependent words and free association of words, including root words and cognates. Instruction should also rely heavily on references to prior knowledge in order to accelerate acquisition of word meaning. Stahl and Nagy (2006) refer to the *knowledge hypothesis* (p. 10), "it is not the knowledge of the words per se that makes one a better reader, but instead the knowledge of the concepts that the words represent." Knowledge of words includes integrating the knowledge the word represents into the reader's reality, or contextualizing the vocabulary. Context clues, cognates, root words, knowledge of affixes and how they relate to the root words enhance the ability of the student to contextualize and acquire vocabulary (for examples, see Table 4.7).

In sum, the incremental process of learning vocabulary, the varying nature of words, and the context of usage make determining when a word is learned a complex task. Despite this complexity, a strong vocabulary is generally recognized as an important part of achieving academic language literacy. The strategies presented in this chapter can help your students develop the type of language skills necessary to build the vocabulary essential to achieving academic language literacy.

Table 4.7 Examples of Teaching Vocabulary Development

1. Build background experiences; then talk about them and focus on relevant new words. (Rupley, Logan, & Nichols, 1998/1999)
   Example: hands-on classroom experiences, Field trips, guest speakers, videos
2. Relate new words to children's background knowledge. (Blachowicz & Fisher, 2000)
   Example: Concept wheel, semantic map
3. Develop relationships between words. (Rupley, Logan, & Nichols, 1998/1999)
   Example: Concept of definition, semantic feature analysis
4. Personalize word learning. (Blachowicz & Fisher, 2000)
   Example: Key words, individual word banks
5. Immerse children in a word-oriented environment. (Blachowicz & Fisher, 2000)
   Example: Word of the day, read-alouds and think-alouds that celebrate words, "Gift of Words"
6. Build on multiple sources of information to learn words through repeated exposures. (Blachowicz & Fisher, 2000)
   Example: Wide reading and writing, speaking, oral groups

CHAPTER 5

Reading Skills Development

1. The more you read, the better you get at it; the better you get at it, the more you like it; and the more you like it, the more you do it.
2. And the more you read, the more you know; and the more you know, the smarter you grow. (Trelease, 2001)

Importance of Reading in the Content Areas

As students struggle with reading academic language in the upper grades, especially in high school, it becomes imperative that reading be explicitly taught in any content area. Current research indicates that many students have trouble with reading comprehension, and this translates into serious difficulty in the content areas. Reading is the key to opening doors to all students. In this chapter, we will first address research which highlights problems with reading and reading comprehension, we will then discuss the issues surrounding reading and content literacy. Next we will present general strategies for helping students with reading comprehension. We will introduce the overall phases that students go through as they read, and present some general strategies and specific tactics for helping students to get through these phases. Finally, we present a sample lesson and analyze it in terms of these phases and strategies.

So we are asking you to do *what*? Teach students how to *read* in my math, science, and social studies classroom? Along with teaching anywhere from 150 to 180 students per day, attending extra training your first several years of teaching, preparing several lessons for the different subjects you teach, disciplining students, addressing the lack of student motivation, conducting afterschool activities, implementing state mandated standards and testing, you are asking me to teach *reading*? Get a grip! Unfortunately for all of us, the reality is that we cannot teach the way we were taught; that is, "Open your book to page such and such, read the chapter, answer the questions for homework, there will be a quiz on Wednesday and a unit exam on Friday," nor would we want to.

Not only do we have to teach students who cannot read on grade level, but we also have to "make it fun"! And we have to make sure the students understand what we are teaching so they can perform well on the state mandated achievement tests. Of course, our ultimate goal is to develop literate students who are productive members of society. Yes, that is a "tall order," but it is not impossible.

Research on Reading and Reading Comprehension

The RAND Study (2002) and the National Literacy Panel (NIH No. 00-4769, 2000) concluded that comprehension is a key missing element in reading instruction. By comprehension we mean reading to learn; learning to read is entirely different. Both learning to read and reading to learn are essential, but reading to learn is the ultimate goal, particularly for content-area instruction. Comprehension refers to how struggling readers "make sense" of the written page in any content area. The emphasis in content-area classrooms should be on student learning—not reading as a separate process. While most teachers are not reading teachers, they must assume the role of making sure that students become effective learners in the content area. Academic language strategies can help teachers accomplish this goal.

It is evident that phonics alone is not effective for struggling students (Hirsch, 2003; Krashen, 2004; Krashen & Brown, 2007). Other teaching methods for reading should be integrated to result in effective learning. Students need subject-specific practices and instructional techniques that tie academic language to the reading process in the different content areas. Textbooks are not written for students to easily comprehend but mainly to store vast amounts of information. Reading methods should allow students to become effective readers to unlock these "vaults of information" in the content areas. Students who have effective strategies for learning from texts will become more proficient readers, and experience more success in the content area.

One population containing many struggling readers that has received extensive study is English language learners (ELLs). Current research indicates that the achievement gap for ELLs has widened between 1998 and 2005. The National Assessment of Educational Progress (NAEP, 2005) provides a more instructive picture of what's going on. It's clear that no statistically significant gains have occurred for both fourth and eighth grade ELLs in reading since 2003. The reading gap between non-ELL students and ELL students persists.

Table 5.1 Differences in Scale Score Points between 4th and 8th Grades Non-ELL and ELL Students in Reading on the 1998–2005 NAEP Tests

Fourth Grade Scores	
Year	Difference
1998	43 scale score points
2000	38 scale score points
2002	38 scale score points
2003	35 scale score points
2005	35 scale score points
Eighth Grade Scores	
Year	Difference
1998	46 scale score points
2000	Data not available
2002	42 scale score points
2003	43 scale score points
2005	40 scale score points

Source: U.S. Department of Education. Institute of Education Sciences, National Center for Education Statistics.

Table 5.1 displays the differences in scale scores between ELL and non-ELL students (National Center for Education Statistics, Nations' Report Card, 2005–2006).

We have also seen average scores stagnate from 1988 through 1992 for non-ELL 17 year olds in reading, and they began to decline in 1994 (Allen, Donoghue, & Schoeps, 2001)). The average reading performance of these students decreased again in 1996 and has been decreasing since. In 2005, the average reading score for high school seniors was 286 on a zero to 500 scale. This was lower than in 1992, although it was not significantly different from the score in 2002. Declines were seen across most of the performance distribution in 2005 as compared to 1992 (NAEP, 2005). Reading continues to be a critical issue in high school.

Literacy and Reading

Literacy was once considered to be the ability to read and understand a simple document. The new, broader definition of literacy is the ability to use, understand, and create "text" to communicate with others flexibly, in a variety of situations, and for numerous purposes. "Text," in this perspective, includes spoken, written, and visual language. Visual language can include such elements as graphics, images, gestures, and body language, as well as messages conveyed through video and electronic technology (Nagy & Scott, 2000). Content literacy, as defined by McKenna and Robinson (1990) is "the ability to use reading and writing for the acquisition of new content in a given discipline" (p. 184). From this we derive the insight that literacy not only encompasses reading, writing, speaking, and listening, but also the ability to transfer and apply knowledge gleaned from reading and comprehending text. In the past, emphasis has been placed on the phonological awareness of reading, the ability to decode text or read out loud. Many of our students, struggling readers, and English learners included, can decode words (read out loud) fluently, but cannot comprehend what they are reading. In order for students to achieve literacy in the expanded sense used here, they need to go beyond reading phonetically to derive meaning from text.

The issue of literacy/reading includes phonics, decoding, fluency, comprehension, and vocabulary awareness. Also heavily discussed is the *whole language* approach to reading versus the *phonological approach*. In the whole language approach students acquire comprehension through multiple exposures to vocabulary and syntax. In the phonological approach, careful and systematic awareness of sounds are taught first, then words, then sentences. Both approaches have their merits and are addressed here only to bring awareness to the reader.

In the content areas, we need to concern ourselves with the students' ability to:

- comprehend text (literal comprehension, simple recall of facts, knowledge),
- interpret text (compare/contrast, basic analysis, and application of knowledge),
- evaluate information from text (construct new ideas after synthesizing information and critique or judge information)

Students who do not have these abilities need specialized, differentiated instruction (Tomlinson, 2003) to understand the concepts taught in the content classroom. Helping these students develop reading repair strategies can significantly improve their ability to learn from text.

The term *reading repair strategies* refers broadly to the use of context clues, root words, cognates, affixes (see chapter 4), and background knowledge to ascertain the meaning of unfamiliar words or phrases. Reading repair strategies are second nature for the experienced or fluent reader, but many struggling readers are not skilled at using reading repair strategies to ascertain the meaning of unknown text. When these students come across a word they do not understand, they may stop in the middle of the sentence. If they are unable to figure out the meaning, they often "shut down" for the rest of the reading selection and become the teacher's worst discipline nightmare because they are not engaged.

The truly struggling reader does not have the ability to "chunk" information (use prior knowledge to scaffold new information); when they try to comprehend unknown words or phrases, they give up, rather than attempting to comprehend the selection as a whole. As stated by E. D. Hirsch, Jr. (2003),

> ... reading comprehension depends on the reader filling in the blanks and silently supplying enough of the unstated premises to make coherent sense of what is being read. Once print has been decoded into words, reading comprehension, like listening comprehension, requires the active construction of inferences that are chock full of unstated premises and unexplained allusions. (pp. 19–20)

Reading repair strategies enable the student to comprehend the general meaning of a passage in order to extract knowledge without full understanding or comprehension of every word or phrase in the text.

Developing reading repair strategies is a complex, difficult task that cannot be addressed in a single, brief section, and sometimes requires individualized tutoring. The strategies presented in chapter 4 and later in this chapter are all strategies that in the long run can be used to help students develop this important skill. As in the development of vocabulary, repeated exposure and practice are extremely important to developing this skill set. Acquisition of reading repair strategies results in more confident, better motivated readers. The quote at the beginning of this chapter really says it all: "The more you read, the better you get at it...", and this includes the development of the ability to use reading repair strategies.

Content Literacy

Meltzer and Hamann (2006), define three important discipline-based practices in academic language literacy development that teachers can use to support content-area reading and learning:

- Recognizing and analyzing discipline-based discourse features: "discourse features" refers to the speaking, listening/viewing, reading, writing, and thinking habits; skills; conventions; and formats used by experts within a content area.
- Understanding text structures: text structure refers to the reading and writing conventions, features, and logic of content-area texts.
- Developing vocabulary knowledge: vocabulary knowledge refers to the essential words and concepts within a particular content area.

Teachers should have students practice discourse in the particular content areas so that they can use newly acquired academic language. Students thus become apprentices in the discourse of the particular content. Students benefit from experiencing discourse through teacher modeling. This includes explicit strategies used by the teacher and assessment of the strategies conducted by both the teacher and student. Students construct their own knowledge through these processes of discourse.

Text structure is the pattern the author uses to arrange ideas in a logical and coherent form. Both narrative and expository text are structured and organized to provide a mental outline for categorizing and processing during reading. The organizational pattern of the text supports the reader in processing information and building relationships that the author intended (Berber-Jimenez, Hernandez, & Montelongo, 2006). Table 5.2 includes examples of how to incorporate instruction of text structures into specific learning activities. The five text structures in Table 5.2 have been identified and adapted from Neufeld (2005–2006).

The reading process is an interaction with the text. Some struggling students have not experienced successful interactions; that is, fluent, comprehensible reading. Students need to experience successful interactions with the text. Ciborowski (1995) has shown that successful content-area reading is not just about specific reading strategies. Successful reading depends upon experiencing quality learning activities that actively engage the student in making sense of the text and task. These activities, which include reading

Table 5.2 Suggested Oral Discourse Activites

Text Structure (expository register from text; author's representation)	Suggested Activites (use everyday oral register to explain text structure)
Sequencing. List of items or events in certain order	-explain or act out order using props, use visuals, recipes, scientific experiments, explain time and history, give example of the school schedule, use visuals
Compare and Contrast Describes or explains differences/ similarities or events	-explain similarities/differences between two things or events, use visuals or pictures that are similar yet different for contrast
Cause and Effect Explains how events cause other events	-explain effect of events using props or real life examples, use visuals
Problem or Solution Explain the development of a problem and one or two solutions to it	-explain how one solves a personal problem i.e. no money, getting to work when car breaks down, etc.
Description A characterization of salient features or events intended to create a mental image of something experienced	-have students describe to each other a favorite place with descriptive words and then have them share with the class

strategies, might involve using anticipation guides, brainstorming activities, and other strategies which elicit student background knowledge and which provide momentum for learning about new material. A variety of interactive learning situations—paired reviews, cooperative groups engaged in summarizing activities, and students defending positions based on support they identify in the text make students interact with text. Student interactions with text also include students questioning the author's premise, synthesizing key information using graphic organizers, and assuming a perspective different from their own as they consider how other people might react to what they are reading. Students often feel intimidated by the printed word and are reluctant to challenge the author or present contradictory evidence. Interactive discourse assists the teacher to scaffold the dialog. The oral academic register is modeled by the teacher and practiced by students. Students begin to construct their own knowledge and express it in the academic register. We will elaborate on these strategies later on in this chapter.

Expository vs. Narrative Text

Students are often not familiar with the types of text structures used in textbooks and other academic text. This lack of familiarity impedes student comprehension of the new information (Bakken, Mastropieri, & Scruggs, 1997; Cook, 1983). This is sometimes due to inadequacies in the materials themselves, particularly the tendency for textbooks, as noted above, to be "vaults of information," often without structures available for students to access those vaults. The American Association for the Advancement of Science (AAAS) project 2061 has taken the lead in evaluating science educational materials, and has the following to say:

> Today's textbooks cover too many topics without developing any of them well. Central concepts are not covered in enough depth to give students a chance to truly understand them. While many textbooks present the key ideas described in national and state standards documents, few books help students learn the ideas or help teachers teach them well. (Roseman, Kulm, & Shuttleworth, 2001, p. 56)

Because the structure of expository text differs from that of narrative text, explicit instruction is helpful in identifying the text structures and application of appropriate strategies. Nearly all the reading on state standardized assessments (with the exception of the language arts content area) consists of expository text that depends heavily on student's prior knowledge, and is very abstract and precise. Narrative text can be abstract as well, but usually is much easier to comprehend.

Narrative text generally follows a story line with a beginning, middle, and end. This structure is familiar to students, and thus easier for them to comprehend. Students know what to expect, and can focus their attention on remembering what they have read.

Expository text differs from narrative text. Expository text presents facts, theories, and dates. The information is largely unfamiliar to the reader, and may not have a coherent "story line" (Cook, 1983).

Brinton, Goodman, and Ranks (1994) have developed the idea of the phases of reading. These phases describe how students progress through a piece of text. They also provide a structure for teachers to use to help students progress through the reading of any type of text, including expository text with dense academic language.

The Phases of Reading: Reading Into, Through, and Beyond

Brinton et al. (1994) describe three stages that teachers often use in assisting students to maneuver their way into, through and beyond in the reading and writing curriculum. Table 5.3 illustrates sample teaching strategies which help students access these three stages of reading. The discovery of meaning is the principle goal in teaching students to read for comprehension. Students should learn multiple ways to approach reading, especially with the multiple mediums of learning content currently available such as the Internet, books, charts, graphs, and extended text literature. Phase 1 ("into": i.e., before or prereading) prepares students for phase 2 ("through": i.e., during reading), which in turn prepares them for phase 3 ("beyond": i.e., after or postreading). Effective lessons in reading model these three stages. They set the stage for reading with a motivating anticipatory set (chapter 2) which taps into their prior knowledge ("into" the lesson), teachers model and students practice reading strategies, including repair strategies, to complete the reading ("through" the lesson) and culminate the lesson with an extension activity ("beyond" the lesson) which not only demonstrates mastery of the curriculum but also takes the curriculum to the analysis or synthesis stage. Ideally, learning a lesson or a chapter is viewed as a thoughtful, well-planned construction of knowledge that continually undergoes the processes of rebuilding, readjusting, and extending that knowledge. All three phases should be generative and interconnected (Ciborowski, 1995). Thus the lines between the phases can be blurred, and many strategies can be useful in more than one phase.

One of the final outcomes for the students is to confidently use reading materials in the subject matter (trade books as well as texts) as a vibrant and dynamic medium to manipulate and learn what is read as they travel "into," "through," and the "beyond" learning phases of the text.

Effective teaching strategies specific to content areas include scaffolding,

Table 5.3 Integrated Literacy Instructional Strategies

These strategies can be taught *Into, Through or Beyond* the lesson.		
Into	**Through**	**Beyond**
Key Vocabulary	Guided Oral Reading	Questioning/Critical
Vocabulary Scaffolding	Jigsaw	Thinking
Anticipatory Set	Guided reading: DRTA/DLTA	Summarization
Text Analysis	Visualization	Reflect & Demonstrate
Generate Hypothesis		Backward Summary
Whole to Part Predication		
Common Text Structures		

support, and practice so students may learn the curricular areas through as many modalities as possible. The teacher maximizes the learning environment by including flexible grouping, visuals and other classroom management tools which help meet individual and group needs. These strategies can help teachers to teach "Into," "Through," and "Beyond" the text. Examples of some of these strategies can be found in many of the lessons included in the appendices.

Strategies for Getting Students "Into" Reading

During the "into" phase of reading, students explore a topic primarily with teacher guidance. Students use their background knowledge and curiosity about what they want to know regarding a subject area or event and engage in preliminary discussions about what is already known. This is a connective stage in reading where the students engage in listening and speaking with their peers and making predictions while engaging with their prior knowledge. The teacher may begin to ask "big questions" (e.g., "Should marijuana be legalized?" (chapter 3) of the students so they may focus on topics and content possibilities before introducing students to text content (e.g., a reading on the pros and cons of marijuana use). Imagery or use of a student's imagination is a key student motivator and channels the student to the "into" phase of reading.

The "into" phase of reading can also include visuals such as pictures, charts, graphs, concept maps, or graphic organizers which engage the student's appetite to know more about what is viewed. Often, some of the activities encountered may include previously learned facts, key vocabulary, and picture cues taken from print resources accessed by the student.

To aid students "into" a reading activity, it is important to activate their background or prior knowledge during participatory activities. Subject matter knowledge, strategy knowledge, personal knowledge, and self-knowledge are all specialized forms of prior knowledge/background knowledge that need to be accessed by students to be successful readers (Strangman & Hall, 2004).

Teachers should read aloud to students to model and support their learning of vocabulary, content understanding, fluency, and comprehension. By reading aloud to the students we do not simply mean reading directly from the text, but also include discussion or modeling of language deconstruction techniques (see Tables 5.3 and 5.4). This helps activate prior knowledge, connect the reading to the students' experience, and motivate them to do well in the activity. Reading aloud has been shown to increase text accessibility for students who are otherwise unable to comprehend the text for themselves (Ivey & Broaddus, 2001). They also found that students saw read-aloud as "… scaffolds to understanding because the teacher helped to make the text more comprehensible or more interesting to them" (p. 367). According to LaBerge and Samuels (1974), reading fluency (the ability to decode words and read fluently out loud) is important because students who recognize words effortlessly can devote more attention to reading comprehension.

Reading aloud in math and other content areas is important because it allows a teacher to introduce key concepts and vocabulary using "text talk," an appropriate register for obtaining academic language literacy. The teacher then brings students back for discussion on the key ideas and terms that need to be learned and practiced. Refer to lesson 3.2 (appendix 3) and you can see that, as part of this lesson, students read aloud to each other to make sure they comprehend the problem. The math teacher in this lesson has read the problem aloud at least twice with emphasis on key academic language and concepts. Reading word problems aloud after modeling by the teacher aids student comprehension. It also models thought processes necessary for problem solving.

Students benefit from oral reading (Ariail & Albright 2006). Among these benefits are increases in students' ability to access texts, motivation, engagement in learning, positive attitudes toward reading, background knowledge in

Table 5.4 Integrated Strategies

Vocabulary Scaffolding	Infer & Analyze	Group Investigation
Referencing Schemata	Compare And Contrast	Project Based Learning
Scaffolding Prior	Asking Why	Literature Circles
Knowledge	Summarization	3 Facts And A Fib
KWL Graphic Organizer	Charades, Pictionary	Truth Or Consequences
Read Alouds	Student Generated Test	Semantic Feature Chart &
Question Clarification	Questions	T Chart
Oral Summaries	Slap Game (Vocabulary/	Collaborative Notes
Cloze Activities	Concept Identification	Cornell Notes
Test Hypothesis	Sorting Cards	SQV3R
	Integration With Text	QAR
		Reciprocal Teaching

content areas, and fluency. How do we accomplish that in the content areas? The teacher can model oral reading from the text, emphasize "text talk," and use academic language and the academic register during oral summaries , discussions, and question and answer sessions (Beck & McKeown, 2001).

"Into" Activities

Anticipatory Set

A student attention hook to focus and gain student interest on the lesson (see chapter 2 for details).

Text Analysis   Familiarize the students with the format of the text. This may include actually giving the students a "walk through" of how to use the text as a resource by directly exploring with them the reasons why an author may have included each section of the book where it is placed.

Generate Hypotheses   Students learn to develop potential explanations about what they observe and are learning about in the curriculum. It may be a "Cause and Effect" statement or a concluding statement but is always presumed true until an evaluation is completed.

Whole to Part Prediction   The teacher provides information to the students about the "Big Picture" for the lesson/text. These may be in the form of visuals and can be delivered by the teacher in the form of listening, speaking, reading, or writing. Students then use their prior knowledge and this information to predict an outcome or what may happen next in the text.

Strategies for Getting Students "Through" Reading

The "through" phase of reading is the point where students affirm and acquire content-area knowledge. Graphic organizers can assist students in this stage to reorder information to accelerate comprehension and retention of content-area material. It is helpful here to construct specific questions for students to answer in order to enable them to read for a purpose. After forming "big questions" in the "into" phase of reading, students predict answers to the questions and then determine the accuracy of their responses in the "through" phase. What might be difficult in this phase is to maintain student motivation and engagement as they actually begin to acquire content knowledge.

Text Organization

Give students a series of questions they can ask themselves as they move through a reading to ensure that they are paying attention to the text organization. For example:

1. Have I looked at the way the text is set up in the content area as to time or sequence, cause and effect?
2. Have I looked at "signal words" that can give a clue to the text structures? (i.e., *sequence-first, second; cause and effect—as a result, nevertheless*; see chapters 3 and 4)
3. Are there any other features of the text (sidebars, glossaries, headings, etc.) that will help me comprehend the content?
4. Have I looked at the how the keywords are presented?

Organizing Your Thoughts and Understanding the New Content

Again, a series of questions students can ask themselves as they move through different parts of the text:

1. How will I organize my thoughts while reading?
2. As I read, what other information do I know about the subject?
3. Can I use a graphic organizer or sticky notes to note key words or ideas?
4. How can I remember the ideas that I am reading and which one(s) do I need more help on?
5. Can I visualize a picture in my head that will help me understand and remember?

Checking Yourself for Understanding as You Read

1. Do I understand what the author is stating in this paragraph or page?
2. Can I see a picture in my head or write a few key ideas to make sure I understand?
3. Do I need more time to read and understand this?
4. Can I read this orally with a partner or in a study group?

"Through" Activities

Jigsaw

Jigsaw activity is a classroom cooperative learning activity from Johnson and Johnson (1975). In the jigsaw activity, groups of four to five students are formed. They initially gather in their "home" group. Each student is assigned a different part of a reading text. Students with the same part from different "home" groups then gather to form "expert" groups to discuss and master their part. Experts return to their "home" group to exchange information. All members of the "home" group should understand the total reading assigned. When you read do the following:

1. Read the passage once for general comprehension.
2. Read the passage again and make sure you know the academic language.
3. Check the academic language and do a summary of the passage; go over this with your expert group.
4. Check with your teacher if there is something you don't understand.
5. Review with your expert group how you will explain the passage or text to the home group.

Guided Reading: DRTA/DLTA

In the Directed Reading Thinking Activity (DRTA; Stauffer, 1969) the procedures include:

1. Students read selection title (and perhaps a bit of the selection) and make predictions about content using background knowledge.
2. Students read to the first stop point—the stop point should be predetermined, either by the teacher or the students. They confirm, refine, or reject their initial predictions and justify their ideas with reference to the text. Students then make new hypotheses.
3. Students read the next section and follow procedures in step 2. This cycle continues until they finish the text assigned.
4. Follow-up activities may be completed after the text is read. The teacher leads the discussion.

The role of the teacher:

- The teacher should facilitate (but not direct) thinking by asking questions such as: What do you think? Why do you think so? Can you prove it? What do you know now about the content?
- The teacher may summarize points that students make during the discussion, but should take care not to let his or her values or interpretations dominate. The teacher's role is to foster thoughtful student participation. Oral discourse is important for student comprehension.

The Directed Listening-Thinking Activity (DLTA), proceeds in the same manner. The only difference is that the teacher reads the text to the students.

Strategies for Getting Students "Beyond" Reading

The "beyond" or phase 3 of learning from text, guides the students to a reflective, demonstrative, and concluding mode where the ultimate goal is to communicate and practice or apply what has been learned. The student relies on the information gleaned from the previous "into" and "through" phases. It is expected that the students have established their own voice at this point and can more clearly express themselves through the multiple modalities of listening, speaking, reading, and writing.

General "Beyond" Activities Reflect and Demonstrate

This is the process or result of seriously thinking over one's experiences regarding a lesson. Teachers model and demonstrate lesson elements so that students view and reflect on the subject matter. For example, after reading about genealogy, students could be told to interview a parent or grandparent, and then write a brief report on the interview, with details on the relationship to the person interviewed and how it relates to the reading.

Lesson Extension

The teacher generates a discussion regarding the topic of the recent reading and guides the students to create a list of potential topics for further study, then assigns students (or groups of students) to collect information on each topic. For example, after reading about a foreign culture or country, students could create a travel brochure, write about the history of the culture, or produce a map of the country.

Table 5.4 lists a variety of strategies that can be integrated across a lesson, and used to get students into, through, or beyond in an integrated fashion. Specific examples of some of the strategies can be found in the lessons provided in the appendices.

Integrated Activities

The following activities are generally longer term and include aspects of all three stages—into, through, and beyond—and are not easy to categorize as any single stage. Some focus more on one stage or another, but all share the aspect of combining two or more stages. They also generally infuse receptive and expressive skills discussed in detail in chapter 3. Many of them have students practice listening and speaking as a way of extending the text-based experience into the realm of oral social discourse. For many of these techniques, introducing a collaborative aspect (for example, have students work in groups to build a T-chart) will add this feature.

The brief descriptions that follow are intended primarily as a guide to get you to think about how to include these types of activities into your specific situation, and not as complete how-to guide for these techniques.

KWL Graphic Organizer

This strategy helps to foster active reading of the text. Students divide a page into three columns. In the first column, they write down what they know, in the second column what they want to know, and in the third column what they have learned as they progress through the lesson. This provides the students with a structure to guide them through the lesson and apply their background knowledge to the new material. Teachers can use the KWL chart to observe and assess the progress students are making in comprehending the text, and if they are targeting the important content.

Read Alouds (Trelease, 2001)

Read alouds are a strategy whereby either the student or the teacher reads a passage. As they listen, students read along. This helps them learn about the pronunciation of words, the pauses, and the emphases on the words in the piece, providing a receptive model of academic language and register. Read alouds can be used to introduce lessons, and demonstrate the critical thinking process.

Group Investigation/Project-Based Learning (Krajcik, Czerniak, & Berger, 2000)

Groups of students are given a specific question or problem to solve and each person is held responsible for a piece of the problem solving, which they then share in a response to the group. This is an inquiry based, long term series of activities where students are responsible for completing goals which allow them to obtain knowledge about a specific topic in small groups or individually. It is intended to increase active student engagement and interest. The teacher models the different stages of the project and monitors the groups to ensure they stay on task and are making appropriate progress. This activity requires students to read from multiple text sources (potentially including textbooks, Internet sources, magazine/journal articles, etc.) and integrate information. Assessment occurs during monitoring and also on the overall finished product.

Literature Circles (Short & Burke 1991)

Students each read the passage, then retell or summarize their understanding to their peers. Each student has a specific task; for example, one student focuses on how to connect the reading to daily life while another is charged with fostering discussion. This activity usually includes specific questions that the students will report on regarding the content and discuss in a group setting. This is a way for them to informally share thoughts on a topic.

Three Facts and a Fib

Students or the teacher construct three facts and a fib related to the topic. The groups debate and decide which statement is the fib, then check their answers. A similar technique is *Truth or Consequences* (based on the game show of the same name) which involves providing students (written or verbally) with invented statements then has them determine which of several historical figures (statesman, scientists, mathematicians, etc.) might have said it.

T Chart (Wormeli, 2005)

This organized structure allows the students to graphically organize notes. Students record words or key points on the left hand side of a "T" chart and place opinions or explanations on the right side of the T chart. Teachers build skill using this graphic organizer by modeling the chart as they teach concepts to students.

SQV3R (Survey, Question, Vocabulary, Read, Respond, Review) (adapted from SQ3R, Wormeli, 2005)

This strategy provides a structure for the students to learn how to read a text for better understanding. Students survey a reading piece (chapter, section etc.) by looking at section titles, figures, etc. They then develop questions based on their survey, and review important vocabulary before actually reading the piece. After reading, they respond to prompts (answer questions or write a summary, etc.,), and finally review the information by going over their responses. This is a comprehensive "Into, Through and Beyond" activity combining many of the "smaller" strategies detailed above.

"Something Happened, But, So" (Peregoy & Boyle, 2004)

The students read a passage or are told by the teacher about an event and then they add a "but" statement and a "so" statement to complete the scenario. This activity gives the students the practice of thinking through and using their creativity toward language construction. For example:

> (*Something happened*) George went to the store to buy 7 apples. His mother gave him a dollar and twenty five cents, which was enough to

buy 7, but not 8 apples. (*But*) on his way to the store, he met his friend who asked him if he could borrow a quarter. George lends him the quarter. (*So*) When he got to the store, how many apples could he buy?

This activity allows the students to not only to use the academic language but also to solve the word problem using mathematics.

QAR (Question, Answer, Response) (Richardson, Morgan, & Fleener 2006)

Ask students where specific information is located in the text. There are four basic answers: Either the information is "right there" in the text (i.e., students can just copy out an answer); the information is in the text, but needs to be thought about ("think and search"; i.e., students must connect information in the text); the information can be developed by connecting to prior knowledge ("You and the Author"; i.e., part of the answer is in the text and part must be supplied by the student); or the information is not in the text at all ("on your own"; i.e., students must supply the information themselves). More potential answers can be added as appropriate for the content area. For example, in math or science, another answer could be "in a graph" or "in a table". This activity assists the student to learn the text structure in specific disciplines.

Reciprocal Teaching (Palinscar & Brown 1984)

In small cooperative groups, students take turns assuming the role of the teacher and work to teach each other information. Teachers model this process by instructing small groups—asking questions, eliciting responses from students and asking students to explain concepts to one another. Students use this strategy as they work together and learn from each other through discussion about content or vocabulary. This often includes generating questions, summarizing content, predicting outcomes, and making clarification statements in dialog sessions with peers.

Sample Lesson: Geometry Proofs

What follows is a sample lesson which incorporates the some of the strategies included in this chapter.

Unit: Proofs
Title: Go With the Flow
Position within unit: Introduction to proofs
Author: Merci Del Rosario

Table 5.4.1 Go With the Flow

OBJECTIVE(S) PURPOSE	Students will be able to: • Use logical reasoning to complete triangle congruency proofs • Analyze triangles in order to identify essential information and postulate to complete a proof	
CA STANDARDS	**Geometry 2.0** Students write geometric proofs, including proofs by contradiction. **Geometry 5.0** Students prove that triangles are congruent or similar, and they are able to use the concept of corresponding parts of congruent triangles.	
MATERIALS	Transparencies of flowchart and worksheets Poster paper and markers Worksheets → Identifying Triangle Congruence, Proofs #1–5	
ACTIVITIES Introduction (Anticipatory Set) R4 (Minutes?) R2 E2 E6, E9	1. "Write a set of directions on how to make a peanut butter and jelly (PBJ) sandwich." Have students exchange directions. 2. Introduce flow chart proof for PBJ sandwich (see below). Emphasize difference between **essential steps and preliminary information**. (identifying givens, assumptions, etc.) Teacher models process of using the flow chart. 3, Introduce "Mall" flow chart (see below) and have students help fill in the chart (guided practice). 4. Ask students to pose their own givens and ultimate goals to their partners and challenge them to complete a flow chart proof. Reading Activities emphasized for lesson: Read aloud and Oral summaries. (Students read the content of Flow chart to one another, then summarize orally for class)	• In this activity, students will become familiar with flow chart format by using them to organize real life scenarios.

Pre-assessment R1, R6, R8	5. Hand out "Identifying Triangle Congruency" worksheet. 6. Teacher reads aloud textbook section introducing proofs while students read along. 7. Students develop flowchart for triangle congruency. 8. Call for volunteers to read their flow-charts to the class. 9. Emphasize the "essential conditions" for the different postulates/theorems (i.e. ASA $\rightarrow$ angle, side, angle).	• Students will review. postulates/ theorems for triangle congruency.
Flow Chart Proofs for Triangle Congruence R6, R8, F.11	10. Model completing "Flow Chart review Link with PBJ and Mall flow charts. Emphasize "essential conditions." ▪What are we trying to prove? ▪What is our ultimate goal? ▪Which parts are congruent? ▪Which postulate could we use? Why?	• Students will use flow chart format to prove triangles congruent.
E2	11. Students work individually to complete additional proofs (just use examples available in your textbook) using	
E1	given templates and cut-outs. 12. Ask students to form groups of 3 or 4 and compare flowcharts with members of their group. Find two different flow charts for the same proof (copy on butcher paper) — "how are they different and how are they similar?" ▪Are they both correct? ▪When does the order or sequence matter? When does it not matter? 13. Ask for volunteers to share flow chart additional proofs. ▪Are there alternative solutions?	
ASSESSMENT E10	Your friend Kelly missed today's lesson. Explain to Kelly how to use flow chart proofs in proving two triangles congruent. You may use any one of the proofs used in class as an example.	
REFLECTION	Reflect on how your lesson went.	

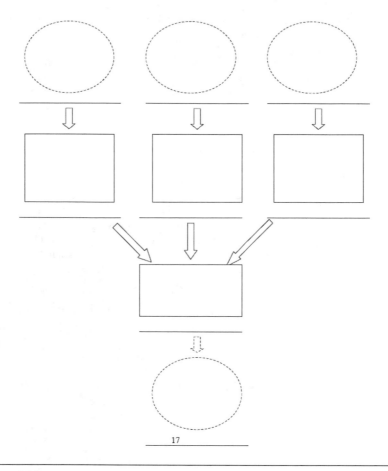

Figure 5.1.1

Given: You have peanut butter in the cabinet and jelly in the refrigerator

Ultimate Goal: to make and eat a Peanut butter and jelly sandwich

Jelly is in the refrigerator	Spread peanut butter on the bread.	Spread jelly on the bread
Need peanut butter for the sandwich	Definition of Sandwich	Eat your sandwich
Peanut butter is in the cabinet	Need peanut butter for the sandwich	You're hungry
Given	Given	

Given: Your mom has money, your dad has a car, and your friends are at home

Ultimate goal: To go to the mall

Get money from your Mom	Ask Dad for a ride	Call your friends
To get to the Mall	So you won't be alone	Go to the mall with your friends
To have fun and go shopping	Given	Given
Given		

The basic activity involved in this lesson is simple and it is necessary for students to use background knowledge and apply it to a graphic organizer so that they begin to understand the goal of the lesson: logical reasoning and analyzing to complete a proof. Below, we analyze this lesson from the perspective of the "Into, Through, and Beyond" phases of reading.

"Into" the Sample Lesson

Students are given an activity that functions as an anticipatory set. This activity involves the teacher modeling the development of a flow chart on the process of making a peanut butter and jelly sandwich, a familiar context for the students to apply the new process. After modeling, students develop their own flow chart on a trip to the mall. In small groups, students will practice all four domains, listening, speaking, reading, and writing as they fill in the flow charts to come up with the logical reasoning that they will use. This thought process, practiced with familiar topics serves as practice for the logical reasoning and the appropriate language for developing a set of instructions or a mathematical proof. It also introduces some of vocabulary needed in the lesson (e.g., givens, essential steps, preliminary information, etc.). The anticipatory set taps into prior knowledge (how to make a PBJ) and prepares students for the main activity of the lesson, developing the flow chart to help them with geometrical proofs. Part of this process should also involve a "translation" from the social register used to initially describe the activities into the academic register. This is necessary for the verbal reading of their flow charts and oral summary for the class.

"Through" the Sample Lesson

Math texts are generally very dense in their use of academic language. Therefore, the teacher helps the students to get through the text by reading the section aloud with the students to model proper pronunciation and academic register. The teacher also uses this opportunity to define new terms for the students in context, when the definitions will be most useful, and to connect these terms with background knowledge. This process can help get students through the text without "shutting down" because they receive immediate help and feedback. Depending on the level of the class, the teacher can also have students take turns reading the passage aloud, during which time corrective feedback can be used for the same purpose.

"Beyond" the Sample Lesson

To push the students beyond the text and reading, additional proofs that can be developed from the textbook are assigned as independent practice. This gives students further practice both with the logic of developing proofs and with the expressive use of academic language. Given the nature of the anticipatory set, further extensions could involve applying the same logical process to other real world applications (e.g., how to fix a small engine, how to transplant a flower).

Summary

There are multiple pathways that teachers may use to enhance student reading abilities and thus, their success. In order for students to be considered literate in today's world, they need to do more than read, they need to be competent in all "communication processes," and teachers must be ready to support students' understanding and learning as they interact with text. The goal, in terms of reading in the content area, is to get students to "read to learn." An understanding of the phases of reading and development of activities that use this knowledge can help students achieve this goal. Educators have to be knowledgeable about academic language and use subject matter reading materials as a vibrant and dynamic medium to teach both content-specific subject matter and the language structures used in the discipline. Teachers should provide multiple opportunities for students to acquire content knowledge in the curriculum. These opportunities help students to learn how to construct meaning through language as they travel the path of learning. It is the authors' intent that use of the activities, concepts, and model lesson provided in this chapter will assist educators in their content-area instruction.

CHAPTER **6**

Grammar and Writing

Just as a home builder converts a set of blueprints or floor plans into an attractive, well-constructed home, we should be able to convert words into a well-constructed piece of writing which conveys purposeful meaning (adapted from Dutro & Moran, 2002). When we write, we build written structures, using words as our materials. Our language is functional, constructed from the world around us, and refined by corrections, just as buildings are built from the available materials, then modified by repairs and adjustments over time (Wong Fillmore, 2004). Just as a competent architect must understand the rules of physics and the properties of her materials to produce a well-constructed building, so must a competent writer understand the rules of language and the properties of words in order to construct a well-constructed piece of writing. In this chapter we turn our attention to helping students construct their own written edifices so they can more effectively share their thoughts and ideas.

We will now focus our continuing study of language on producing coherent written work within the content areas. We start with a brief description of the research on the importance of grammar to language acquisition, and how that research has been applied to the teaching of grammar, and why content-area teachers need to be concerned with grammar instruction. We will then turn our discussion back to the relationship between academic language literacy and students' writing abilities, building the case for using the connection between oral and written expressive language as a tool for teaching writing and building student's academic language skills by teaching them to use the academic register in both oral and written expression. We provide some strategies for assessing student writing in ways that are formative (i.e., assessment as a teaching tool that allows students to progress in their abilities) rather than simply evaluative. We briefly provide a series of potential writing activities that can be used to get students to write at several different levels. Finally, we will close the chapter by presenting a sample lesson in history that utilizes several of the strategies over time to help students build both their writing skills and their ability to express themselves using the appropriate language, structures, and conventions in specific content areas.

The Importance of Grammar to Language Acquisition

Scarcella (2003) notes that, "In the last twenty years grammar has often been ignored or under-emphasized in public school instruction" (p. 61). We could take that a step further and state that it has been underemphasized in college preparation instruction as well. As an English education major at State Teacher's College in Buffalo, NY, only one class in linguistics was required, no classes in grammar preparation were required. Wong, Fillmore, and Snow (2001) concur that this is true for most teacher preparation programs; teachers are not taught grammar. When we say they are not taught grammar, do we mean that aspiring teachers do not study the structure of language? Not necessarily. The study of linguistics is commonly required even for a liberal arts degree. Linguistics is the study of language, which includes descriptive linguistics (expression systems), historical linguistics (study of changes in languages), comparative linguistics (study of deviations of languages of a common origin), geographical linguistics (regional language study), sociolinguistics (study of social discourse), and applied linguistics (the study of forms and structures of language) (Gleason, 1967). Thus, when we study grammar, we are, in fact, exploring the world of applied linguistics, the morphology and pragmatics of a language, or how the forms and structures of a language form syntactic structures or measures of meaning. Without becoming overly technical, grammar investigates language unit functions and how they are used in a sentence to convey meaning.

For those of us in the "peanut gallery," this means the study of nouns, verbs, adjectives, other parts of speech, and their functions. This includes how they convey meaning in communication; reading, listening, writing, or speaking. Grammar deals with morphemes and the word combinations used to form meaning. The study of grammar is very often connected to rules of grammar. In teaching adult English learners an instructor is frequently asked for the rules. The response is standard: "There is no rule save one: there is an exception to every rule." The study of grammar rules is also referred to as transformational grammar, which was once a cornerstone for teaching any "foreign" language (French, Spanish, German, etc.). This has also been labeled the "grammar translation method" whereby we learned how to conjugate verbs, the "cases" of nouns, prepositions, syntax, and pattern responses, in order to learn the language. This is also evident in the instruction of sentence diagramming (remember those days?) when we had to label every part of speech in each sentence. What, exactly, did diagramming propose to teach us?

Through diagramming sentences we were supposed to learn sentence structure and syntax: how the words "fit together" in a sentence. We isolated each word and learned what part of speech it was. But that knowledge did not really assist us in understanding the basic structure of English. We learned the forms of words, but did not really learn the functions of words. If one were "lucky" enough to study Latin, one would have learned not only parts of speech, but what role each part of speech plays in a sentence. Knowledge of Latin grammar requires us to study the role of each part of speech to the extent that no matter where a word is located in the sentence, the ending of that word indicates what part of speech it is and therefore what meaning the word carries. For example, Julius Caesar always began his sentences with the nominative case, which is the subject of the sentence, and the last word in his sentences was the verb. Knowing the ending of the words, in addition to the role the part of speech plays, is crucial to understand the meaning of the sentence in translation. Latin, a language not normally spoken now, was the forerunner for the language translation method. In learning Latin through this method we also learn the intricacies of English grammar. However, this method does not help us in learning grammatical structure in other languages.

How Should Grammar Be Taught?

Now we see a trend where "foreign" language teachers employ language acquisition strategies in their classroom—students learn a second language much like second language learners here learn English. "Rules" of grammar, which have previously driven how we learn grammar, are still very important, but they are secondary to understanding the concept of what role words play in sentence syntax and the resulting meaning of the combinations of those words. Isolated words do not form the entire context of meaning, how they are used in a sentence or paragraph conveys meaning. This leads us back to an emphasis on content based language instruction for understanding.

Diaz-Rico and Weed (1995) state that, "Grammar is the organizational framework for language and as such has been used as the organizational framework for language teaching" (p. 79). However, they agree that grammar taught in isolation is not effective for developing knowledge of language structure. Language should be taught thematically and organized around topics, ideas, and basic content. The structure of language should be taught as the need arises. Rules should be taught through the negotiation of meaning, as students comprehend context, and as they acquire the language and negotiate the understanding of communication (Weaver, 1996). Students will then be able to restructure the language based on this negotiation of meaning. Students often do not understand the relationship between the structure of a piece of writing and its meaning. They don't understand that an ill-conceived piece of writing may not communicate what the author intends because it either does not use the correct vocabulary (semantics) or because it is not structured properly (grammar).

Teaching grammar through isolated worksheets where students identify parts of speech does not assist them in understanding the function those words play in the syntax, not only of specific sentences, but also in the meaning of essays, lab reports, research, and other expository forms of writing. To assist students to acquire the grammatical structure of language, we need to teach the role of grammar in the context of language meaning. As we instruct students in what we expect from an essay ("Write a five paragraph essay on the major causes of the Civil War. Paragraph one will address…"), we could also state in the grading rubric that a specific number of points will be allocated for proper ending punctuation, proper capitalization, and appropriate subject/verb agreement. Or, we could point out how improper subject/verb agreement would cause us to err in conducting a science experiment. Modeling for students and then leading them through guided practice of proper grammatical structures in the context of the content area they are studying is more effective than asking the students to apply basic rules of grammar to isolated sentences.

How Are Writing Skills and Grammar Related?

According to Krashen (1984), there is no relationship between formal grammar instruction and effective writing skills. He also emphasizes the importance of wide reading in improving writing. Natural exposure to language through conversation and reading enhances our ability to communicate more effectively than learning the rules of grammar out of context. We learn grammar to improve communication, writing, or speaking. Here we return to Chomsky's language acquisition device (LAD), mentioned in chapter 4. We learn by listening and reading. The more exposure we have (listening and reading) to correct usage of the language, the more likely we are to use correct grammar. Fountas and Pinnell (2001) also discuss how we construct meaning with text and how the predictability of sentence structure and repeated patterns of language structure improves our ability to replicate those patterns. How we communicate is as important as what we communicate.

Betty Azar (2007) talks about "Grammar-Based Teaching," which is the need to teach grammar simultaneously with language acquisition. She distinguishes the two approaches by identifying the difference between academic instructors who teach the research and theory of language or the analysis of language and those practitioners who teach the synthesis of language (explicit instruction vs. communicative exposure). She also states that teaching explicit grammar works well when teaching grammatical structures in the context of the content area. That is to say that explicit teaching of isolated grammatical rules is not effective, but the instruction of grammatical rules when they appear as concerns in student writing is effective.

Halliday (1985b) stresses the importance of language learning through the knowledge of the forms and functions of words and their subsequent meaning. Scarcella (2003) refers to a continuum for learning grammar via forms and functions. Forms and functions relate to the parts of speech (noun, verb, preposition, etc.) and what meaning the function has in the sentence (Table 6.1). Consider the following example:

> We were expected to *produce* five varieties of vegetables for our art project. The various *produce* we brought to class were then used as models for a drawing. (The word *produce* appears as both a verb, to bring something forth, and as a collective noun, i.e., vegetables.)

Table 6.1 Basic Forms and Functions of Language

Forms	Functions
NOUN	• Names people, places, and things • Acts as the subject of a sentence or the object of a verb or preposition
PRONOUN	• Takes the place of a noun
VERB	• Shows action or a "state of being"
ADJECTIVE	• Describes nouns • Answers the questions "How many, How much, What kind"? • They compare
ADVERB	• Describes verbs • Answers the questions "How" and "When"?
PREPOSITION	• Shows placement or location • A prepositional phrase includes the prepositions and an object and it also shows placement or location
SUBJECT	• Who or what is doing the action in a sentence
PREDICATE	• What action is being accomplished • Action can just "be"
POSSESSIVE	• Shows something belongs to someone
CONTRACTION	• Combines a helping verb with a main verb
CONJUNCTION	• Connects words, phrases, or clauses

Scarcella's continuum includes a method where students:

1. Learn the rule of grammar,
2. Use the rule, produce output,
3. Use output as input (they personalize the example) and, ultimately,
4. Acquire the new grammatical feature.

However, even through the process of learning the rules of grammar, Scarcella states, "Knowledge of grammar without the ability to apply it is useless" (p. 61). This reference reinforces the need for students to learn grammar in context.

Brick and Mortar Words

The home builder must understand how the plumbing system works in order to lay the foundation of the house and to build the framework for the house. Students need to understand the forms (parts of speech) and functions (the meaning those parts of speech convey) of language to construct effective writing.

Dutro and Moran (2002) state that general utility vocabulary, as opposed to content specific vocabulary, should also be classified as forms of language. They use the metaphor of building a structure to develop the idea of "brick" and "mortar" words, If you use too many "bricks" (heavy, dense, content specific vocabulary) and not enough "mortar" (connecting words, prepositions, pronouns, signal words; see Table 4.6, forms of the verb "to be," etc.), the foundation will collapse. For the most part we all know that we need to teach the brick words—the content specific vocabulary—but some of us do not realize that our students are also unaware of the meanings of some of the mortar words, which are the everyday vocabulary words that indicate what the text organizational pattern is; they also give us "signals" as to what information we can expect to read next. They are the context clues which assist us in deciphering meaning of the unknown "bricks" and they are also the words which "connect the dots" or the meaning in a paragraph, and assist us in transitioning from one idea or thought to the next. Some signal words indicate that there is a conclusion coming (moreover, thus, finally, etc.), some indicate a time or sequence (first, next, before, etc.), and others may indicate location. Knowledge of the meanings of *both* brick and mortar words is essential to understand meaning. However, with limited knowledge of content specific vocabulary (bricks), a student may be able to ascertain meaning if they know all the signal or mortar words and have a healthy knowledge of root words and affixes. Imagine a student attempting to choose the correct word in parentheses:

When the temperature of water _____ to 0°C, it will begin to (*condense, evaporate, freeze, or melt*).

If the blank is replaced with the word *increases,* is the brick word required to complete the statement different than if the word *decreases* is substituted in the blank? Is there any context which might allow the student to determine which word belongs in the blank? If the student is unfamiliar with these important mortar words, even with a solid knowledge of the vocabulary of changes in state, their ability to answer the question is reduced to 50/50 at best.

Just to drive home the point, look at what happens to the statement if we replace all of the mortar words in this simple statement with blanks:

____the temperature of water _____ to 0°C, it will _____to (*condense, evaporate, freeze, or melt*).

On the other hand, removing the brick words from the statement actually causes fewer problems given the same level of knowledge on the vocabulary of changes in state:

When the _____of water increases to 0___, it will begin to (*condense, evaporate, freeze, or melt*).

We often assume that students know these "everyday" words, but it is not uncommon to find that words like *increase* and *decrease* are not part of their everyday language. Students have to possess this knowledge in order to successfully communicate their ideas, especially in writing.

The conclusion of 90 years of research is that teaching grammar in isolation does not seem to have an effect on the writing of more than a few students (Weaver, 1996). Teaching grammar through writing activities, where students learn how to effectively manipulate syntax for optimum meaning is more helpful than traditional grammar instruction (i.e., rules instruction). Teaching students how to edit work is another useful tool in the acquisition of grammar, but difficult at best. If students demonstrate the ability to write well enough to be able to recognize errors in other students' work, then this is a very useful strategy for reinforcing grammar instruction in the content areas. When teaching students how to peer edit work, they need to be explicitly taught what types of structures they are looking for and how to offer suggestions for correction to improve both meaning and syntax.

Why Should Content-Area Teachers Teach Grammar?

Each content area has its own characteristic uses of grammar and syntax that students must learn in order to write effectively in that area. Thus, not all of the skills they learn in English classes are readily transferable to effective writing in the content area. Because of this, if we want our students to write effectively in our content areas, we must teach them how to do so. However, grammar is a topic that many content-area teachers probably feel least qualified to teach. Many teachers do not write well themselves, and therefore have difficulty teaching grammatical conventions within their content area. However, if we design instruction to meet the needs of students as we see concerns arise from their content-area writing (for example, proper subject/verb agreement, proper use of ending punctuation, etc.), we can make our instruction more effective. To clarify: grammar is the set of rules we use to determine the endings we put on words; syntax is the structure of the sentence and how it is used to create meaning. In order to write well and to communicate effectively we need to understand and be able to apply the forms and functions of words, which necessitates using appropriate grammar and syntax.

Appendix 7 is a complete grammar reference handbook. Because our study of grammar has been somewhat limited, the authors felt that inclusion of a grammar guide would assist most content-area teachers. True, this handbook might be a bit more detailed than what content-area teachers might use on a regular basis, but we felt that more, not less, is better. This will also serve as a personal reference for us as teachers who venture out into the world of publishing research. This appendix serves as a guide or handbook only—we do not intend that it be used to teach grammar, per se. When issues or concerns in student use of grammar arise in the classroom, here is where you can turn for assistance! To illustrate—a question arose (when writing this text) as to the use of *produce*, a collective noun, and proper subject/verb agreement. In the example given in this chapter we use the plural verb *were*. To follow the rule given in the grammar handbook section of this chapter, collective nouns usually require singular verbs. However, in some cases, especially where the members of a group (collective noun) are acting as individuals, the plural verb form would then be used. This is a good example of the exception to every rule. We hope that you find this guide to be a handy reference.

Writing and Academic Language Literacy

When we discuss the writing component of academic language, we usually refer to the density and complexity of the language (Schleppegrell, 2004). Academic language is dense in the use of abstract, content specific, and dependent vocabulary, and it is also complex in sentence structure and other syntactical expressions. Often we have to deconstruct dense academic language in the reading phase to clearly understand the meaning of the text (see example in Table 6.2). In deconstructing language, we simplify the syntax and grammar and try to use vocabulary that is easier to understand, but we should not "water down" or "dummy down" the content-area information. Instead, our job is to teach students to decipher this dense language for themselves.

We deconstruct receptive language (listening and reading) in order to

Table 6.2 Deconstructing Dense Academic Language

Science Text Language—High School Earth Science*	The Same Text, Deconstructed (simplifying vocabulary and sentence structure)
A hurricane begins when very warm, moist air over the evaporating ocean rises rapidly. When moisture in the rising warm air condenses, a large amount of energy in the form of latent heat is released. This heat increases the force of the rising air. Moist tropical air continues to be drawn into the column of rising air, releasing more heat and sustaining the process. An average hurricane has an energy content equal to the total amount of electricity used in the United States for six months.	A hurricane begins when warm, moist air over the ocean rises rapidly. The air over the ocean is moist due to evaporation of water from the ocean into the air. When the water in the rising air condenses — that is, when the gaseous water in the atmosphere becomes liquid water and forms raindrops — it releases heat, which warms the air surrounding it. When a gas becomes a liquid, it releases heat. The more heat in the air, the faster the air will rise. As the air above the ocean rises, it draws in more moist air from over the surrounding ocean. As the water in this moist air condenses, more heat is added to the column of rising air, making it rise even faster. This is what generates the high winds found in hurricanes. This change of state (when a gas becomes a liquid) converts enough energy to run all the homes in the US for six months.

*Taken from *Modern Earth Science*, Sager, Ramsey, Phillips, and Watenpaugh, 2002, p. 505.

construct or express ideas using academic language (speaking and writing). Speaking can act as a precursor for writing and is generally a less formal register of academic language. Academic language literacy in writing can be defined as the use of content-area (math, science, social studies, etc.) vocabulary with complex syntax appropriate to the academic register and content area to demonstrate the knowledge of the subject or to organize information learned in the content area.

The Relationship between Verbal and Written Language

In teaching writing to high school students we have noticed a trend that emulates that of reading: students read less, therefore comprehend less, and consequently write less and are less able to write well. It is not uncommon for students to complete an essay, proofread it, edit it, and then turn it in, thinking that not only is it grammatically correct, but also that it is a coherent piece of writing and the rationale in it makes perfect sense. How many essays have you read that make no sense to you whatsoever, but perfect sense to the writer? When you read a problematic essay (out loud) to a student, so that they may "hear" their mistakes, they typically become very agitated and exclaim, "But I didn't write that!" They may then proceed to yank the paper from your hands and read their essay to you in not altogether perfect format, but in a more comprehensible format than is on the paper. In other words, students are able to fictionalize their work when verbalizing it and to use appropriate grammar, even when it is not on the page. They actually add words where words are missing and appropriate syntax and grammar as they are reading. It is really amazing to watch, and you have likely experienced a similar problem while editing your own work. It is very easy to miss your own errors simply because you know what you *meant* to write, even if you actually wrote something different.

This disconnect between oral and written discourse is a major difficulty. While students generally speak with reasonably accurate (or at least understandable) grammar and syntax, they often have difficulty translating their speaking skills into written language. In part, this is because of the discrepancy between the oral register and the academic register. If students wrote in the same way they speak, they would probably make fewer grammatical errors, and be more comprehensible. However, they would also lose vocabulary and end up writing in a much less formal register than is necessary for academic success and effective written communication.

Most writers have a tendency to write in a way that is similar to their speech, but in accomplished writers it is generally the voice that is similar, while the register of the language becomes more formal when it is written. It is this translation between registers that causes difficulty, and, as discussed above, the difficulty, especially when reading your own work, of recognizing the differences. Students don't necessarily "see" that what they are writing does not match what they are saying. One way to overcome this problem is to actually type or write exactly what the student is saying so that they can "see" their words in print. Novelist E. M. Forster (1927, p. 39) stated it well when he said, "How do I know what I think until I see what I say?"

Student Writing Skills

We expect a higher level of achievement in writing when students arrive at high school than we actually do in reading. In actuality students' writing ability will be much lower than their ability to read. Oglan (2003) describes three levels of writers: reluctant, developing, and independent. Most of the students we work with would most likely fall into the reluctant writers' category. Reluctant writers often write in the first person, have a great deal of difficulty with content and organization, and barely write in complete sentences, much less coherent paragraphs. Developing writers have the ability to organize an essay properly, use the appropriate conventions, use concrete evidence, and vary their sentence structure. We seldom see independent writers at the high school level, but there are some. These writers are well-read and advanced in their use of conventions, organization, evidence, and sentence structure. Writing skillfully includes the ability to competently address proper language conventions (as well as more complex syntax and sentence structure), use appropriate organization in the text, and reference detailed evidence to reinforce the topic.

The reason we have overly high expectations is probably because we don't like to teach writing. If we don't write skillfully ourselves, we will have a problem teaching writing. We, as teachers, may need to shore up our own writing skills before we can effectively teach them. A review of the research regarding best methods for teaching writing, however, indicates that teachers should be proficient writers in order to effectively teach writing (Dickey et al., 2005). Keith Caldwell, a Fremont, California, high school teacher who spent many years conducting in-service training workshops on writing for the Bay Area Writing Project and National Writing Project, reported that he began each session "with this question: 'Could you please tell me what institution of higher education taught you how to teach writing?'" The response, Caldwell said, was silence, "because the participants—elementary, secondary, and college teachers—[could] give no answer" (cited in Neill, 1982, p. 11). This tells us that teachers need more practice in effective writing skills in order to be able to train students how to write.

Building the Academic Register for Writing

Writing does not occur in a vacuum, but is dependent on the student's ability to comprehend information and express it. Writing needs to be taught explicitly as students express their understanding of content using expository writing. We also know that struggling readers and English language learners are limited in both oral and reading skills (Brice, 2004). Students in early writing phases write the way they speak. Vygotsky (1978) believed that meaning and understanding are derived from the ability to conduct social interactions with teachers to present information within the student's zone of proximal development—the area between the student's actual development level (what student can currently do independently) and the potential development that can be achieved with teacher guidance. Teachers can help students make the transition from oral language discourse to writing through the use of scaffolding, modeling, and guided practice, helping students become more proficient in the process of expressing their thoughts verbally and in writing. These are opportunities for them to use and practice their everyday register as they acquire the academic register necessary to prepare them for the expressive activity of expository writing. This expression begins with oral explanation and moves to a written form in a series of specific steps in the writing process.

Oral language opportunities using appropriate register related to the content such as open ended questions, guided discussion, modeling, and any other oral language activity need to be carefully planned and explicitly taught in the content area by teachers (Kinsella & Feldman, 2005). Oral language is a common register used to communicate or express ideas about the content in order to expand understanding and thinking. Students need to be able to construct their own meaning from their understanding of the content information. Table 6.3 displays how receptive and expressive language functions can be established so that students can practice and learn content using their own everyday register. The teacher can set up the activities to make sure that students practice, use, and learn the appropriate academic language register which then supports the writing skills. Research indicates that "teacher talk" about student's writing is highly correlated to student achievement (Dickey et al. 2005).

Assessing Writing in Order to Develop Writing Skills

We have a problem with assessing the ability to write. Writing is not as easy to assess as content-area skills or reading ability, nor is it assessed as often. Writing is much more subjective to evaluate and requires more of our time. We cannot evaluate a student's writing ability by giving him or her a multiple choice test. We think we can assess student grammar ability this way, or by using a worksheet where they fill in the blanks, or by asking them to underline the subject once and the verb twice in sentences, but that is debatable.

Table 6.3 Academic Oral Language Use in the Context Areas to Support Writing

Receptive Language Functions (Teacher Talk)	Expressive Language Strategies (Student Talk)	Examples for Writing Process Activities
As teacher presents content these can be used to make content comprehensible:	As students respond, these skills need to be practiced using oral language:	1. Classroom discussion of open-ended questions for prewriting
	Repeating	2. Pair share for prewriting
Explanation	Elaborating/Amplifying	
Description	Clarifying	3. Teacher explicitly
Comparison	Specificity	models oral responses to
Assessment or	Paraphrasing	questions about content
Summary		then students practice.

An eighth grade teacher once bragged that her students were experts in grammar. Challenging her, the principal told her to have the students identify just the subjects and verbs in the sentences on the first two pages of the first chapter in their literature book. Students claimed that this was going to be easy and began. About half way through the first three sentences the students began moaning, "Miss, I don't understand!" Knowing how to identify subjects and verbs on a worksheet is completely different from identifying them in a literature piece (in context) and different again from having the ability to recognize when sentences you have written are run-ons or fragments. We have to assess the writer's use of conventions, evidence, and their organization. It is not uncommon to have three people evaluate a writing piece (written by a teacher or a student), using the same rubric, with the same training on how to use the rubric, and end up with three completely different results. In spite of such assessment problems, standardized tests (the California High School Exit Exam, the SAT, etc.) now include a writing sample as part of their assessment.

In assessing or grading student essays, we often have a tendency to correct the work for the students instead of focusing on correcting one issue at a time (i.e., subject–verb agreement or ending punctuation). This promotes a tendency to "bleed all over" a student's paper. Instead, we need to focus on their ability to use their language acquisition device (LAD), as mentioned in chapter 1 to "hear" the problems in their writing. If students can verbally correct their written mistakes by reading their work aloud, we should use this ability to assist in proofreading their papers. If they will read their work, word for word, they will eventually be able to hear their mistakes, especially run-on sentences, fragments, and incorrect verb tenses. The main difficulty is that getting students to actually read their written work, rather than what they think they wrote, can be a struggle.

Assessment of writing should be a formative, not a summative, process where we pay careful attention to the process as well as the product. If we focus on one criterion (organization, content, syntax, etc.) where the expectations are clearly defined and modeled for the student, we can expect a higher success rate on the writing assignment. As we progress through the term, we add more criteria, until, ideally, by the end of the year, students are aware of, and including, most of the criteria we want them to address This technique has two major advantages: (1) it makes expectations clear for the student and focuses them explicitly on one aspect of writing and the content area, and (2) it makes grading a much easier task. Collaborating with students to improve their work, rather than simply judging them for what is wrong with their work, will also foster success and participation in the writing process. Teacher conferences with the students are an effective method to achieve student collaboration and "buy-in" where students are actively involved in the assignment and desire to seek success in communicating their ideas on paper. Conferencing with the students individually or in groups does take a lot of time, but can be accomplished in conjunction with other anchor assignments in the content-area classroom, where students may be working on other aspects of the writing project (including gathering information on the topic and peer editing one another's work). The teacher's connection to the student is personal and important to ensure that the student is "on the right track" and to give the student input not only on the format of the writing but the content of the project as well. This is assessment versus evaluation (where assessment is a formative process and evaluation is a summative process), where the analysis of a student's work is performance-based and ongoing, as opposed to a final analysis of the completed work, which can be considered evaluation (Olson, 2007).

The assessment versus evaluation notion promotes the use of scaffolding in the teaching of writing. The very definition of scaffolding is to offer a support system. As we model and conduct guided practice to demonstrate effective methods for constructing meaning in writing, we are incrementally sculpting student s' ability to express themselves. The writing process itself is a lesson in scaffolding:

- Step 1 is the brainstorming phase where students gather information on the topic they will write about.
- Step 2 is the draft stage where students begin to put their thoughts down on paper in a rough format.
- Step 3 is the revision stage where we revisit the work again after the brainstorming draft, to make sure we are "on task" and fulfilling the requirements of the assignment.
- Step 4 is the editing phase where students seek input to improve and finalize their draft.
- Step 5 is the publication, or final draft of the project.

Or, as a teacher candidate in one of the author's classes stated:

1. Prewrite: Think, stupid.
2. Draft: Now write it down.
3. Revise: That's a start, now sober up and make some sense of it.
4. Edit: Thank God for spell check.
5. Postwrite (publish): Attaboy! Now share it. Don't be shy…

Note that the steps are not mutually exclusive in that students may revisit any one of them, even up to the final publication, at any time. If students are not satisfied with the final publication of their project, they may return to the drafting stage or even the brainstorming phase to redesign the project. Again, it is important to explicitly teach, model, and practice each stage of the process in order to ensure that students are fully aware of what is expected of them and that they are aware of how to produce what is expected. Students will need to practice peer editing several times, with explicit guidelines, in order to be able to effectively critique each other's work (see also the Writing Rubric, appendix 4). The guidelines could involve asking students to respond to the following: Check sentences for subject–verb agreement or capitalization. Has the writer included evidence for his factual statements? Are the facts noted sequentially—first, second, third? Are the statements made clear and easily understood using the appropriate academic language required in the content area? If not, what questions does the reviewer have? See Table 6.4 for a sample peer editing worksheet which can be modified to meet the needs

Table 6.4 Peer Editing Feedback Worksheet (with Sample Topics)

Format	Yes/No	Evidence (When a "NO" response is indicated, show evidence of where or why the writer did not demonstrate the skill)
1. Most words are correctly capitalized?		
2. Most sentences are complete, with a subject and verb?		
3. Most spelling is correct?		
4. Some sentences show complex structure? (Show evidence)		
5. All verb tenses are correctly used and subjects/verbs agree?		
6. The writer demonstrates a clear beginning, middle and end to their composition?		If not, what does the writer start and end with? What evidence does the writer need to support the middle of their composition?
Content		**Evidence**
1. If this is a persuasive essay, clear evidence for each statement is given?		
2. Has the writer stated a clear hypothesis?		
3. Clear arguments are stated both for and against the topic given?		
4. (Other topics as related to specific subject area assignments….)		

of the content area and specific assignment. This movement from modeling to guided practice to actual application of strategies is another example of scaffolding information and instruction for students where students can apply academic language and concepts.

Writing is interactive. We ask students to discuss topics and information learned in the content areas and then request that they either report back or reflect on the learning process. In doing so we move them from highly interactive, guided writing activities to the final draft which can be individually or group produced, depending on the specific goals of your assignment. As they refine their writing ability and their writing projects we should maintain interaction with students, modeling and reinforcing use of the proper register. Please see the end of this chapter for a model lesson which demonstrates the aforementioned strategies.

Writing: "Into, Through, and Beyond"

Writing in the content areas is, for the most part, expository. We use writing to explain, inform, reflect, interpret, compare, and contrast and occasionally, to persuade. Students make connections to the reading by predicting what the author will write, questioning what the author did write, generalizing what the author wrote, and evaluating the result (Olson, 2007). In parallel with the sequence of teaching students how to read text, expository writing can be taught in three stages: "Into," "Through," and "Beyond" (chapter 5).

When students begin reading text (the "into" phase) they should be introduced to the format of the writing project (description, summary, process, etc.). In this phase students gather information to support their writing task. Teachers model the activity for students and lead them through guided practice of what they will expect on the draft and the final product. This is also the organizing or outlining phase where students could make good use of graphic organizers and note taking systems (see chapters 3 and 4). For this phase, teachers can use group discussion regarding the "big questions" (questions which drive the concept being taught), teacher led discussion, and other clustering or organizing strategies. Quick writes are also useful in this stage, as students connect the new knowledge to prior knowledge. For example, Unrau (2008, p. 230) tells his students he wants them to play "DEAD" (Drop Everything and Draft) in order to assess how well students can relate to the topic he wants them to learn (which parallels DEAR—Drop Everything and Read—a sustained silent reading strategy, chapter 5).

During the "through" phase, for example, students would be asked to write notes, draw diagrams, and fill in graphic organizers, which assist them in completing the writing assignment. The draft of the assignment would be completed during this phase, as well as preliminary summaries, reports of information, description of information, journals, and logs.

During the final phase of writing ("beyond"), the students would be asked to analyze or summarize the text in order to complete the writing project. Some of the brainstorming and annotation in the "through" stage can be accomplished through group activity which would assist in differentiating instruction to meet the needs of struggling readers and other special needs students in the class. Reports, summaries, directions, research papers, and observational essays are good examples of expository writing; see Table 6.5 for more examples. In this case, student writing is used to assess what they have learned; it also assists students in the application and acquisition of new knowledge.

Activities that Develop Writing Skills

Other types of writing, such as narrative, descriptive, and persuasive essays, can also be introduced in content-area writing. This could include, for example, comparisons, letters to famous figures, journals, text reviews, lab reports, travel brochures, interviews, learning logs, biographies, autobiographies, and observation reports. These types of writing can supplement expository writing by including more academic language and more density in their syntactic and grammatical structures.

Writing activities range from simple reaction papers to process projects. They include double entry journals where students reflect on *what* they learned and demonstrate *how* they learned in I-Search papers, three-search papers, research reports, essays, and position papers. In process projects students need not only to report information learned, but also to analyze and synthesize that information. For example, when writing a position paper, information is gathered, then it is discussed in class to determine the feasibility of taking a stand either for or against a theory or issue. This can range from discussing in biology whether or not viruses are alive, in history debating euthanasia, or in math comparing individual to population probability predictions.

The "I-search" paper was developed by Ken Macrorie (1988). It differs from the regular research paper in that it allows the writer to use a narrative style of writing as they research a topic they are familiar with through primary sources and through interviews. Students actually tell the story of their research in four parts: the summary of what they know, a discussion of what they want to find out and why, a report of what they discovered, and a reflection of how they learned the information.

The "three-search" paper was developed by Terry Phelps (1992) in a quest to have the students write a research report which included student comments and reflections and not just a string of quotations from different sources. It is similar to the I-search paper in that it asks the students to write their opinions and it involves four steps. First the students read past students' papers on the topic chosen, after which they brainstorm and annotate whatever experiences they have had with the topic. In groups of three, students discuss what should be added or eliminated from the already established list of ideas. Then the students interview an expert on the topic and a peer to obtain more information and other viewpoints about the research topic. The final step asks the students to conduct a now focused search of primary sources to assist the writer in the completion of the paper. Phelps intended for the final stage, which is normally the first stage in the research process, to be more focused and narrow because the students are now very familiar with their topic and do not need as wide an array of information.

RAFT is an organizing concept which directs the learner to identify the *Role* of the writer (reporter, letter writer, researcher, narrator, etc.), the *Audience* the writer is writing to (newspaper reader, corporate sponsor, home owners, etc.), the *Format* of the writing (news article, persuasive letter, how-to manual, etc.), and the *Topic* (current event, changing the method for manufacturing a toy, lab report and directions, etc.) in their writing activity. Unrau (2008) compares using the RAFT graphic organizer to Huck Finn floating down the Mississippi as students explore their content area. He explains that students need instruction in "RAFTing" before leaving shore as we explain and model the components of the RAFT organizer. He recommends that the teacher "RAFT" along with their students as they use the rudder to decide what their topic will be, the audience, their role in the writing process, and the format of their writing.

There are many different types of activities for writing in the content areas (Table 6.5), but the focus is always on gathering information and then summarizing and analyzing it. Special attention is directed to the writing process and how to assess student writing to facilitate the effectiveness of their communication. As we mentor students in the writing process through extensive modeling and guided practice, we need to be sure to focus on improving writing incrementally, one step at a time.

To illustrate the strategies described in this chapter, we insert a sample lesson here: *"Three-Search" Research Paper on the Holocaust*—(end of first semester).

Sample Lesson: Three Search Papers on the Holocaust

In this lesson students are introduced to a concept (the Holocaust and the historical, social, religious, political, and economic issues and causes leading to the "Final Solution"), and then discuss the concept briefly with the

Table 6.5 Suggested Writing Projects for the Content Areas

Content Area	Projects
Science	• Observations/Description of Events (sight, sounds, events) • Methods • Notebooks • Lab Reports
Math	• Description of procedures • Process • "How to" • Practical Applications • Word Problems
Social Studies	• Description of Events • Interviews • Biographical Sketches • Historical Fiction • Advertisements
All Content Areas	• Journals • Research Projects • Report of Information • Learning Logs

teacher. The teacher then asks them to research the concept using a set of "big questions" (see the Expressive and Receptive Academic Language list, chapter 3) in order to build background knowledge for the concept. In the first activity the teacher and students review vocabulary using strategies outlined in chapter 4. Vocabulary cards can then be used to create cloze activities, daily oral language activities, or for a "Slap Game," to promote multiple exposures to the words students are not immediately familiar with. To complete building background knowledge, the teacher models a semantic feature analysis graphic organizer so that students can sort the information in the beginning stages of the writing process (see Table 6.6). This is also the draft stage of the writing process.

The next step involves a guided group discussion (see the "Three-Search" research paper, described earlier in this chapter) of the issues involved in the Holocaust. At this point, students are still writing, but they are elaborating on the information given regarding the issues mentioned. They also receive feedback from their peers and the teachers regarding researched facts. The

Table 6.5.1 Three Sample Papers on the Holocaust

OBJECTIVE(S) PURPOSE	• The student will investigate and evaluate the historical, social, religious, politica,l and economic issues which resulted in the "Final Solution" or forced immigration and near extermination of the Jewish race during the Holocaust (WWII).
CA STANDARDS	• (10.8 #5) Analyze the Nazi policy of pursuing racial purity, especially against the European Jews; its transformation into the Final Solution; and the Holocaust that resulted in the murder of six million Jewish civilians.
MATERIALS	• Overhead transparencies & pens, computers, textbooks—research regarding World War II, paper, pencils, graphic organizer outlines, materials for illustrations • Vocabulary lists
ACTIVITIES: Introduction (Anticipatory Set) R3, R4, E3, E4, E6, E11	INTRODUCTION: The Allied forces are going to hold a hearing to determine if the Nazi's should be charged with the murder of six million Jews during World War II. The Nazi's claim that there are valid historical, social, religious, political and economic reasons for forcing the Jews into concentration camps and consequently their murder. The Allied proponents feel that even though the German claim to a superior Aryan race might be justified in the eyes of the Nazi's, the near extinction of the Jewish race was not justified. Your group of four students will be assigned either to defend or prosecute the German Nazi's. In their defense or prosecution you will need to outline and historical, social, religious, political and economic issues surrounding the Holocaust and answer the following questions: 1. What were the Nuremburg Laws and why were they implemented? 2. What other procedures did the Nazi's impose to limit further production of the Jewish race? 3. What political measures did the Nazi's use to further restrict the Jews? 4. Why didn't the Jews just leave Germany and German occupied territories? 5. Describe the Nazi's rationale for proclaiming Nordic non-Jews as Aryan. 6. What were the major events which led to the "Final Solution"? 7. What were the social and economic results of the laws they implemented to protect the Aryan race?

ACTIVITY #1:

[Activity #1
Vocabulary]

Ghetto   Concentration   emigration   immigration
Quarantine Acquiesce   Plaque   Holocaust
(Add to this list any words which students identify as
problematic and which the teachers identify.)

R5, R6, R8, E5

- Teacher models root words, cognates, prefixes, suffixes
- Students work in groups to finish list on vocabulary cards

ACTIVITY #2:

[Activity #2
Graphic Organizer]

- The teacher begins by modeling a graphic organizer.
  A T-Chart, Flow-Chart or Semantic Features Analysis format
  can be used. (See attached sample)
- The students finish the chart in their groups of six students—
  two readers, two recorders and two reporters for each group.

R1, R2, R3, R7,
E1, E2, E6, E8,
E9, E10, E 12

ACTIVITY #3 PREWRITING:

- The teacher assigns a "defense" or "prosecution" position
  to each group. The teacher brainstorms with the class the
  development of a list of three rationales or charges for each
  of the historical, social, religious, political or economic issues
  which led to the "Final Solution". The groups then each

[Activity #3
Prewriting]

  complete their list.

ACTIVITY #4 GROUP DISCUSSION:

R2,R3, R7, E1,
E2, E6, E9, E11,
E12
[Activity #4
Group Discussion]

- The teacher splits the class up into a defense and prosecution
  group and the individual groups share their lists with one
  another. They then decide on a common list of charges/
  defenses to present.

ACTIVITY #5 MOCK TRIAL:

R1, R2, R8, E6,
E10, E12

[Activity #5
Mock Trial]

- The class conducts a mock trial with the charges and defense
  chosen from each group, with most of the class members
  given a role in the trial. The students take notes during the
  trial as to whether they will charge the Germans with
  murder or not.

ACTIVITY #6 PRE-WRITE:

R1, R2, R8, E6,
E10, E12

- After the teacher models what the paper should look like,
  the students now consult primary research to write an
  opinion paper of why they think the Allied Forces should
  file charges against the Nazi's for the murder of nearly six
  million Jews and the historical, social, religious, political
  and economic reasons why the Germans committed these
  crimes.

[Activity #6
Pre-write]

- A grading rubric is established for the paper which includes
  content issues (organization, evidence and structure) as well
  as mechanics issues.

(*continued*)

Table 6.5.1 Continued

	ACTIVITY #7 PEER EDITING:
E2, E8, E13	• The teacher models filling in a peer editing feedback worksheet (see sample worksheet) and the students work with a partner to peer edit their writing. Because this is the end of the first semester, it is assumed that the students have already reviewed complete sentences, proper ending punctuation, capitalization, and subject verb placement and agreement. The focus for grammar will be on using more descriptive sentences and language. The teacher assists students by holding individual editing sessions as well. Students first read their partner's writing out loud, then proceed to peer edit their work. Discussion sessions follow
[Activity #7 Peer Editing]	the peer editing so that each partner understands the other partner's concerns.
	ACTIVITY #8 FINAL DRAFT:
E2, E8. E13	• Individual students (or pairs, depending on the writing ability of your class) produce a final product which is then graded according to established rubric.
Activity #8 Final Draft E2, E8, E13	
ASSESSMENT	• Students write an opinion paper exploring the historical, social, religious, political and economic issues which resulted in the "Final Solution" or forced immigration and near extermination of the Jewish race during the Holocaust
REFLECTION & EXTENSIONS	• Other public speaking or writing activities can be assigned as first, the teacher determines whether or not their students have mastered the major issues concerning the causes of the Holocaust and second, as time in the class permits.

mock trial, which is the next activity, is a further refinement of the draft stage of writing and the discussion of gathered information, clarifying the information for veracity.

The next two activities cover steps 3 and 4 of the writing process (and the "through phase") where the students write their draft of the final paper and ask a partner to peer edit it. Note that the peer editing is modeled by the teacher and guided by the peer editing feedback worksheet (Table 6.7). This provides the students with interaction and feedback from their peers and the teacher regarding their progress on the writing assignment.

The last activity is the final draft of the paper which will then be evaluated

Table 6.6 Events Leading to the "Final Solution" During the Holocaust: Semantic Features Analysis

Issues	Actions by Nazis	Possible Charges from Allied Forces
HISTORICAL	1. Nuremburg Laws	
SOCIAL		
RELIGIOUS		
POLITICAL		
ECONOMIC		

based on a common rubric to be established by the teacher with the students' input. This is step 5 of the writing process and the "beyond" phase of writing. A few of the really good papers that are produced can be sent to an online journal or published in the school newspaper. Another idea might be to ask students to write a summary of the mock trial's proceedings to be published in the school or local newspaper or in a paper produced by the class. There are many other ways to model the strategies suggested in this chapter; the authors have selected a select few to demonstrate implementation for you.

Inherent in any writing instruction is the need to address the needs of different learners. Activities should be structured to accommodate the English learner, struggling reader, accelerated student, and students with other needs. In this sample lesson, the final product can be completed by a group,

Table 6.7 Peer Editing Feedback Worksheet (Holocaust)

Format	Yes/ No	Evidence (When a "NO" response is indicated, show evidence of where or why the writer did not demonstrate the skill)
1. Most sentences are complete and vary in structure with many sentences containing independent and dependent clauses.		
2. The vocabulary used is near grade level with multi-level descriptions of events and some figurative language used. Adjectives and describing phrases are used.		
Content		**Evidence**
1. Clear evidence for each statement is given.		
2. The writer clearly establishes a stand describing in detail why the charges against the Germans should hold up.		
3. The historical, social, religious, political, and economic issues are all addressed.		
4. The conclusion is viable and relates to all the items discussed.		

a pair of students, or individually, depending on the writing and language abilities of your learners.

Summary

Developing the writing skills of our students incrementally is the most effective way to improve their writing. If our students do not arrive in our rooms with the ability to write well, to communicate fluently, then we should nurture that skill through collaborative efforts which build upon their innate ability to express their ideas and thoughts.

CHAPTER 7

Summing Up

In chapter 1 the authors presented an overview of the history of the term *academic language*, a definition of academic language, and why we have to teach it in the content areas. In chapter 2 we offered ideas for motivating students, along with some research on what students claim motivates them. Chapter 3 offers insight as to why we began writing this text. The term *academic language* has been on the table for a number of years, but we have yet to see organization of the application of strategies that upper grade teachers (4–12) can use to facilitate the teaching of language in social studies, math, and science. That is where we have placed the Es and Rs list and the observation protocol checklist. The remaining three chapters address academic language in the major domains of vocabulary, reading, and writing.

In receiving academic language students will benefit from reading repair strategies (see chapter 5) particularly when deconstructing dense academic language passages. Their increased awareness of root words, affixes, cognates, and signal words (see chapter 4) can assist them to develop confidence in their reading to the point where unknown vocabulary will not cause undue stress. Instead, they will be able to approximate the meaning of the unknown word and continue on with their reading. This skill is very helpful when taking state or national standardized tests.

Grammar acquisition is also a critical factor in the ability to use the appropriate expressive or receptive register. Without knowing the correct grammatical forms and functions, students will not be able to effectively use the formal academic register required in classrooms. While this is not emphasized in the Es and Rs list as a specific teaching strategy, it is nonetheless, important to include in the teacher's bag of tricks. Teaching writing so that students will have full knowledge of complete sentences integrated with complex sentences, proper use of adjectives, adverbs, and appropriate paper organization and content are also strategies the content teacher needs to be aware of. These skills are explained in full detail in chapter 6.

The text was written not only for self-edification, but also to assist preservice and in-service teachers. Our approach has been very straightforward and somewhat informal. We have not included formal exercises or questions at the end of each chapter; but we have included the sample lessons in a format which easily lends itself to further practice of the application of the strategies. The Professional Input and Feedback Form (Table 3.2, in chapter 3) can be used as a checklist for observing teacher use of academic language instructional strategies and behaviors, along with the Es and Rs list located in chapter 3 (Table 3.1) and in appendix 1. There are also four additional lesson plans located in appendix 3, where the reader can practice identifying the expressive and receptive academic language strategies and behaviors within a lesson. These lists are by no means an exhaustive list of those strategies and behaviors which define academic language. They are what the authors believe to be a set of strategies which will assist teachers to build academic language in their classrooms in order to assist students achieve and acquire content-area knowledge. There are more strategies and teacher behaviors delineated in chapters 3 through 6 which will assist teachers to improve their delivery of academic language.

We expect that the text will be a major contribution to the field, especially in improving secondary school performance at a time when student achievement is critically important for all stakeholders. The intention of the authors was to fill a gap for secondary stakeholders as the current field of research, rich in the development of strategies to improve literacy with English learners and for lower grade students, is not replete with information to assist secondary school teachers. We hope that this text has been useful in offering an array of ideas and effective instructional strategies which teachers can use in the classroom.

Glossary

Affixes: Prefixes and suffixes.

Anchor assignment: Assignment given to students which is usually completed individually and is reinforcement for skills already learned.

Brick words: Usually content-area vocabulary; dense or difficult vocabulary indigenous to the content area.

Cognates: Words which look almost the same in English and Spanish (can be any Latin-based language); i.e., transportation (English), transportacion (Spanish).

Constructivist approach: Students, through the processes of *accommodation* and *assimilation*, construct new knowledge from their experiences. This derives from Piaget's theory.

Content literacy: Use reading and writing to acquire new knowledge in a discipline.

Context-embedded language: Concrete language.

Context-reduced language: Abstract language.

Decode: The ability to sound out words with intonation and pitch.

Dense language: Refers to the difficulty of the text—multiple concepts may be written with complex sentences and unfamiliar vocabulary.

Differentiated instruction: Catering to the individual needs of the learners in a classroom—giving the higher level students more challenging work and restructuring a lesson so that struggling students will acquire the intended content without "dumbing down" the information.

Domains of language: The four primary uses of language. Specifically, listening, speaking, reading, and writing. (see also "Expressive Language" and "Receptive Language")

Expository text: A type of written discourse that is used to explain, describe, give information, or inform.

Expressive language: Language that an individual produces (i.e., expresses). Speaking and writing are the primary expressive language skills. (see also "Domains of Language" and "Receptive Language")

Formal register: Formal language used in teaching content and usually found in content textbooks.

Fourth-grade slump: The documented reduction in language skills development that occurs after the primary grades.

Graphic organizer: A graphical depiction of the relationships between concepts, words, etc. A very widely used graphic organizer is the Venn Diagram.

Higher order questioning strategies: The higher level of Bloom's taxonomy for questioning that involves analysis, synthesis, and evaluation; i.e., "Can you see a possible solution to this dilemma?"

Information dense: Refers to the density of language and the use of academic vocabulary.

Language acquisition device (LAD): Theoretical mental processor that enables unconscious acquisition of correct grammar usage.

Literacy: Ability to read and write and acquire new knowledge by that means: reading to learn vs. learning to read.

Mortar words: High frequency words that "glue" content-area vocabulary together.

Narrative text: A type of written discourse that tells a story or account of events, experiences, or the like, whether true or fictitious.

Operational definitions: Definitions that develop after exposure to context. That is, instead of "front-loading" or defining a word in a vacuum, the student is first exposed to a hands-on experience (a lab or other activity). Then the new vocabulary is used to label some aspect of that experience. Ideally, the student thus has an understanding of the concept and the new vocabulary is learned as a label for prior knowledge, rather than learning the concept and the word simultaneously.

Operationalizing words: Students are able to use new vocabulary in oral discussion or in writing in the content area.

Pair/share: When two students complete an assignment together (i.e., reading a selection from a text) and then discuss the results.

Personalizing words: Students build new vocabulary into their schemata or background information.

Phonics: The study of the sounds of a language.

Quick game sets: Short, interactive games that focus students on content. These are particularly useful for providing multiple exposure to vocabulary.

Reading repair strategies: Instructional techniques in reading that add to comprehension; for example, rereading or using context clues to understand unfamiliar vocabulary.

Receptive language: Language that is received by an individual. Listening and reading are the primary receptive language processes. (see also "Domains of Language" and "Expressive Language")

Register (of language): The accepted norms (forms, functions, and usage) of language within a specific context, whether oral or written.

Root words: The Latin or Greek base for a word—the etymology of a word, its derivation.

Schemata: Using prior knowledge or knowledge from the immediate environment to acquire new information.

Signal words: Mortar words in expository writing which usually indicate location, comparison/contrast, time, emphasis/summary, or sequence.

Social discourse: Verbal expression in speech or writing determined by social practices.

Sponge activity: Quick activities that can be implemented on the spot on those rare occasions when your lesson ends earlier than anticipated, or students end up being held in class. These activities are generally extras, designed to "soak up" the extra time in these situations to prevent students from sitting around doing nothing.

Strategized assistance: Strategic tutoring or specialized instruction to assist students who lack specific skills.

Visual language: Graphics, images, body language, video, etc.

Zone of proximal development: The difference between what a learner can do without help and what he or she can do with help; concept developed by Lev Vygotsky—moving the student out of his or her comfort zone to learn something new, which is scaffolded on prior knowledge.

Expressive and Receptive Language Strategies and Model Lesson Plan Format

The following tools were developed as part of the CALLI Project mentioned periodically throughout the text (see also the preface).

The first sheet is a checklist of academic language strategies to look for both when developing and when evaluating a lesson or lesson plan. This is also presented as Table 3.1, and see chapter 3 for more explanations of the individual strategies mentioned here.

The lesson plan template shows the model lesson plan format that the teachers in the CALLI project were asked to use in order to standardize between teachers to make sharing easier. This is also the format used to present our model lessons in appendices 2 and 3. Note the inclusion of California content standards, which simply reflects the fact that the template was developed in California: Obviously, whatever standards you require can be substituted.

Academic Literacy in the Content Areas: CALLI Project—Funded by CPEC

Academic Language: a variety or a register of English used in professional books and characterized by the specific linguistic features associated with academic disciplines (Scarcella, 2003):

- It is the language used by teachers and students for the purpose of acquiring new knowledge and skills.
- It assists in imparting new information, describing abstract ideas, and developing students' conceptual understanding (Chamot & O'Malley, 1994)

- It focuses on understanding, using and reflecting on written material to develop new knowledge and potential—read to learn and build conceptual knowledge.
- Academic Literacy is the use of metacognitive strategies—"thinking about thinking"—using thinking skills to acquire new knowledge.

Table A.1.1 Receptive Academic Language vs. Expressive Academic Language

DECONSTRUCTING LANGUAGE (Analysis of how listening and reading is used to create knowledge for the student)	CONSTRUCTING LANGUAGE (Using speaking and writing to demonstrate knowledge)
R1. Teacher identifies similarities and differences: students and teachers read passages to analyze and organize information	E1. Students identify similarities and differences by discussing comparisons and writing them down on graphic organizers to later expound on information
R2. Teacher guides students through appropriate note-taking and summarization of information (graphic organizers)	E2. Students summarize information using notes and graphic organizers they created
R3. Teacher conducts 'whole to part to whole' instruction: big picture first, then parts, then reassemble	E3. Students experience 'whole to part to whole' instruction and are able to perform appropriate assessments
R4. Teacher uses prior knowledge to create anticipatory sets which capture students' attention	E4. Students create "big questions" or problems to answer regarding the anticipatory set
R5. Teacher models and students (through guided practice) conduct intensive vocabulary development: using affixes, cognates, root words and context clues to understand text	E5. Students operationally define words by relating them to steps in a sequence or by using them appropriately in writing
R6. Teachers ensure that students have multiple exposures to new vocabulary	E6. Teachers and Students speak using the appropriate register
R7. Teachers conduct text analyses: reviewing subtitles, graphics, titles, predicting and identifying difficult vocabulary	E7. Journal Writing
R8. Teachers and students personalize new vocabulary by building the new vocabulary into their background information	E8. Students generate and test hypotheses/math word problems
	E9. Students and teachers interact formally and informally to express knowledge
	E10. Teachers use higher order questioning strategies to conduct ongoing assessment and students use the appropriate register to answer
	E11. Teachers scaffold information to build on prior knowledge
	E12. Teachers model corrective feedback for speech and writing
	E13. Projects, portfolios and other assessments are differentiated to match student ability levels

- Teacher has high expectations and gives positive feedback to students when appropriate

Lesson Plan Template

Unit:
Position within Unit:
Title:

Table A.1.2

OBJECTIVE(S)	What should they learn by the end of the lesson?
PURPOSE	How will achieving the objective benefit them?
CA STANDARDS	What Standards are addressed by the lesson?
MATERIALS	List and include all materials you will using. *Attach the files of materials in electronic form.* Presentation materials: Copied materials (Handouts, worksheets, tests, lab directions, etc.): Pages in textbook: Book title: _____ Pages: _____ Laboratory materials: For the teacher or the class as a whole: For each laboratory station: Other materials:
ACTIVITIES Introduction (Anticipatory Set) (Minutes?)	Describe the activities that you and your students will be doing at three stages in the lesson: Introduction, one or more Main Activities, and Conclusion. **Make sure that your Introduction and Conclusion help to connect this lesson with the lessons before and after.** Briefly describe how you will: • Get the class interested in the day's lesson & off to a well-managed start • Make conceptual connections with previous lessons (Prior knowledge/scaffolding)
[Activity #1 Name] (Minutes?)	• Help students anticipate problems and activities of the class Briefly describe what and how you will teach, including: (via Modeling/Guided Practice) • Key examples, patterns, models or theories to help students understand • Key questions you will use to start discussions
[Activity #2 Name] (Minutes?)	• What the students AND the teacher will be doing • Embedded assessment activities to show students' understanding • References to materials you or the students will be using • Procedural details, including transitions, materials management, etc.

(continued)

Table A.1.2 Continued

Conclusion (Minutes?)	▪ *Precise examples of how you will incorporation cademic Literacy into your lesson* See directions for Activity #1, above. If there are more than two activities in a lesson, continue this format. Describe concluding activities that will: • Help students review or summarize what they have learned • Make sure students and materials are in order before students leave • Help students anticipate problems and activities of future classes
ASSESSMENT	Describe how you will assess students' understanding of your most important objective. This task might be a question or a series of questions. It might take many forms, including: (a) embedded assessment tasks such as worksheets, journal questions, or lab reports, (b) class/group work, and/or (c) formal assessments such as homework, test, performance-based assessments, or project. *How will you differentiate assessment for your special populations?* **Include the actual task; don't just describe it**. If it requires special materials that cannot be copied into this section, attach them as Appendices or separate files.
REFLECTION	Write yourself some notes about impressions of the lesson, key student difficulties, and ideas for improving the lesson the next time you teach it.

Literature cited: Zang, Z. (2006). The language demands of science reading in middle school. *International Journal of Science Education* 5(28):491–520.

Sample Lesson Plans Including Expressive and Receptive Language Prompts

The lessons in this appendix follow the lesson plan format and the expressive (E) and receptive (R) language strategies provided in appendix 1. The strategies are presented in the left-hand column of the lesson plan where they occur. These lessons can be used as initial examples of how to include these strategies into specific, discipline-based lessons. Appendix 3 expands on this demonstration lesson set, but without explicitly identifying the strategies used. The purpose of this is to allow the reader to practice identifying these strategies independently, following the basic strategy of modeling and guided practice presented in chapter 2.

Sample Lesson Plan 2.1: Sentence Analysis and Rephrasing (Earth Science)
Sample Lesson Plan 2.2: Using the Text (Algebra)
Sample Lesson Plan 2.3: Classifying the Elements (Chemistry)
Sample Lesson Plan 2.4: Using a Science Notebook (General Science)
Sample Lesson Plan 2.5: Stem-and-Leaf Plots (Graphing)

Sample Lesson Plan 2.1: Sentence Analysis and Rephrasing (Earth Science)

Unit: Earth Structures
Position within Unit: Introduction
Title: Sentence Analysis and Rephrasing (C. T. Kloock)

Table A.2.1 Sentence Analysis and Rephrasing

OBJECTIVE(S) PURPOSE	To guide students to an understanding of some of the syntactical conventions of scientific language, provide multiple exposures to scientific vocabulary, and introduce some of the basic language and concepts of Earth structure.
CA SCIENCE STANDARDS	No California Science Standards address analyzing language. The context that this example is embedded in addresses: Grade 6, 1b: Students know Earth is composed of several layers: a cold, brittle lithosphere; a hot, convecting mantle; and a dense, metallic core.
MATERIALS	Handouts located at the end of the lesson plan.
ACTIVITIES Anticipatory set: ~5 minutes (Link to prior knowledge, introduce importance of language and the idea of a science "accent": a.k.a. register.) Strategies: R4 [Activity #1 Deconstructing referents] Strategies used: R1, R5, R6, R8 E3, E5, E6, E12	Ask students: Have you ever noticed that people from different parts of the country, or from different countries, speak differently? If you want to talk to somebody from England, for example, they might use different words, or say the same words differently, or even use the same words with different meanings: In England, they don't have elevators, they have lifts, and not apartments, but flats. Anybody know any other things that have different words or meanings to people from other places? (give students a bit to throw out different ideas, add a few of your own if they slow down). What if I told you that I "took a torch to my classroom"? Scientists also have their own accent, and it carries over into their writing: not just the vocabulary they use, but the way they phrase their sentences and use language is often different from "everyday" speaking. If you talk to most scientists they sound perfectly normal, but when they write it is like trying to understand someone with a very heavy accent. This activity is designed to help you unpack this tightly packed accent and begin to learn how to deal with it. We will also start trying to teach you how to condense your writing so you can learn the scientific accent. Page 1 on the sample handout provides students with a simple worksheet that asks them to identify the referent of the relational pronouns identified in each sentence. Work through an example with them (i.e. modeling) to show students how to decode the referent, then have them work through the rest of activity 1. They may need some help with the first few (guided practice). This gives them a chance to see the scientific writing in context (notice that in this example all of the sentences relate to basic earth structure) and forces them to spend time decoding the syntax of scientific writing. Please note that this example activity is very brief, for demonstrative purposes only. You could do the same activity, in a much longer lesson, by

[Activity #2
Constructing
Referents]

Strategies used:

R1, R5, R6, R8
E3, E5, E6, E12

Conclusion

E3

having students deconstruct a section of their textbook in this fashion. This gives the students multiple exposures to any new vocabulary in context and is a way to force them into active reading.

Page 2 of the sample handout is basically the same example in reverse. Instead of decoding the scientific writing, students take some highly repetitive sentences and make them more information dense by substituting referring pronouns for the long, repetitive noun-phrases used. This will be harder to do in an "off-the-shelf" manner as above because very few science textbooks construct their language in this fashion. One possibility is to use some very low-level science textbooks (grade 3 or lower), which sometimes use these simplified, repetitive constructions — but also simplified vocabulary. A better way will be to produce sentences like these is by deconstructing passages from your text, and then having the students construct sentences from those.

The last questions summarize the main points of the activity: that there is actually a good reason that scientific writing is constructed the way it is, and students need to be made aware of this. This dense construction helps pack a lot of information into a relatively short space: that is, it is concise. In scientific writing, concision is a major goal. After they answer the last questions, discuss with students which style (question 1–5 vs 6–10) is easier to read, and make them compare the meaning of the original with the modified sentences (there should be no difference). In order to get the most out of your textbook, students need to be able to understand the scientific "accent". Note that the last question also shows substitution of vocabulary for long phrases, again making the writing more concise.

| ASSESSMENT | If you use a worksheet like this, the worksheet can be used as an assessment. If you make them unpack sentences from a textbook, you can have them turn in their unpacked sentences. |

| REFLECTION | This lesson is based on a simpler, non-context-embedded sentence completion activity presented in Zang (2006), which provides a complete treatment of the differences between scientific writing and "everyday" language. |

The high information density of scientific writing makes for a much more concise writing style that avoids repetition of vocabulary — which of course goes against much of what this book has told you about student learning (i.e. multiple exposures, repetition is a good thing!). This activity, as well as introducing the students a little to the syntax structure of scientific writing, makes the students spend time with the

(continued)

Table A.2.1 Continued

vocabulary of the content they are studying in context. This provides them with multiple exposures, both receptively and expressively.

The sample activity here shows a "beginning" stage. As students progress you can get away from underlining the words and have them underline and explain noun-phrases, referring pronouns etc. An interesting twist for more advanced students would be to have them write a brief paragraph, trade them with one another, and identify vocabulary, noun-phrases and relational pronouns used, or identify where they could be used in each other's writing. The editing process they would go through here again gives them extra exposure.

Sentence Analysis (Earth Structure)

Activity 1 In order to keep scientific writing concise, it is common to use a variety of writing structures to avoid repetition and reduce the number of words used. In the following sentences, replace each underlined word with the phrase to which it refers.

Example: The Earth's structure consists of four basic layers, the inner core, outer core, mantle, and crust. *This* forms the basis for plate tectonic theory *which* explains earthquakes, mountain building and other important geological phenomena.

This: The fact that Earth's structure consists of four layers
   Which: Plate tectonics theory
   1. The inner core is composed of dense, solid iron and nickel. It also contains heavy, radioactive materials. This supplies some of the heat that keeps the Earth's interior very hot.
It:
   This:
   2. The outer core consists of molten iron and nickel. It is less dense than the inner core, which is why the inner core sinks within it.
It:
   Which:
   3. The mantle is also molten and contains some iron and nickel, but much more silicon than the core. Because of this, it is even less dense than the outer core.
This:
It:
   4. The least dense portion of the Earth is the crust. Because it is less dense than the mantle, it floats on top of the mantle in much the same way that ice floats on the surface of a pond or in your soda.

It (#1):

It (#2):

5. There are two types of crust: oceanic crust and continental crust. Normally <u>these</u> are side by side, but when <u>they</u> push against one another, continental crust tends to end up on top of the oceanic crust. Based on <u>this</u>, which type of crust do you think is less dense?

These:

They:

This:

Which type of crust is less dense?

Activity 2 The following statements are written in expanded form, which scientists (and your textbook) rarely use. Replace each italicized phrase with one or two words that accurately refer to the phrase. For convenience, each phrase is referred to by a subscripted letter (for example$_a$) for identification. Read each sentence after the substitutions to make sure they still make sense.

Example: When you boil water, the hot water near the flame becomes less dense than the colder water near the surface. *The relatively low density of the hot water$_a$* causes *the hot water$_b$* to float over the more dense, cold water. *The movement of water in a pot of boiling water$_c$* is called convection.

    a. *This*

    b. *It*

    c. *This*

6. Convection also occurs in the Earth's mantle. The lower portion of the mantle is heated by the radioactivity of the core. The warmed, lower portion rises, pushing the cooler, upper mantle out of the way as *the warmed mantle material$_a$* rises, but much more slowly than water in a pot.

    a:

7. Remember that the crust is floating on top of the mantle as the cooler surface mantle is being pushed aside. *The motion of the cooler surface mantle being pushed aside$_a$* causes motion in the crust as well.

    a:

8. The crust is not a solid piece of rock, as noted above. The crust consists of both oceanic and continental crust, and *oceanic and continental crusts$_a$* are each broken into several, very large pieces. *Pieces of oceanic and continental$_b$* crust are known as plates.

    a:

    b:

9. The motion of the magma is transferred to motion in the crust through the force of friction. *The motion of the crust$_a$* is opposed by force applied to the crust in regions where two or more plates meet. *These regions where two or more plates meet$_b$* are known as faults.

a:

b:

10. *Regions where two or more plates meet*_a are categorized primarily by the relative direction of the plates that meet. When two plates meet and are moving toward each other, the *region where they meet*_b is called a convergent fault. *Regions where two plates meet and are moving toward each other*_c are often associated with mountains, due to the stresses of the collision of the plates.

a:

b:

c:

Compare the lengths of the passages before and after substitution of the long phrases with shorter phrases that refer to them. Why do you think scientists (and other writers) frequently use these sentence structures?

How heavy do you think your science textbooks would be if they used the writing style exemplified in passages 6–10? Would you really want to carry that around?

Sample Lesson Plan 2.2: Using the Text (Algebra)

Unit: Translating expressions into numeric equations
Position within Unit: General mathematics
Title: Using the Text/Coaching Lesson (Dr. E. Garza, June 2006)

Table A.2.2 Using the Text/Coaching Lesson

OBJECTIVE(S) PURPOSE	What should they learn by the end of the lesson? The basic activity is for the students to translate written expression into mathematic expressions using oral and logical reasoning. Students will learn the value of reading academic language carefully to completely understand how to translate written expression into mathematical numeric equations. Simple expressions will be introduced; then simple equations.
CA STANDARDS	What standards are addressed by the lesson? Grades 7-9 Students make decisions about how to approach problems. 1. Use a variety of methods, such as words, numbers, symbols, charts, graphs, tables, diagrams, and models to explain mathematical reasoning. 2. Determine when and how to break a problem into simpler parts and solve it. 3. Write an algebraic expression for a given situation.

MATERIALS	List and include all materials you will be using.
	Textbook
	Handouts
	Chart paper
	Some overheads

ACTIVITIES	INTRODUCTION
Anticipatory set	Anticipatory Set would be that the teacher poses a general question on how many students have often translated from one language to another.
R4 R1	Ask someone to tell you what process they went through.
	Put some examples on the chart paper on going from one
R8	language to another.
	Try to personalize the situation and the language if possible relating back to math terms, i.e. Spanish to English is the same as ax=2 (algebraic) or a number times another number equals 2 (regular English).
	Explain why this is important in mathematics. Explain to them how this will help them do better in their understanding of
R6	math. Explain algebraic versus English words or phrases.
	Teacher will model (read) examples from word expressions into algebraic expressions and tell them that it is like another language. Teacher will explain all the academic vocabulary that is key in translating these expressions. (List comes from example problem teacher models. Put these words on chart paper and explain them using academic language
E 2	techniques, i.e. say the word aloud , have them repeat it, talk about the structure of word and its spelling, compare to any cognates, use it in a sentence, and then have them repeat it.) Teacher will do guided practice with all the class and then check for understanding.
	Closure: Teacher will ask students to translate orally a few of the leaned expression with a partner. They will be asked to volunteer their answer.
	Teacher will assign the students independent practice on their own. Handout will be given to complete. They will practice and if they do not finish it, they will do it as homework.
	Note: The most logical and probably easiest way to format this assignment is to follow the standard math assessment with multiple opportunities for them to use the language both orally and in writing.

ASSESSMENT	The main point is for students to translate mathematical language into mathematical reasoning. Using algebraic equations. This is an opportunity for them to analyze any type of math reasoning as they develop higher level processing. They will have to do this to solve real life problems and translate words into their own reasoning.

REFLECTION

Sample Lesson Plan 2.3: Classifying the Elements (Chemistry)

Unit: Periodic table.

Position within Unit: After introduction of atomic structure, before introducing properties of elements (metals, nonmetals, etc.). This activity is an introduction to the periodic table and its structure, and also to ionic bonds. Extension can include covalent bonds, and possibly begin discussion of properties of elements (noble gases are touched upon, but you could add others). Please note that this activity is intended as an introduction. Further elaboration of concepts such as electron orbitals, the octet rule, etc., can be done, but are not included here; exceptions to simple patterns are also left for later. The basic goal of this lesson is to understand that the periodic table's structure is based on patterns that affect the chemical properties of atoms. Similar patterns can be seen in a variety of other properties (e.g., electronegativity, melting point) but to keep things simpler for the students, only a single pattern is used here.

Table A.2.3 Classifying the Elements

OBJECTIVE(S):	To develop an understanding of the periodic table and its structure. In particular, to understand that the periodic table is structured as a way to organize the elements according to chemical properties that vary in a periodic fashion, and that this organization is based on natural patterns that effect chemical bonding. Also serves as an introduction to the concept of ionic bonds.
CA STANDARDS:	Main activity: Grades 9-12: Chemistry, 1; a, d: Chemistry 2; a (in part)
	Extension adds: Chemistry 2; a (complete), b
MATERIALS:	3cmx3cm paper squares
	Per group:
	6 green
	7 Yellow
	3 Blue
	2 White
	Handout (attached)
	Optional:
	Samples of various elements within the first 18: e.g., sulfur, carbon.
ACTIVITIES:	
Anticipatory set (5 minutes):	Use some examples of ways that organization can make their lives easier. For example, you could have some materials scattered randomly around the classroom and have students collect them, then have things organized and make the students

R4, E11

collect those to compare the difference in ease. Make the connection between this physical organization and organizing information. Ask students if any organization works, or if there might be some ways of organizing information that make more sense. Again, an example might help: How is a dictionary organized? Could you organize by subject instead of alphabetically? (yes) — but which is more useful?

The main activity is students working their way through the attached worksheet, which you should provide students. The worksheet has the specific details for the activity; additional information is provided below.

R6, R8

Activity A: (5 min)

The first activity has the students organize the first 18 elements based solely on physical properties, provided in the table. Students will generally lump them into a few groups (either solids, liquids, and gases; or by color). It doesn't matter how this comes out and don't spend much time on this: Use this as an opportunity to remind them about atoms and elements.

Activity B: (30 min)

Next, students will organize the 18 elements based on their tendency to gain and lose electrons, following the details in the handout. Walk them through one example of filling out a card for an element, then let them do it in their groups to finish all the cards based on the table. When they are done with this, they can start trying to organize the cards as directed.

R1, R2, R5, R6

They should, after some trial and error, end up with a structure that looks like the top 3 rows of the periodic table. The biggest problem students tend to have with this is the idea of allowing gaps, so you may need to help them get this.

E2, R8

(**Note:** only the first 18 elements are used to keep the numbers manageable and also because beginning in the 4th row, some new patterns emerge that would be very difficult to approach in this fashion.)

Don't tell the students that they'll be building the periodic table! The whole point is that the patterns are easy, and lead naturally to the table. They should be able to build it just by following the simple rules provided. You should avoid any mention of the periodic table. If there is one up in the room, take it down, preferably at least a day before the lesson so as not to draw attention to its absence. Students who realize they are building the periodic table tend to try to remember what it looks like and reconstruct it from memory, rather construct it using the patterns — and therefore get less out of the activity. The teacher must resist the urge to show students the "right" solution as long as possible. Give students time to

(continued)

Table A.2.3 Continued

E9, E10, R3	try a bunch of alternatives; just point out where the solutions don't match and offer simple suggestions and hints, but don't fix it for them. One thing that happens here is that as the quicker students get it, others will see it and the idea will spread through the room like an infection. This is OK (and speeds up the process), just try to get to each group and make sure they see the patterns as outlined below.
E12	
	After they have the basic structure, ask students in their groups to show you where all the atoms that tend to gain one electron are (or gain 2, lose 1 etc.) until they see the pattern — don't just show it to them, ask them questions that will make them discover it for themselves.
	There is one big **possible misconception** — and this is why students should not put + & - on the cards when they fill them out. Electrons have a negative charge, so an atom that gains an electron forms an ion with negative charge, while an atom that loses an electron becomes a positive ion. This "backwardness" is sometimes tough for students to deal with, and this activity doesn't help much on that front. One possible correction is to have them actually put the correct charge, based on a simple formula like (protons – electrons) assuming
E4, E8	the atom has gained or lost those electrons. This is reasonable if you have already done some work on ions, but may be too much to add if they haven't already got this concept.

Introduce Ionic Bonding: (10 min)

R3   The questions at the bottom of the page require the students to use the periodic table they have built and examples of stable, ionically bonded compounds given, to determine the pattern of simple ionic bonds (you can express this as either gaining or losing electrons in the outermost shell, or simply try to get them to notice that the number of electrons gained by one atom always equals the number of electrons lost by the other atoms).

Conclusion:

Show students a complete periodic table and explain to them that the patterns they saw as they completed the lab are why the periodic table has the strange shape it has: it is a way of classifying the elements that is extremely useful for predicting which atoms can form different kinds of chemical bonds. With this introduction the students are now primed to look for patterns in the periodic table and you can continue to introduce the many patterns within this structure.

ASSESSMENT	Basic assessment is done as they work, the ultimate goal being to build the periodic table. The answers to the questions on the

worksheet can also serve as assessment, especially question 5. You can also give them some novel combinations of atoms to determine whether they will form ionic/covalent bonds. Notice that they do not have a card for Potassium (K) – they need to figure out where in the table K belongs based on its atomic #.

Questions 1–5, Answers:

1) What do all of these compounds have in common? (Hint: look at the total number of electrons gained/lost). Note: This pattern holds true for **ionic** bonds, but not necessarily for **covalent** bonds. **The number of electrons gained by one atom always equals the number of electrons lost by the other atom: electrons gained-electrons lost=0**

2) Which classification scheme, A or B, provides you with an easier way of determining which elements might bond easily with each other? **B, the classification based on electron gain/loss, works much better than A, the classification by physical properties.**

3) Are there any elements that you think would be unlikely to form bonds with any other elements? Which classification scheme (A or B) did you use to identify these elements? **The elements that tend to neither gain nor lose electrons (i.e. the noble gases); Classification B makes these obvious and groups them together.**

4) Which classification scheme is more useful for predicting chemical reactions? **B again**

5) Use one of your schemes to predict which of the following compounds should be stable:

MgS; HCl; ClS; CN; NH; MgK, KCl. (The atomic # of potassium, K, is 19)

> **Stable:** MgS; HCl; KCl
> **Unstable:** ClS; CN; NH; MgK

REFLECTION	This lesson is an adaptation of an idea in Wright and Mitchell (1998).

There is an alternative pattern that works given the basic parameters of the lesson, except that it isn't symmetrical: The alternative pattern places the noble gases on the left side of the table rather than the right, and shifted down a row. Students who get this aren't really wrong! Depending on where you are going with the lesson, you may want to just leave it like this and readjust later (a nice way to show alternative solutions — As in most science, one right answer just doesn't exist) or "fix" it right away (generally by trying to get the student to make it symmetrical, or sometimes just by moving helium to the right place, then have the students re-align everything). This tends to happen a lot because students seem to prefer asymmetry to leaving gaps. This is a good time to work on the meaning of symmetry.

(continued)

Table A.2.3 Continued

Extension:

Page 3 of the handout extends the basic structure and pattern searching behavior to covalent bonds: student find the basic pattern of covalent bond formation follows a slightly different, but related rule for "good" bond formation. This can serve as a basic intro to the Octet rule. You could extend the basic idea of this to most of the periodic properties of elements so that, instead of showing students the patterns, they discover them for themselves.

Extension Answers:

1) Could the molecule N_2 be stable? **YES** If so, how many electrons must each atom gain (share)? **3**
2) What about CN? **NO** If so, how many electrons would each atom have to gain (share)? **No answer needed, but: Carbon needs 4, Nitrogen needs 3. Hydrogen Cyanide, HCN, is relatively stable.**
3) Is it possible for the element Lithium (Li) to form stable covalent bonds? **NO** Why or why not? **Lithium would need to share 7 electrons, but only has one available to share: an atom cannot share more electrons than it has available to share under most conditions.**
4) Is it possible for the element Phosphorus to form stable covalent bonds? **Yes** Why or why not? **Needs 3 electrons and has five to share.** Now is not the time to get into why phosphorus can sometimes form 5 covalent (but not very stable) bonds — save that for organic chemistry and after they know a lot more about electron configuration!

The last question would be a good opportunity to have your students produce a Venn diagram of the similarities and differences of Ionic and covalent bonds.

1. In your notebook, sort the elements in the table above according to their physical properties.
2. Now we will sort them differently. Use the colored cards provided to help you.

You will use the four different colors to represent what happens to the electrons of each element:

a. Use green for all elements that gain electrons.
b. Use yellow for all elements that normally lose electrons.
c. Use white for all elements that can either gain or lose electrons (i.e., those labeled "+ or –").
d. Use blue for all elements that neither gain nor lose electrons.

Table A.2.4 Mendeleev Periodic Table

Element	Symbol	Atomic Number	# Electrons normally gained (+) or lost (-)	Physical Properties (under normal conditions)
Aluminum	Al	13	-3	Silver Solid
Argon	Ar	18	0	Colorless Gas
Beryllium	Be	4	-2	White Solid
Boron	B	5	-3	Brown Solid
Carbon	C	6	+ or – 4	Clear crystal
Chlorine	Cl	17	+1	Greenish-yellow Gas
Fluorine	F	9	+1	Greenish-yellow Gas
Helium	He	2	0	Colorless Gas
Hydrogen	H	1	-1	Colorless Gas
Lithium	Li	3	-1	Silver/white solid
Magnesium	Mg	12	-2	Silver-white solid
Neon	Ne	10	0	Colorless gas
Nitrogen	N	7	+3	Colorless gas
Oxygen	O	8	+2	Colorless gas
Phosphorus	P	15	+3	White, waxy solid
Silicon	Si	14	+ or – 4	Grey solid
Sodium	Na	11	-1	Silvery, waxy Solid
Sulfur	S	16	+2	Yellow Crystal

Source: Wright, D.W., & Mitchell, S.B. (1998). *Mendeleev Periodic Table Simulator.* Burlington, NC: Carolina Biological Supply Company.

Label each card with the symbol for an element in the center, the atomic number for that element in the upper left-hand corner, and the number of electrons gained or lost by that element in the upper right-hand corner. Do *not* use a + or – sign; remember to use the color-coding system above as you label cards (see sample).

Once your labeling is complete, arrange your cards so that their atomic numbers are in sequence *and* the elements are grouped together by their colors (i.e., tendency to gain or lose electrons).

You may use multiple rows, and you should try to arrange your cards in a symmetrical pattern.

Check with your lab instructor before copying your arrangement into your notebook.

Some easily formed, stable compounds are:

NaCl, BeO, HF, and LiCl.

Atomic number → 3 1 ← electrons lost

Li

Since Lithium tends to lose 1 electron, this square should be yellow

1. What do all of these compounds have in common? (Hint: look at the total number of electrons gained/lost). Note: This pattern holds true for *ionic* bonds, but not necessarily for *covalent* bonds.
2. Which classification scheme, A or B, provides you with an easier way of determining which elements might bond easily with each other?
3. Are there any elements that you think would be unlikely to form bonds with any other elements? Which classification scheme (A or B) did you use to identify these elements?
4. Which classification scheme is more useful for predicting chemical reactions?
5. Use one of your schemes to predict which of the following compounds should be stable:

   MgS; HCl; ClS; CN; NH; MgK, KCl. (The atomic # of potassium, K, is 19.)

Extension: covalent bonds:

Some covalently bonded molecules follow the pattern you determined previously. For example: H_2O, CH_4 and CO_2 are all stable, covalently bonded molecules that follow the same pattern (if your pattern doesn't work in this way, go back and revise your thinking until you see a pattern that does).

Other covalently bonded molecules don't follow this simple pattern (for example, hydrogen peroxide, H_2O_2; ethane C_2H_6; Glucose, $C_6H_{12}O_6$). There is another pattern that these molecules follow that is also quite simple. Use the clues below and the scheme B you developed to help you figure out this pattern.

Clue 1. Remember that the elements He, Ne, and Ar are chemically unreactive what property do they share?

Clue 2. In ionic bonds, you looked at the number of electrons gained or lost. Number of electrons is still important in covalent bonds, but atoms involved in covalent bonds don't gain or lose electrons. Instead, they *share* electrons—each atom must share one of its own electrons in order to get an electron from the other. These shared electrons can be "double counted"; that is, each atom involved in a covalent bond gets to count the pair of electrons shared (one by each atom) as if it belonged exclusively to itself.

Clue 3. If we look at the ability to covalently bond to hydrogen we see the following pattern:

Ne cannot bond any hydrogen atoms.

One F atom can bond stably to one hydrogen atom. (HF)
One O atom can bond stably to two hydrogen atoms. (H_2O)
One N atom can bond stably to three hydrogen atoms. (NH_3)
One C atom can bond stably to four hydrogen atoms. (CH_4)

Count the number of electrons each of the above atoms has (remember, they get to count one extra electron for each H atom they bond with)—what do the atoms in each of these covalently bonded compounds have in common? Which atom do all of these resemble in their number of electrons (their own plus shared) when they are stably bonded?

Now look at the number of electrons each hydrogen atom has. Remember that each hydrogen atom can get a maximum of one electron from its partner because that is all it has to share. Which atom do they resemble in their number of electrons when they are stably bonded?

Clue 4. More hydrogen patterns:
Ar cannot bond any hydrogen atoms.
One S atom can bond stably to two hydrogen atoms. (H_2S)
Which atom do they resemble in their number of electrons when they are stably bonded?
How many hydrogen atoms do you think silicon will bond with (Si)?

Clue 5. Here are some other covalently bonded molecules: Do they fit the pattern identified above?
F_2 (two atoms of fluorine bonded together), Cl_2 (2 atoms of chlorine bonded together)
How many electrons must each atom gain (share) in order fit the patterns identified above?
F_2O and NOH are also stable: How many electrons must each atom gain (share)?
O_2 and S_2 are also stable: How many electrons must each atom gain (share)?

Use your new hypothesis about how covalent bonds work to answer the following questions:

1. Could the molecule N_2 be stable? If so, how many electrons must each atom gain (share)? If not, why not?
2. What about CN? If so, how many electrons would each atom have to gain (share)? If not, why not?

3. Is it possible for the element Lithium (Li) to form stable covalent bonds? Why or why not?
4. Is it possible for the element phosphorus to form stable covalent bonds? Why or why not?

Look back at the pattern identified for ionic bonds and compare it to the pattern identified for covalent bonds. What are the similarities and differences (remember to focus on the electrons!).

Sample Lesson Plan 2.4: Using a Science Notebook (General Science)

Unit: Scientific method/ Introduction to science
Position within Unit: Early: Introduction to using notebook and writing scientific paper
Title: Using a science notebook

Table A.2.5 Using a Science Notebook

OBJECTIVE(S) PURPOSE	The basic activity is for the students to complete a "recipe-driven" chemical reaction and take notes on it. Then they will be asked to propose modifications of the recipe and conduct an experiment to determine if their modification improved, reduced or had no effect on a simple property of the substance. This is, by design, a 2-day activity. The first "day" will be used to introduce the lesson and the vocabulary. (See attached vocabulary sheet) Vocabulary cards can be created by the students in groups and the sentences can be used the next day as an introductory activity. Have a set of note cards with the names of the words on them and with the definitions on the board, play a short slap game as part of the multiple exposures to the vocabulary.
	Students will learn the value of maintaining a notebook and how to use it to produce a more "finished product." Secondary learning goals can include some basic Chemistry concepts (see CA Science Standards) and, with suitable modification, some understanding of the nature of polymerization.
	How will achieving the objective benefit them? By being forced to use their own written notes to accomplish a task (self-feedback), this will force them to come to terms with their limitations in written communication and help them improve their overall communication skills.
CA STANDARDS	Grade 6, 7d: Communicate the steps and results from an investigation in written reports and oral presentations.

Grade 8, 3c. Students know atoms and molecules form solids by building up repeating patterns, such as the crystal structure of NaCl or long-chain polymers.

Grade 8, 5a. Students know reactant atoms and molecules interact to form products with different chemical properties.

With Extension:

Grades 9-12, Chemistry:

10. The bonding characteristics of carbon allow the formation of many different organic molecules of varied sizes, shapes, and chemical properties and provide the biochemical basis of life. As a basis for understanding this concept:

a. Students know large molecules (polymers), such as proteins, nucleic acids, and starch, are formed by repetitive combinations of simple subunits.

b. Students know the bonding characteristics of carbon that result in the formation of a large variety of structures ranging from simple hydrocarbons to complex polymers and biological molecules.

MATERIALS	Laboratory materials:
	For each laboratory station:
	    2 250 ml beakers (preferably plastic)
	    Graduated cylinder
	    Stir rod (preferably plastic)
	Other materials:
	    White glue (30 ml/lab gGroup)
	    Borax (~ 10 ml/lab group)
	
	IMPORTANT SAFETY NOTE: While commercially available Silly Putty™ is non-toxic and can be used to lift images off of some types of paper, the substance made with this recipe is different. Do not allow students to ingest it, and keep all paper products away from it as well. It is not dangerous for this to come in contact with paper, just impossible to remove it.

ACTIVITIES Academic Literacy Strategies R2, E2, E7	Anticipatory set. Day 1: The best introduction for this lab is to be as dry and boring as possible! The substance that will be made will generally provide the spark that will draw students in — if you try to get them all excited about it beforehand you run the risk of elevating their expectations, which can actually decrease their interest level. Start by simply telling them that today they will be conducting a simple chemical reaction in their lab groups (Don't tell them anything about it), and that they will be expected to conduct the same reaction on their own later so they had better take good notes in their lab notebook. Then provide students with the following recipe. As you present the *(continued)*

Table A.2.5 Continued

recipe, be sure to have the students write down observations about the properties of the ingredients (color, texture, state, etc.), and tell them you want them to write down observations of the product of the reaction. (Use outlines as necessary for EL's and struggling readers.) Introduce Vocabulary Sheet and use a simple slaps game with the students after they have finished making the stuff. This way you can use the material itself to help with some of the definitions of properties, ingredients, etc.

Recipe:

Ingredients

30 ml saturated Borax solution

Make by placing ~5 ml of Borax into a beaker, then filling with water to 30 ml and stirring vigorously)

30 ml white glue

Be sure to have students measure this in a beaker, not in a graduated cylinder, as it is very time consuming to clean glue out of the graduated cylinder if it is allowed to dry.

30 ml water

A few drops of food coloring (if desired) — be forewarned, it may stain the student's hands a bit, but it does make the product a bit nicer to look at.

Instructions

Add water (and food coloring) to glue and stir the glue solution until well mixed. Observe properties of this solution

Add Borax solution to glue solution. It is important to add the borax solution to the glue solution and not the glue to the borax!

Stir vigorously.

Do NOT tell the students what will happen. As the product clumps up and turns into a disgusting lump, walk over to one lab group and pull the lump out of the breaker and knead it with your hands a bit — then hand it to the students and tell them to do the same until it dries out a little (basically stops dripping water off). Students need to observe the properties of the substance and write down this info in their notebook. Move on until all of the students are playing with the stuff, and let them play for awhile. Most students will play with this stuff for as long as you'll let them, so you'll need to bring them in at some point, but they'll be willing to listen.

E4: E5:

Introduce and hand out the assignment: Their job, next class period (or even better next week, but whenever it fits into your schedule), will be to make some modification to the recipe see how it affects the properties of this stuff.

Students can change the proportion of ingredients, delete ingredients or add ingredients You'll need to provide some limits here — what is readily available or students can bring in themselves, and is safe — Don't let them add strong acids or bases or anything that is not safe to touch. They can add things like different kinds of glue (NOT superglue!), different laundry detergents, or water with various additives (sodas, sugars, etc). Another variable you can play with is temperature. In general, if you're not comfortable with them adding something, don't let them. Give them what's left of the period to discuss in their groups what they want to test. Students need to keep track of their modifications.

Depending on the level of your students, you can constrain their dependent variable (which makes grading easier), give them a few options, or make them come up with their own procedure. Some easy ideas:

E2: Students summarize info

Test viscosity by timing how long it takes to ooze a given height (say 10 cm) under standard conditions (i.e. start with same volume of stuff in the same shape etc.).

E9: Interact to express knowledge

Test elasticity by measuring the height a ball of the stuff will bounce given a drop from a certain height (at least 1 m to get a decent bounce).

Extension: With higher level students, present information on the chemical structure of polymers and, in particular, the fact that the polymer subunits are held together with hydrogen bonds – how might the addition of a weak acid or base (e.g. vinegar) affect the structure? Low level students can just test the physical properties, but high level students could potentially be moved into testing hypotheses.

Assignment: See assessment, below.

Day 2: Entire period. Allow and help students to mix up new batches: control + modified. Test physical properties of silly-putty and record data. Paper due sometime later.

ASSESSMENT

Design and conduct an experiment to determine if your modification to the recipe changed one or more of the properties of the substance. You will write up your experiment using the notes you've taken in class and the notes you will take on the experiment day. Your lab write up must include:
An introduction to the substance and its basic properties.
The original recipe used.
The modification you made to the recipe
What property you tested and how you tested it.
Your data (and statistical analysis if appropriate).
A brief discussion of whether or not your modification changed the properties of the final product.

(*continued*)

Table A.2.5 Continued

If there was no change, try to explain why not.

If there was a change, do you consider this change to improve or damage the final product? Be sure to describe a purpose toward which you are considering this judgment.

Remember: The quality of your assignment will depend to a large extent on the quality of the notes you take in class, so make sure that your notes are complete and easy to understand — you will eventually have to read your own notes, so write them so that you aren't guessing about what happened when you are writing up your results.

Note: The most logical, and probably easiest way to format this assignment is to follow the standard science format: An introduction, materials and methods, results and discussion, the basic structure of which is easy to see in the list of instructions above. However, other formats are certainly possible and you should use whatever makes the most sense in your situation.

REFLECTION	The main point of this activity is to get the students using their notebook and providing their own feedback by forcing them to read their own notes. The basic structure, having them conduct an experiment and record their methods and results, can be applied to pretty much any activity you might like. This reaction is fun and gets the students engaged. The activity can also be returned to later in either a chemistry or biology class when the topic of polymers is addressed. The web site www.sillyputty.com has some history and science of silly putty, including details on the chemical structure and polymerization reaction.

Sample Lesson Plan 2.5: Stem-and-Leaf Plots (Graphing)

Unit: Comparing sets of data
Position within Unit: Introduction to plotting data.
Title: Stem-and-leaf plot lesson (Janet Tarjan, Ed.D., Mathematics Professor, CALLI Grant)

Table A.2.6 Stem-and-Leaf Plot Lesson

OBJECTIVE(S) PURPOSE	Students will be able to accurately read and interpret Stem-and-Leaf Plots that are presented. They will make stem-and-leaf plots for a given set of data or when given two sets of data to compare. Students will correctly identify the minimum and maximum values of a data set. They will learn the terms increasing and decreasing and the terms ordered and unordered as they apply to the data and the stem-and-leaf plots. They will strengthened their reasoning skills and their ability to make sense of numerical data, look for patterns, and read data that others have organized.
CA STANDARDS	SDP 1.1 Use a stem-and-leaf plot to display a single set of data or compare two sets of data. SDP 1.3 Understand the meaning of the minimum and maximum of a data set.
MATERIALS	Pictures of plants or real plants or flowers, papers, pencils, and handouts. Data sets for high temperatures, urban population of Western states, and NFL data after two games. Presentation materials: Board and chalk or white board and markers Copied materials: handouts Pages in textbook: Book title: Mathematics: Concepts and Skills Pages: 253–257
ACTIVITIES Anticipatory Set: Flower Drawing) (4 Minutes) R3, R4 R2	INTRODUCTION: Welcome! We've been working with numbers a lot lately. You have been working with percents, decimals, and fractions and learning how to move back and forth between the different representations. Today we will be doing some new activities with sets of numbers. That means that instead of just working with ONE number at a time, we will be working with a group of numbers (or set of numbers) all at one time. The set of numbers will be interesting pieces of information about people or cities or countries! We will call the sets of numbers data sets. … BUT FIRST ….a biology lesson. How many of you know what a flower is? Close your eyes and imagine a flower. NOW, open your eyes and very quickly on a piece of paper in front of you draw a picture of a flower! No peeking at anyone else's flower! (Wait a minute!) OK! Finish up. Now, do I have a volunteer to stand, share his or her picture and describe it in words? (IF no volunteers, the teacher can do his or hers.) Okay, pass them in! Quickly! (I review them quickly and if they match mine, I say "we drew" instead of "I drew" in what follows. IF the pictures are not silly, I will display them in class

Table A.2.6 Continued

E4 (optional)	to remind students about the meaning of the words "stem-and-leaf.")
	Teacher Led Discussion:
	Here's how I drew mine! I have a flower, a stem and a leaf! Every time I draw flowers, this is the first one I think of.! If I get fancy, I draw more than one leaf, but my flower is still pretty simple. Let's review the parts of my flower: flower, stem, leaf. Here are some other pictures of flowers. Every stem has leaves coming off of the stem. (Share any pictures or real plants brought from home!)
	Today, we will borrow the vocabulary of stem-and-leaf and use the mental picture of a stem and leaf to create organization from a messy set of data. Let me explain by doing a quick example. Then I have a handout for you to practice the concepts. Then, we'll get a little more complicated, more practice, more discussion, and you will be experts today in creating and reading STEM-AND-LEAF PLOTS.
R5, R8, E11	Here we go!
	ACTIVITY 1:
	First let's use the data for High Temperatures from around the world for Friday, September 22, 2006 according to the Bakersfield Californian. (Obviously you can update these with data from your local paper.) We will use the data from
High Temperatures Data Set	these 40 very influential cities to create our first stem-and-leaf plot and examine the important feature of our first stem-and-leaf plot.
(5 minutes)	
R2, R6, R7, R8	Distribute Handout #1: High Temp Data
	As you are distributing the paper, review the meaning of the words, increasing and decreasing. Talk about heights for school pictures. Talk about ages of siblings in a family. Talk through the following comments and fill in the blanks as you distribute paper. Students should respond. If they don't, explain that they should!
	Vocabulary: "De-" means down. "In-" sometimes means not but in this case means adding to!
	Please note that Increasing means getting bigger!
	Decreasing means getting smaller!
	The total number of deaths in IRAQ is increasing!
	The number of days until Halloween is decreasing!
	The number of species found on earth is _____
	(decreasing).

The number of daylight hours is _____
(decreasing) as winter approaches.
The number of E. coli cases reported since January is
_____(increasing).
Your understanding of the word increasing is _____
(increasing).
E2, E9, E10, E11   Your understanding of the word decreasing is _____
(increasing).

SPEND TIME WITH THE High Temperature
HANDOUT…follow the directions there for discussion and
Urban Population   development of the first stem-and-leaf plot.
Data Set
(5 minutes)   (Return to this document when finished!)
E2, E9, E10, E12
E11   ACTIVITY 2:
Now let's do the same thing with data from your
textbook about urban population in states in the Western U.S.
Football Data Set   I have it ready for us on another handout. Distribute this as
(5 minutes)   you answer questions from the first handout.
E2, E3, E4, E5, E6,
E9, E10, E11, E12   ACTIVITY 3:
More complicated:
After two NFL games, here are the data for Points For
(PF) and Points Against (PA) NFL teams according to the
Bakersfield Californian Sports page C8 Look at the handout
Conclusion   that has this data!
(5 minutes)
CONCLUSION:
E3   Let's review what we've learned! Go back through the
stem-and-leaf plots that have been made and remind students
of the patterns that become obvious when the data is organized
in this fashion.

Sometimes we need to look for patterns in a lot of
data. Patterns may be hard to see before we organize the data.
Making stem-and-leaf plots can help us see patterns in sets of
numbers. They can be the final product OR they can help us get
more refined information.

ASSESSMENT   Questions and answers during class.
Worksheets (Handouts) done together.
Homework.
Quiz the following day (a problem from the homework to be
done either independently or in groups).
Test questions.
In order to differentiate instruction, I may use different levels
of assignments (from the homework set #1-21) depending
(continued)

Table A.2.6 Continued

E13	upon success in the following bulleted activities in the order presented here.

- Finding the minimum value and maximum value from a data set.
- Building a basic unorganized stem-and-leaf plot from a small set of data.
- Building a basic unorganized stem-and-leaf plot from a larger set of data.
- Discussing observed patterns and trends in the data. (Which group is the biggest?)
- Building an organized stem-and-leaf plot from a small set of data.
- Building an organized stem-and-leaf plot from a small set of data.
- Building a histogram from a stem-and-leaf plot.
- Building Back-to-Back stem-and-leaf plots.

REFLECTION	Possible Extension: Building Double Stem and leaf plots This was not discussed in this lesson, but it is a natural extension of the ideas presented and could be used as enrichment. IF there are LOTS of leaves in the categories and not very many numbers in the stem, each number in the stem can be written twice! It would the represent half of the original category. If "5" represented "50-something" then one "5" would represent the numbers 50–54 while the other "5" would represent the numbers 55–59, thus splitting the intervals in half. Beautiful and fun to do with the advanced students or quick finishers.

Contributed by Janet W. Tarjan, Ed.D.

(Bakersfield Californian, 9/23/06 on Page B8)

City	High*	Here are some questions to ask and answer first!
Acapulco	87	1. What is the minimum temp.? _____
Anchorage	49	2. What is the maximum temp.? _____
Aspen	37	3. What numbers should be included on the stem?
Bakersfield	81	Numbers from____ to ____

Why?_____

City	High
Bangkok	82
Bogota	68
Buenos Aires	68
Cabo San Lucas	95
Cairo	86
Calgary	53
Delano	82
Dublin	62
Ensenada	73
Frankfurt	78
Fresno	81
Guadalajara	78
Havana	91
Hong Kong	89
Jerusalem	84
Lima	68
Lisbon	71
London	66
Los Angeles	77
Madrid	71
McFarland	82
Mexico City (D.F.)	75
Minneapolis	59
Montreal	62
New Delhi	95
New Orleans	90
Olso	66
Paris	73
Rome	80
Salt Lake City	55
San Francisco	78
Tijuana	73
Tokyo	75
Toronto	62
Vancouver	61
Washington D.C.	70

*Degrees, Fahrenheit

Shall we write the numbers on the stem from low to high going top to bottom (decreasing) or from high to low going top to bottom (increasing)? As math artists we get to choose. I definitely want to have the numbers get smaller as I go from the top to the bottom (decreasing order) in this case. Can you guess why? (Think about thermometers!)

High Temperatures for 9/22/06

9

8

7

6

There are some important features to notice. The dotted lines above are to help us be neat on our FIRST stem and leaf plot. It is VERY important to write the information neatly so that numbers line up both vertically and horizontally. Otherwise, we would not learn as much from our plot! What if we want to include Baghdad with high of 107?

Figure A.2.1 Bakersfield Californian 2006. Weather from international cities, September 22, 2006. Retrieved from http://weather.baskersfield.com/auto/bakersfield/geo/IntlCityList/index.html on Sept. 22, 2006.

Population Census Data for the Western United States

1. Let's first make a stem-and-leaf plot.
   What is the minimum value in the data set?_____
   What is the maximum value in the data set?_____
   What numbers should be included in the stem?_____ to _____
   Shall we do increasing or decreasing data? This is our choice as artists!
   Let's choose INCREASING ORDER for this stem-and-leaf plot.

2. Now let's organize the data in each row in increasing order from the stem. This is called an organized stem-and-leaf plot. The first type is therefore "unorganized" because "un-" as a prefix in English means "not." The data within the leaf area was not organized. Therefore we say the plot was an unorganized stem-and-leaf plot.

Western Urban

State	Pop (% of state).	I. Stem-and-Leaf Plot
AK	68	
AR	54	
AZ	88	
CA	93	II. Organized Stem-and-Leaf Plot
CO	82	
HI	89	
IA	61	
ID	57	
KS	69	
LA	68	
MN	70	
MO	69	
MT	53	
ND	53	
NE	66	
NM	73	
NV	88	
OK	68	
OR	71	
SD	50	
TX	80	
UT	87	
WA	76	
WI	66	
WY	65	

3. Read and answer the following questions and we'll discuss them in class.
   (a) What did you notice you thought about as you did the work? (b) Can you name every state in the list, spell it correctly, and find it on a map? (c) Was the effort to make the organized stem-and-leaf

plot worthwhile? (d) What did you gain? (e) Could you skip making the unorganized stem-and-leaf plot and go directly to the organized one? (Yes, but it would take a *long* time. Don't do it! Just make the unorganized one first!)

Population Census Data for the Western United States, cont.

4. Now, let's make a histogram from the data! I'll explain what it is as we make it. But, we can begin by imagining that we are turning the stem-and-leaf plot on its side so the stem is on the bottom.

   The stem numbers 5 6 7 8 9 become 50 60 70 80 90 on a numberline! Instead of writing all the detail in the leaves, we just count how many leaves each part of the stem has. For example, how many leaves begin with 5 (for 50)? We call this the frequency of the class 50–59. We need to find the frequency of each class or interval. Frequency just means the number you get when you count how many of something there are so that you can answer the question "How many?" We use f to represent frequency on the vertical axis of the histogram. Fill in the missing numbers on the vertical axis.

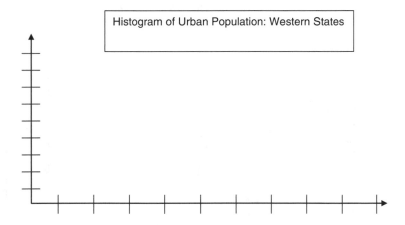

5. More discussion! When we made the histogram, did it help to have the data organized in increasing order along the stem? Why? Was it necessary? Is it possible to leave the numberline from 0–49 off because we don't need it? (Yes, but you have to be careful to put "…" to indicate that you've removed part of the numberline. Otherwise people reading it expect that 0 is included.)

6. Comments: The stem-and-leaf plots are very useful for initial organization of data so that the researcher can start to see patterns and groupings of numbers. It is sometimes the final project. But, very often, making a stem-and-leaf plot is done as a very quick first step in examining data!

After two NFL games in 2006, here are the data for Points For (PF) and Points Against (PA) NFL teams according to the Bakersfield Californian Sports page C8. Look at the handout that has this data!

Let's do a stem-and-leaf diagram to compare PF and PA data.

First let's think about some important ideas.

- What is the minimum of the PF data?_____
- What is the maximum of the PF data?_____
- What is the minimum of the PA data?_____
- What is the maximum of the PA data?_____
- What numbers should be included on the stem?___ to ___
- What will the "Key" say?
- Shall we do increasing or decreasing? _____

(Either is fine. We are the artists! Shall we vote?)

Team	PF	PA
New England	43	34
Buffalo	33	25
NY Jets	40	40
Miami	23	44
Indianapolis	69	45
Jacksonville	33	17
Houston	34	67
Tennessee	23	63
Cincinnati	57	27
Baltimore	55	6
Pittsburgh	28	26
Cleveland	31	53
San Diego	67	7
Denver	19	24
Kansas City	16	32
Oakland	6	55
NY Giants	51	50
Dallas	44	34
Philadelphia	48	40
Washington	26	46
Atlanta	34	9
New Orleans	53	41
Carolina	19	36
Tampa Bay	3	41
Chicago	60	7
Minnesota	35	29
Detroit	13	43
Green Bay	27	60
Seattle	30	16
Arizona	44	48
San Francisco	47	47
St Louis	31	30

Back-to-Back Stem-and-Leaf Plot
Points *for* Points *against*

Sample Lesson Plans without Expressive and Receptive Language Prompts

The lessons in this appendix follow the lesson plan format and the expressive (E) and receptive (R) language strategies provided in appendix 1. The strategies for these lessons are not provided. See appendix 3 for lessons with strategies explicitly included.

Sample Lesson Plan 3.1: Unit Analysis (Math and Science)

Unit: Introduction math and science
Position within Unit: Early
Lesson Plan Title: Unit analysis (C. T. Kloock and J. W. Tarjan)

Table A.3.1 Unit Analysis

OBJECTIVE(S) PURPOSE	To teach the tool of unit analysis (a.k.a. dimensional analysis), in order to help students successfully deal with the many conversion problems they will encounter in the sciences in particular, but in many other field as well.
CA STANDARDS	Science: Grade 8, 9f: Apply simple mathematic relationships to determine a missing quantity in a mathematic expression, given the two remaining terms (including speed = distance/time, density = mass/volume, force = pressure*area, volume = area*height). Grades 9–12: Investigation and experimentation 1a: Select and use appropriate tools and technology (such as computer-linked probes, spreadsheets, and graphing calculators) to perform tests, collect data, analyze relationships, and display data. Grades 9–12: Investigation and experimentation 1f: Solve scientific problems by using quadratic equations and simple trigonometric, exponential, and logarithmic functions (a bit of a stretch, but solving problems using math, if not these specific types of equations) Math: Algebra 1 1.0 Students identify and use the arithmetic properties of subsets of integers and rational, irrational, and real numbers, including closure properties for the four basic arithmetic operations where applicable: 5.0 Students solve multistep problems, including word problems, involving linear equations and linear inequalities in one variable and provide justification for each step. 12.0 Students simplify fractions with polynomials in the numerator and denominator by factoring both and reducing them to the lowest terms. 13.0 Students add, subtract, multiply, and divide rational expressions and functions. Students solve both computationally and conceptually challenging problems by using these techniques.
MATERIALS	Presentation materials: Attached overheads (optional) 2 Rulers and/or metersticks A small item that you can assign a price to and that students are likely to "want": Something that will grab your students' interest

Copied materials: See attached handout.
Laboratory materials:
  None
Other materials:
Disclaimer: We are aware that some people teach conversions using the "T" or "Box" model rather than as equations. The main ideas of this lesson do not depend on the format, and it will work in exactly the same way in those formats. We prefer this format because it makes the mathematical nature of the process more explicit.

ACTIVITIES	Anticipatory set: Bring out a small item, preferably something your students would find desirable that is pretty inexpensive — A dessert or treat, for example. In my example I'll use a $1.50 chocolate bar, but use whatever will best get your students interested
Introduction	
(Anticipatory Set)	
(5 Minutes?)	On the board (or overhead) write down the price and announce: This chocolate bar costs a dollar and a half. Now if you only have pennies to pay with, how many pennies would you need to give me to buy this candy bar?

(*Optional motivation technique: You could give the first student with the correct answer a small reward. I never recommend giving students candy, but that is a possibility. If you have a reward system in place, use it; if not, some ideas are extra points, homework passes, maybe a free ticket to the next football/basketball, etc. game if you can wring them out of your athletic department. Repeat and vary the reward randomly as you ask questions so students will never know when they might get something for participating in class.*)

Once you get a correct answer, write it out, including the units, pennies. Continue presenting the students with similar, slightly more difficult scenarios: If you only had dimes, how many dimes would you need? What if you only had half dollars? Quarters? Nickels? As each of these is answered, write it down.
  (Here you are setting the stage for scaffolding on previous knowledge — most students can do at least some of these conversions in their heads)

After you've gone through this simple exercise, ask students how they figured out the correct amounts — go back to the students who answered first and ask them to explain their logic. For pennies and half dollars let the students just explain verbally, but for quarters move to the board to "do the math". As the student explains their logic, you write down the key aspects (see example below, repeated with numbers only on attached overhead). Note that it is **crucial**

[Activity #1
Money conversions
explained]

(*continued*)

Table A.3.1 Continued
(15 minutes,
teacher led)

to include units as you do this, and it is generally easier for the students if you do not abbreviate the units and if you express fractions in $\frac{a}{b}$ format rather than $^a/_b$ format.

To convert \$1.50 to # of quarters (for lower performing students, convert the \$1.5 into 150¢ for them to avoid the decimals, at least to start):

You know that the candy bar costs 1.50 Dollars and you know that there are 4 Quarters per Dollar. You can write 4 quarters per dollar as $\frac{4\ Quarters}{1\ Dollar}$. Whenever anything is expressed using "per", you can express it as a fraction like this. For example if there are 12 eggs per dozen you can use $\frac{12\ Eggs}{1\ Dozen\ Eggs}$. You can just read the division bar as the word per, or the word per as the division bar — they are interchangeable.

This is good practice for all word problems: students should always write down what you know before you start.

We want to know the number of quarters in 1.5 dollars.

Multiply: $\frac{1.5\ Dollar}{} * \frac{4\ Quarters}{1\ Dollar}$.

This gives you 6, but six what? How do you know it is quarters?

At this point, depending on the class, some students may come up with the idea that the dollars cancel out. DO NOT just accept this; ask the student why the dollars cancel out. From my experience they cannot tell you, they just know that it is true, or say something along the lines of "'cuz there's a dollar on top and a dollar on the bottom." To get them to understand the basic idea behind Unit analysis you need to get them beyond this rote memorization. If no one gets this far, just move straight to the next section.

Let's take a break for a minute and do something easier: (see overhead 1, attached) What is 1 divided by 1? What about 5 divided by 5? How about 1,326 divided by 1,326? What general rule are you using? Try to get a student to express the idea that a number divided by itself is always equal to one. If they don't, give them a few more questions like these until they do, or you feel the need to move on and just tell them this rule.

If it is true that any number divided by itself is equal to one, then if we use X to stand for any number, what is X divided by X? What if we let a word act like a number? What do we get if we divide a dollar by a dollar, as in the equation on the board? And any number times 1 is equal to? This is why we can cancel out dollars: dollars divided by dollars equals 1, and multiplying by 1 doesn't change the number, so we can get rid of it. In the same way, remember that any number divided by 1 is itself, which is what allowed us to write our 1.5 dollars as a fraction over one (and write in the one under the fraction). If we cancel out the dollars, what does that leave us with?

> *Here students will generally say "Quarters". Remind them that they still need to multiply the numbers 1.5 *4 to get "6 quarters".*

Now look at the term $\frac{4\ Quarters}{1\ Dollar}$. All by itself, what is this equal to? Remember that 4 Quarters = one dollar, so these are just two different ways of expressing the same number, and what did we just say a number divided by itself is equal to? So, when we multiply the 1.5 dollars by this fraction, did we change the amount of money?

What if we have a number of quarters, say 18, and want to know how many dollars that is? What can we do? Write down 18 Quarters and wait for suggestions — It is not uncommon for students to want to just multiply by 4. If they make this suggestion, go through it as below, if not reverse parts I and II below so all students get a chance to see why it works one way and not the other.

Part 1: The wrong way (Show students the math):

$$\frac{18\ Quarters}{1} * \frac{4\ Quarters}{1\ Dollar} = \frac{72\ Quarters^2}{1\ Dollar}$$

Does this make sense? What do we need to do to get rid of the quarters so our answer is in Dollars?

Part II: The right way (Again, show the math)

$$\frac{18\ Quarters}{1} * \frac{1\ Dollar}{4\ Quarters} = \frac{4.5\ Dollars}{1}$$

Notice here that we can invert (i.e. "flip over") the **conversion factor**, $\frac{4\ Quarters}{1\ Dollar}$. The conversion factor equals one, so it doesn't matter which unit of measure (i.e. quarters or dollars) is on top (does it matter which 5 is on top of 5/5?).

Now that we've spent some time with money, The fun begins, because it turns out that we can do the same thing with any units. If dollars divided by dollars is one, what is meters divided by meters? seconds divided by seconds? grams divided by grams?

Look at this meterstick. It is one meter long. It is also 39.37 inches. What is 39.37 inches divided by 1 meter? Not sure? What if I ask you what is this distance (show the length of the meterstick) divided by this distance (Show the

(continued)

Table A.3.1 Continued

length of a 2nd meterstick)? The distance is the same, so it equals one. What about 1 meter divided by 39.37 inches? Remember, **units matter**. If I tell you someone is 100, what does that mean? What if I tell you that it was 100 Pounds, what does that mean? 100 Years?

Remember, doing conversions is all about knowing two things:

First of all, you need an appropriate conversion factor. This is just a way of expressing the number one using the units you have and the units you want. For example, if you want to convert feet to inches, you need to know the number of inches per foot $\frac{12\ inches}{1\ foot}$:

[Activity #2
Student practice]
(till end of class)

The second thing you need is to know which goes on top and which goes on the bottom of your equation. Just remember your units. Always put the one on bottom that you want to get rid of, and the one on top that you want to change to. If you want to convert 6 inches to feet. You need to know the number of feet per inch and then

$$\frac{6\ inches}{1} * \frac{1\ foot}{12\ inches} = 0.5\ feet$$

If you want to convert 6 feet to inches, then

$$\frac{6\ feet}{1} * \frac{12\ inches}{1\ foot} = 72\ inches.$$ Notice that the conversion factors for these 2 problems are the same, one is just the **inverse** of the other. Who can tell me what an inverse is? *Remind students of the definition of an inverse.*

Conclusion
(10 minutes)

The worksheet for this lesson contains a variety of conversion factors, and some simple conversion problems.
As an extension, or for use in higher level classes, there is a second section with some multi-step conversions.

Provide students with the attached worksheet. Let them work in groups to help each other understand conversions. Move from group to group checking on the work and helping groups that have problems. As always, encourage students who "get it" to explain to those who don't — this is good for both students.

The worksheet is set up so that for each conversion factor given there is a "right-side up" and "upside-down" conversion. The first 3 columns of problems use the three types of units (length, mass, volume) "in order", while the last column has them mixed so the students have to work a bit harder to figure out the correct conversion factor. Probably a few too many metric problems, for just a lesson on conversions, but it is to help them see some patterns in metric conversions and convince them that metrics really are the way to go.

The next set of problems has multi-step conversions. There is nothing special about these problems; feel free to assign as many or as few as you need to meet your time-frame and student level — you may want to skip the multi-step conversions with low level classes or cut down the number of metrics problems for high level students to make room for more multi-step conversions.

Wrap up class by demonstrating a multi-step conversion:

How many seconds are there in a day?

Start by asking students what they know about day length (ask how many hours in a day if they need prompting) — Now what do you know about hours? (ask how many minutes per hour if they need prompting) and about minutes? (sec/minute, if prompting needed) Build the equation below as they help you answer these questions

$$\frac{24\ hours}{1\ day} * \frac{60\ minutes}{1\ hour} * \frac{60\ seconds}{1\ minute} = 86{,}300\ seconds/day$$

A second example: How many meters in a football field;

$$\frac{100\ yard}{1} * \frac{3\ feet}{1\ yard} * \frac{12\ inches}{1\ foot} * \frac{2.54\ cm}{1\ inch} * \frac{1\ m}{100} = 91.44\ meters$$

(Of course, if you have a conversion factor that goes straight from yards to meters you can do it in one step, but this shows how you can build a conversion from known conversions when you don't have one that will work directly.)

This method of doing conversions will allow you to do any conversion that is possible, but it will not allow you to do any conversion where it is not possible to find some quantity that is equal to one. For example, while you can convert between any two measures of length (feet, meters, inches, miles, even light-years) you cannot convert between units that measure different things – you cannot convert, for example, mass (i.e. kilograms) into length (i.e. kilometers) because there is no way to express kg/km in terms that equal one. There is no method that will allow these conversions.

> *In a physics class, this can serve as a good springboard (for another class period) into the difference between mass and weight (force), and why we can sometimes convert between these two: we can make the conversion as long as acceleration remains constant (since F=ma), but NOT if acceleration is not constant.*

ASSESSMENT	Collect worksheets. We suggest collecting one worksheet per group as a "check-off" assignment to make sure they've done the work, then assigning a few questions for them to complete individually in the last few minutes of class or as homework

(continued)

Table A.3.1 Continued

(see attached assessment). I like to give a challenge problem to take home as well.

Example challenge problems:

For a "general" class:

Calculate the number of hours in 2 weeks. Remember that there are 24 hours in a day and 7 days in a week.

For a higher level class.

Calculate the number of inches in a mile. There are 1760 yards in a mile; the rest of the conversion factors you should already know: How many feet per yard and how many inches per foot? *(63,360 in)*

In the metric system, the comparable measurements are centimeters and kilometers. How many centimeters are there in a kilometer? (ask yourself: how many meters per kilometer? How many cm per meter?) *(100,000 cm)*

Which system, the English system (miles and inches) or the metric system (centimeters and meters) use easier conversion factors? *(Metric)*

Just another:

Convert 55 mile/hr into km/hr. (55mile/hr *1.609km/mile = 88.495 km/hr)

For a physics class:

In crash tests, cars are driven into a solid wall at a constant speed of 35 mi/hr. What is the absolute value of the force of a 1,800 kg car hitting the solid wall? It takes 0.2 seconds for the car to come to a complete stop. (Hints: Convert everything to metrics to begin; acceleration = change in velocity/time; look at the units of Newtons, N; watch your units of time — make sure they match; only round your final answer).

Answer: Using F=ma, where m=1,800 kg, and a=(35 mi/hr)/0.2 s. The units of Newtons are $Kg*m/s^2$, so you need get all of the units into either meters, kg, or seconds. In the equation below, the first two terms are Mass and acceleration, respectively. The next 3 terms are just conversion factors. 1609m/mile converts miles to meters and the 2 time fractions convert hours to seconds:

$$F = 1800 \, kg * \frac{\dfrac{35 \, mi}{hr}}{0.2 \, s} * \frac{1609 \, m}{mi} * \frac{1 \, hr}{60 \, min} * \frac{1 \, min}{60 \, s}$$

First , Fix the complex Fraction :

$$\frac{\dfrac{35 \, mi}{hr}}{0.2 \, s} * \frac{\dfrac{1}{0.2 \, s}}{\dfrac{1}{0.2 \, s}} = \frac{35 mi}{0.2 \, s * hr} \quad \textit{Then substitute this for Acceleration in the equation}$$

$$F = 1800 \, kg * \frac{35 mi}{0.2 \, s * hr} * \frac{1609 \, m}{mi} * \frac{1 \, hr}{60 \, min} * \frac{1 \, min}{60 \, s}$$

$$= 140{,}787.5 \frac{kg * m}{s^2} = 140{,}787.5 \, Newtons$$

but be careful of rounding error

REFLECTION

You may want to add some of your own problems or substitute some other conversions for the many metric ones in the worksheet as it stands. Here are some other important conversion factors for you to use. I should also point out that the temperature conversion requires a little more than the others. This is simply because the meaning of zero is different in the two systems (i.e. 0 °C=32°F), unlike in most other units of measurement (e.g. 0m=0ft, 0 l=0 Gal etc). I suggest you introduce this conversion later, after students are comfortable with the idea of conversions in general.

Force(F=m·a)
1 Newton (N) = 0.2248 lb
1 Newton (N) = 1 kg·m/s²

Energy: (E=F·d)
1 calorie = 4.184 Joule
1 ft·lb = 1.356 Joule

Speed or velocity
km/hr = 0.62 mi/hr
m/s = 3.3 ft/s

Pressure: (=Force/area)
1 atm = 101325 N/m2

Temperature
°C = 5/9·(°F-32)
°F = (9/5)·°C + 32

Time
60 min = 1 hr
60 sec = 1 min

Contributed by Janet W. Tarjan, Ed.D.

$$\frac{4\,Quarters}{1\,Dollar} = \text{"4 Quarters per Dollar"}$$

$$\frac{1}{1} = \underline{\quad}?\qquad \frac{5}{5} = \underline{\quad}?\qquad \frac{1{,}326}{1{,}326}\underline{\quad}?$$

$$\frac{X}{X} = \underline{\quad}?\qquad \frac{\$}{\$} = \underline{\quad}?\qquad \frac{Feet}{Feet}\underline{\quad}?$$

$$\frac{1.5\,Dollar}{} * \frac{4\,Quarters}{1\,Dollar} = \underline{\qquad\qquad}?$$

$$\frac{4\,Quarters}{1\,Dollar} = \underline{\qquad\qquad}?$$

$$\frac{18\,Quarters}{} * \frac{?}{?} = \underline{\qquad}\;Dollars\,?$$

Figure A.3.1 Conversions Lesson Overhead 1.

$$\frac{6\,Inches}{} * \frac{1\,Foot}{12\,Inches} = \underline{\qquad\qquad}?$$

$$\frac{6\,Feet}{} * \frac{12\,Inches}{1\,Foot} = \underline{\qquad\qquad}?$$

Invert: To turn upside down

Inverse: a Fraction that has been inverted

If: $\quad \dfrac{1\,Foot}{12\,Inches}\qquad$ What is the inverse? $\qquad\underline{\qquad}?$

Multiple conversions can be chained together

$$\frac{24\,Hours}{Day} * \frac{60\,Minutes}{1\,Hour} * \frac{60\,Seconds}{1\,Minute} = \underline{\qquad}?$$

$$\frac{100\,Yards}{} * \frac{3\,Feet}{1\,Yard} * \frac{12\,Inches}{1\,Foot} * \frac{2.54\,cm}{Inch} * \frac{1\,meter}{100\,cm} = \underline{\qquad}?$$

Figure A.3.2 Conversions Lesson Overhead 2.

For this worksheet, assume all conversions involving pounds are on Earth.

Which type of units are easier to deal with: American Units (ft, in, lbs, gals, qts) or Metric Units (m, km, cm, mm, g, kg cg, mg, *l*, kl, cl, ml; also known as SI, for Systeme International).

Which is larger?

1m or 3 ft?   1 l or 1 qt   1 g or 1 oz   1 cm or 1 m   35 oz or 1 kg?

Length	Mass	Volume
$\dfrac{1\,Foot\,(ft)}{12\,inch\,(in)}$	$\dfrac{1\,Pound\,(lb)}{16\,ounces\,(oz)}$	$\dfrac{1\,U.S.Gallon\,(Gal)}{4\,Quarts}$
$\dfrac{1\,Inch\,(in)}{2.54\,centimeter\,(cm)}$	$\dfrac{2.2\,Pound\,(lb)}{1\,Kilo\,grams\,(kg)}$ ON EARTH ONLY	$\dfrac{1\,Gallon\,(Gal)}{3.786\,Liters\,(l)}$
$\dfrac{1000\,meters\,(m)}{1\,Kilometer\,(km)}$	$\dfrac{1000\,grams\,(g)}{1\,kg}$	$\dfrac{1000\,Liters\,(l)}{1\,Kiloliter\,(kl)}$
$\dfrac{1\,m}{1000\,Milli\,meters\,(mm)}$	$\dfrac{1\,g}{1000\,Milli\,grams\,(mg)}$	$\dfrac{1\,liter\,(l)}{1000\,Milliliters\,(ml)}$
$\dfrac{1\,cm}{10\,mm}$	$\dfrac{1\,centigram}{10\,mg}$	$\dfrac{1\,centiliter\,(cl)}{10\,milliliter\,(ml)}$

Which is larger?

1 inch or 1 cm   1 Gal or 1 l 1 lb or 1 kg

Solve the following conversions:

12 in= _____ ft   357 oz=___ lbs   4 qts=_____Gal   50 kg=_____lbs*

6 ft = ____in   2 lbs* = _____oz   7 Gal=_____qts   100 m=_____km

7 cm = ____ in   100 kg=_____lbs*   2 l=_____Gal   5 gal=_____qts

3 in = _____cm   150 lbs*=____kg   1 Gal=_____l   2000 lbs* = ___kg

3517 m =____ km   15 g = _____kg   7 l=_____kl   27 l =_____ml

7 km=_____ m   17kg=_____g   12 kl=_____l   15 cm = ____mm

3 m = _____ mm   1235 mg = ____g   750 ml =_____l   23.6 l=____Gal

7mm–_____m   37g=_____mg   3 l =_____ml   300 mg=___g

25 cm=_____mm   1.5 cg = _____mg   7 cl = _____ml   300 ml=____l

27 mm=_____cm   13 mg=_____cg   12 ml = _____cl   300 mm=____m

---

Figure A.3.3 Conversion Factors.

Sample Lesson Plan 3.2: Word Problems (Math)

Unit: Solving systems of equations, word problems, mixture problems
Position within Unit: Toward the end of the unit; but enough time should be spent on this so that there is still time to practice solving equations after they are set up and putting the solution back into the context of the problem. (May be used in a variety of courses)
Lesson Plan: Word problems (math)
Title: Mixture problems (Janet W. Tarjan, EdD., Mathematics Professor, CALLI Grant)

Table A.3.2 Mixture Problems

OBJECTIVE(S) PURPOSE	What should they learn by the end of the lesson? Students will be able to read and set up equations to represent the situation described in words in Mixture Problems. Students will learn to read a given problem multiple times in order to identify important features of a problem. Students will learn to identify the difference between "Work Problems" and "Mixture Problems." Students will gain practice in solving the resulting systems of equations for homework. The emphasis for the lesson is the setting up of two equations in two unknowns for a given verbal description of the "Mixture Problem" type. Students who achieve the objective will benefit greatly by strengthening their reading skills, their reasoning skills and their ability to do word problems.
CA STANDARDS	What Standards are addressed by the lesson? Write an equation that represents a verbal description. Also, interpret the solution of the equations in the context in which it arose and verify the reasonableness of the result. (AF 4.1)
	Students add, subtract, multiply, and divide monomials and polynomials. Students solve multi-step problems, including word problems, by using these techniques. (Algebra I 10.0)
	Students solve system of linear equations (in two or three variables) by substitution. (Algebra II 20.0) and more!
MATERIALS	Pictures of Thing One and Thing Two (from Dr. Suess' "The Cat in the Hat") and newspaper ads.
	Presentation materials: Board and chalk or white board and markers
	Copied materials: handouts
ACTIVITIES Anticipatory set	INTRODUCTION Welcome students and tell them that during the next few days, they will become experts at setting up and solving many word problems! Write "I love word problems!" on the board and have students practice saying it out loud as if they mean it! Explain that after a few days, we'll return to that statement and hope that it will be absolutely true! One more time! "I love word problems!"
Activity 1	Class discussion: Yesterday, we put a lot of formulas on the board. Today, I'll just emphasize the few we'll be using this week. They are the following:
	(Rate)(Time)=Distance
	(Value of one Coin of a certain type)(number of that type of coin)=(Value of that type of coin)
	(Strength of "alcohol" solution)(Quantity of solution)=Total amount of "alcohol"

Activity #2	[NOTE: The word in quotes may be changed for another word (e.g. acid, salt or saline).]
Graphic Organizer	
	ACTIVITY 2
Chart to help keep track of Thing One and Thing Two	Re-introduce the chart to help keep track of information. Now use x- and y- variables as needed to represent unknown quantities.
Activity #3 Worksheet problems	ACTIVITY 3 Distribute a handout for Mixture problems. Practice 3 in class. Then, turn time over to students to practice!
Activity #4 Book Reading and Problems	ACTIVITY 4 Turn to page 675 in your book Algebra I Practice setting up problems. Solve the first one together. Then, emphasize the set up! Do many.
Activity #5	ACTIVITY 5 Use examples from the beginning of class to make up our own problems.
Use examples from the beginning of class to make up our own problems.	How much information is required? What information may be left out. In pairs, make up one problem together from your ads. Get ready to say it out loud if asked. Discuss as a group.
Conclusion	CONCLUSION Let's review what we've learned!
	Please read the book, page 673 and do problems 51–55 on pages 675–676 and problems #13–15 on page 677.
	There will be a quiz tomorrow! Are there any questions before you leave? Do you have all the materials you need to be successful on the homework?
	I hope it goes well for you! Ask questions tomorrow on any problems that are difficult.
ASSESSMENT	Questions and answers during class. Homework. Quiz the following day (a problem from the homework to be done either independently or in groups). Test questions.
	I would review the lesson the next day and bring in additional problems made up from the examples given in class the day before. Also, I would provide more problems than the book has on the first night of homework.
REFLECTION	Take time to think about whether to continue on this topic or whether you should move on.

Contributed by Janet W. Tarjan, Ed.D.

Sample Lesson Plan 3.3: Scientific Method (General Science/ Biology)

Unit: Experimental method

Position within Unit: After introduction of basic cycle of the experimental method, including hypothesis, prediction, experiment, and conclusion. This can be used as either an introduction to basic statistical techniques or application if they have already been introduced.

Title: Why do snakes digest so slowly?

> *Assignment*: Students should design their own experiment involving a hypothesis developed in the lab. The format below can help them.
>
> *Hypothesis*: (i.e., Potential Explanation) Provide a potential explanation of why snakes digest their food more slowly than humans. This potential explanation is your hypothesis.
>
> *Prediction*: Your hypothesis can be used to develop a prediction about **what might happen** given a particular new situation. Your experiment should bring that situation about.
>
> *Experiment*: Provide the following information detailing the experiment that tests your hypothesis.
>
> *Method*: A brief description of each treatment, and how you would collect the data. The basic idea is that someone should be able to read this and repeat the experiment.
>
> *Independent variable*: a.k.a. treatment variable. The variable you manipulated in order to test the hypothesis. Give both the variable and the two categories of the variable used in the experiment. Include the units it was measured in, if appropriate.
>
> *Dependent variable*: a.k.a. response variable. The variable you measured in order to test the hypothesis. This must be a variable you expect (correctly or not) to be influenced by the independent variable. Include the units it will be measured in.
>
> *Factors to be held constant*: List here factors that were held constant in all treatments. Don't just randomly list factors here; limit your list to those factors that you actually think could cause an effect on the outcome of your experiment, and do not put your dependent or independent variables here — after all, they should, by definition, vary.
>
> *Control group:* Identify the control group, if the experiment had one. If the experiment did not have a control group, state this and explain **why** it did not have a control group.

Table A.3.3 Why Do Snakes Digest so Slowly?

OBJECTIVE(S)	Learn to apply the experimental method and the concept of reductionism to get a partial answer to a complex question. Break down a complex question into a series of simple ones that experiments can easily answer.
CA STANDARDS	Grades 9-12: Investigation and Experimentation 1 a, b, c, d, g, j, k Grades 9-12: Chemistry 8 b
MATERIALS	For a lab of 30, working in 2 person teams 15 mortars and pestles (or any way to crush the antacids) 30+ Calcium Carbonate antacid tablets (1 bottle) 1 L 0.1 M HCl acid labeled Note: dilute vinegar can be substituted for HCl; I suggest a 10% or 20% dilution. 30 100 ml beakers 30 forceps 15 Grease pencils (or label tape to ID beakers) 30 50-100 ml Graduated cylinders (ideal #, but can be shared) 30 pH test strips (0-14 range works well, 0-7 can be done) or a pH meter.

ACTIVITIES
Anticipatory Set
	Introduction (Anticipatory Set) (5-10 min).
	Observation:
	Questions to open lab: *How many of you have seen snakes eat? When they eat, about how long does it take for their food to digest? How long does it take you to digest your food?*
	   The answers to these questions should lead students to the observation that snakes digest their food more slowly than humans (exactly how much longer isn't critical; snakes generally take several days, sometimes weeks, humans generally ¾-1½ days. Make sure that they realize that this is an observation, based on the past experience of at least some of the students in the classroom. Then ask:
	What are some other differences between snakes and people?
	   Students generally come up with ideas like: swallowing food whole vs. chewing it, differences in body temperature, differences in digestive juices, eating fur/scales, moving after eating vs. staying still — and a variety of others, some good, some bad. You may need to guide them to the factor(s) you intend to test, but these ones generally pop up without too much coaxing. Again, point out that these are all observations, based on past experiences. Collect a list of the differences as the students develop them.

(continued)

Table A.3.3 Continued

Developing Hypotheses: (10–15 min)	**Main Activities:** Major question: *What makes snakes digest their food more slowly than people?*
I suggest that you work on developing hypotheses, predictions, and beginning to design the experiment on one day. Finish the design and conduct the experiment the next day. Extensions can carry this lab through as many additional periods as you like.	Students will immediately throw out some ideas. As they slow down (or if they never get started) guide them by returning to the list of differences you made earlier; explain that each of these differences contains a simple hypothesis potentially explaining why snakes digest their food more slowly than humans (e.g. snakes digest their food more slowly because they don't chew their food). For each difference the students identify, ask whether they think it is likely to affect the rate of digestion, and ask them to explain why. Eliminate ideas that nobody thinks will effect digestion, but also point out that these hypotheses are not mutually exclusive, nor are they all-inclusive. Explain the concept of reductionism and how it works in science — tell students that you will break down the rather complicated question about digestion in these two different organisms into a series of simple predictions, based on simple hypotheses about which of the factors they identified influence digestion. You can then test these simple predictions one-at-a-time to begin developing your answer to the more complicated question.
Developing a Prediction: (5 min.)	Pick any of the differences students have identified as possibly affecting digestion (I'll use chewing as an example throughout), and ask students: If (chewing) affects the rate of digestion, what kinds of predictions can you make? Almost invariably, some students will predict that snakes will digest their food more slowly than humans. This gives you the opportunity to point out how useless it is to predict your initial observation, and why this circular reasoning doesn't work. Point out that if your prediction and your observation are the same, you can justify any hypothesis: for example, I can hypothesize that little green men retard the digestion of snakes and make the same prediction — can my hypothesis be falsified? Move them beyond this by asking: *What would you predict would happen if we set up a digestive process using chewed food, and compared the rate of digestion to the rate in the same process using unchewed food?* Once you have a valid prediction move the students on to designing a simple experiment to test their hypothesis.
Designing an experiment: (10-20 min)	Usually, the students will get to the prediction that chewed food will be digested faster than unchewed food, all else being equal. You may need to spend some time convincing

them that "all else being equal" is important and allows you to be non-circular in your predictions.

Ask students: how can you make "all else equal"?

Students generally get stuck on the idea that they need to compare a snake and a human to answer the question. A common idea that they develop is to make someone swallow a mouse whole, and compare their digestive time to a snake that eats a same-sized mouse (or similarly, they want to force a snake to eat a chewed mouse). Once they stop being disgusted by this suggestion, you get to point back to your list and point out all those other differences and the fact that they are still different — so any difference in digestive rate you might find with such an experiment doesn't mean much — you can't separate out the different factors this way. Next, someone will usually venture that you could use two people (or two snakes), one chewing the food, one swallowing it whole. Point out 1) this could work, but you'd need a bigger sample size and 2) logistically it's not really feasible. At this point you can guide them to the idea of doing an experiment in an artificial stomach, where you can keep all those other factors constant. Good questions to use through here typically involve starting to show them some of the materials. For example, you can ask questions like:

What if we could make digestion happen in this beaker? How might we be able to do that, given that we have hydrochloric acid, a common stomach acid, and antacids sitting right here on the table?

At this point at least some of the students get the idea and will volunteer information which you can use to develop a simple experiment. Put the steps of the experiment on the board as they volunteer possibilities, and have students discuss the pros and cons of different steps and procedures. As you do this you will get to see — and correct — a number of misconceptions that your students have about snakes, digestion, and the experimental method. As you start putting up the method, ask questions like:

What is the independent variable? (the antacid's state: chewed or whole)

Does it matter if there is more acid in one beaker than another? Why? What about the concentration (Molarity) of the acid — should it be the same? Can we chew up the antacids and spit them in the beaker? Why not? How should we go about crushing them?

Do this to get them to tell you that they need to hold everything constant except for the independent variable. I make 2 lists, which I make the students fill out: one with

(*continued*)

Table A.3.3 Continued

everything that needs to be done with the "chewed" antacids, one with everything that needs to be done to the whole antacids. These lists should go through a series of revisions as you progress, but eventually the 2 lists end up being identical except for the state of the antacid. The important thing is that the students are forced, as a group, to think their way through the problem. Act as a guide, but make them tell you how to fix problems you point out. Then ask:

What is the dependent variable?

Typically they want to time how long it takes for the different antacids to dissolve. This makes sense, but is a logistic nightmare — the antacids crumble and float and discolor the solution, and it is very difficult to tell just when, if ever, the antacids completely dissolve. It also takes a long time. For this experiment using pH indicator paper to determine the change in pH after 10 minutes of "digestion"

Conducting the experiment: (Day 2, 20–30 min, plus analysis)

works well. Simply measure the pH before adding the antacid and again after ten minutes, and use the change in pH as the dependent variable to indicate how much antacid dissolved. There is no need to try to convert this into a mass.

In this part of the lab, there are several things you could ask the students, but they may not have enough experience to give reasonable answers, so they may just need to be told things like: A good volume of acid to use is 30 ml; a good time for measuring the change in pH is 10 min; you need to stir the solutions briefly because the crushed antacid tends to float (ask them if they should stir the whole antacid solution as well). You can just supply this information as opportunities arise.

Once the experimental design is on the board, conducting the experiment is just a matter of getting the students to follow the directions they've developed. In small classes, every student can do both a crushed and a whole antacid; in larger classes they can work in groups. You want a sample size of 10–15 per treatment so any statistical analysis you want to do will work well without taking too much time for the students to collect all of the data. Depending on the class, you may want to be the "timekeeper" and make everyone do the experiment simultaneously — I find that this reduces the number of mis-timed experiments and reduces variation in the data. Have everyone put their data on the board to share. The TI calculator performs a t-test that can be used as a nice quick way to analyze the results. If students have experience with TI's this should take 5–10 minutes. If not, a while longer.

Conclusion: Use data collected to answer the question: does chewing account for at least some of the difference in digestive rates? Then go back to the list and ask if the experiment we did helps us support or falsify the other hypotheses — point out that many times, hypotheses are not mutually exclusive.

ASSESSMENT	Assessment can be done by having the students design their own experiment on the topic of digestion using the basic setup, but testing another hypothesis. This can be done by having them actually carry out experiments (if you have time and supplies) or by having them just design the experiment without actually conducting it. See attached assignment.

    Lower level students can just be asked to provide this information on the experiment already conducted.

REFLECTION   **Extensions:**

    Repeat! Once they have finished the first experiment, go back to the list of hypotheses you generated, select another one, and go through the procedure again from that point. This reinforces a lot of the ideas that were introduced the first time around. Students will generally go through it the 2nd time much faster and with more confidence.

Suggestions for other tests to conduct:

These are primarily limited by your imagination (or better yet, your students' imaginations). The methods all follow the same basic outline, the tough part is usually figuring out how to manipulate the system to test different variables. Below are just a few ideas, based on differences between snakes and humans that students frequently come up with:

Acid concentration/type: Students often want to know how different concentrations or different types of acid affect digestion. This can be easily experimented with using this system (e.g. 0.1M vs. 0.2M HCl). Snakes actually have a more concentrated stomach acid than we do, so this is a good opportunity to demonstrate falsification of a hypothesis)

Temperature: Place beakers in water baths at different temperatures (room temperature vs. 37°C makes sense) to test whether or not temperature affects digestion rate.

Activity levels: Snakes sit around after eating, mammals move around. Stirring vs not stirring can simulate this difference, but don't stir the entire ten minutes.

Food content: Students always want to test the differences in diet between snakes and humans (i.e. meat vs vegetables, cooked vs. raw, with bones and fur vs without, etc.). In general I don't recommend this, since digestion is much slower with these materials. If you are adventurous, try increasing the digestion times (overnight?) and/or acid concentrations to test these types of questions. You'll want to test out new materials before performing them to make sure they work well and don't stink too much.

Sample Lesson Plan 3.4: Linear Equalities in 2 Variables (Math)

Unit: Graphing Inequalities
Position within Unit: After introduction to graphing inequalities in one variable.
Lesson Plan: Graphing linear inequalities in 2 variables
Title: Graphing linear inequalities in 2 variables (Janet W. Tarjan)

Table A.3.4 Graphing Linear Inequalities in 2 Variables

OBJECTIVE(S) PURPOSE	What should they learn by the end of the lesson? They will learn to graph linear inequalities in two variables.
	How will achieving the objective benefit them? This is an important skill in algebra and future work. The next section will be to solve systems of equations and inequalities. This skill is used in finance and business calculus as well as in advanced work in linear programming. This, with prior work on linear functions in two variables, will make it possible for students to solve a new set of real life problems from linear programming applications.
CA STANDARDS	What Standards are addressed by the lesson?
	Standard AF 4.0 Solve inequalities over the rational numbers.
	Standard AF 1.5 Represent quantitative relationships graphically and interpret the meaning of a specific part of a graph in the situation represented by the graph.
MATERIALS	List and include all materials you will using. *Attach the files of materials in electronic form.*
	Presentation materials: Vocabulary list, overhead projector and pens, graph paper overhead slide of Cartesian Plane (the xy-plane), graph paper for students, notebooks
	Copied materials (handouts, worksheets, tests, lab directions, etc.):
	Laboratory materials:
	For the teacher or the class as a whole: Graph paper, straight edges
	For each laboratory station: N/A
ACTIVITIES Introduction (~5 Minutes)	Describe the activities that you and your students will be doing at three stages in the lesson: Introduction, one or more Main Activities, and Conclusion. **Make sure that your Introduction and Conclusion help to connect this lesson with the lessons before and after.**

Briefly describe how you will:
- In order to get the class interested in the day's lesson & off to a well-managed start, I jump right into reviewing the prior days' material. That lesson includes graphing equations in two variables. While the review seems long, it moves rather quickly because of the recency of the material in Review Part I and the simplicity of the material in Review Part II.

The teacher explains that there are two prior sets of information that are important to review thoroughly before introducing the new lesson. As the teacher discusses the ideas and writes, the teacher should ask students to take good notes in their notebooks so that they will be able to refer to them as they do homework. Because it is review of material covered recently, questions should be used to prompt students to give answers that will be used to fill in information as planned in the table below for the first review part.

Review part 1 (~5 minutes)

[It is important to plan ahead to write the following review of prior material on the board in a position where it can stay for review during the current lesson. A sample summary table is provided for the material in the first part of the review. Much of what follows is said out loud with the summary being written in the table as presented below. It is very important to read through the whole lesson plan prior to giving it to make adjustments for individual classrooms and sets of students. There will be three sets of information on the board by the end of the hour that should not interfere with the overhead projection of information. Again, prior to beginning, the teacher should plan three large areas that will not be covered by an overhead screen. These may be thought of as REVIEW PART I, REVIEW PART II, and the new material: GRAPHING LINEAR INEQUALITIES IN TWO VARIABLES.]

REVIEW PART I

Possible prompting questions are given here.
- What are three forms of an equation of a line? (Answer: Standard Form, Slope-Intercept Form, and Point-Slope Form)
- What is another name for an equation of a line? (Answer: A linear equation in two variables. Note: Students will probably not offer this answer, but it is a good question and answer to provide anyway…it will help introduce the day's lesson and connection to the day's work.)
- Tell the students to think about what they have learned about graphing lines when the equations are given in the different forms. (The following information should have been presented in prior lessons in order to be reviewed now!) Then ask:

(continued)

Table A.3.4 Continued

- If you are given an equation of a line (or a linear equation in two variables) in STANDARD FORM, what is the quickest way to graph two points and find the graph of the line? (Note: As you ask about standard form, write ax + by = c in addition to writing "standard form." Answer: Find the intercepts (or the x- and y- intercepts).)
- If you are given an equation of a line (or a linear equation in two variables) in SLOPE-INTERCEPT FORM, what is the quickest way to graph two points and find the graph of the line? (Note: As you ask about Slope-Intercept Form, write $y = mx + b$ in addition to writing "slope-intercept form." Answer: Find the y-intercept (0,b) [emphasize two coordinates for a point and the y-intercept is a point with x = 0]. Then use the information about the slope $m = \frac{m}{1}$ two find another point or other points. Then draw the line through the points you've found.)
- What about Point-slope form? (Answer: First rewrite in either standard form or in slope-intercept form and then follow the directions we've just reviewed!)

The following table may be used to summarize the above information. (This is what could be written a little at a time as each of the above questions is asked and discussed briefly. Remind students to copy the table down as discussion happens!)

Form of an equation of a line	Quickest method for graphing the line	Sample graphs: Provide a quick example of each!
Standard Form $ax + by = c$	Find Intercepts! Remember: y-intercept ➜ x=0 ... (0, ?) Remember: x-intercept ➜ y=0 ... (?,0)	
Slope-Intercept Form $y = mx + b$	Find y-intercept (0,b) Then, use information about slope m to find a second point! Rewrite m as $m = \frac{m}{1}$ if it helps!	

Point-Slope Form $y - y_1 = m(x - x_1)$	Rewrite in either standard form or Slope-Intercept Form and follow above instructions!	See above.

Review Part 2
(~15 minutes)

REVIEW PART II

I put this on a different part of the board. It should also remain visible during the rest of the hour.

Teacher intro: Long ago, you learned how to graph inequalities in one variable. In order to review these possibilities, let's begin with a linear equality (called an equation) in one variable. What is an example of this type of equation? (Answer: 3x+2=14 or x = 7 or 5-x = 11.) What does it mean to solve the equation? (Answer: Find the value of x that makes the equation a true statement!) What does the graph of the solution look like? (Answer: a point on a number line.)

Now, to extend the ideas to inequalities in one variable, let's just use one such equation as the basis for our discussion. I'll pick: x=7 (Pick any one you'd like. I want to work through the examples that follow very quickly!) How could we rewrite x = 7 so that we have x and 7 still but we do not have an equation? (Point out the prefix "in" means "NOT." So inequality means "Not Equality" or "not an equation."

(Allow students to come up with IN-Equations, or, if they don't respond quickly, continue with pauses for them to jump in with answers.)

Possibilities include the following:

$$x \leq 7$$
$$x < 7$$
$$x \geq 7$$
$$x > 7$$
$$x \neq 7$$

Let's study what we do when we graph each of these linear inequalities in one variable!

We can anticipate that the graph of each solution set will be part of the number line.

- With $x \leq 7$, I first find x=7 because that acts as the **boundary** point that cuts the number line into three parts. The point is the part that is equal! Is that included in my final solution? (Answer: Yes!) How do we know that? (Answer: x "less than OR EQUAL TO" 7 includes x=7 as part of the values that make the inequality true!

(continued)

Table A.3.4 Continued

The symbol "≤" tells us!) Now what do I need to do? (Answer: shade one side of the boundary point.) Which side of the boundary point should I shade and how can I decide? (I can look at another number on the number line and decide if it is less than or equal to 7.) I'll **check the point** x=9. No it doesn't work x ≤ 9 is a FALSE statement. So I shade the "other" side of the boundary point. I'll summarize.

(Note: I talk through all of the above words quickly for each of the possible inequalities. Each time emphasizing using the equation that looks like the inequality with the equals sign replacing the inequality to find the boundary and a point (not the boundary) to use as a check point to decide what side of the boundary to shade. These examples are done rather quickly because students do not find them threatening or difficult. But, they are important to do because they set the stage for the new material.

- Now let's graph the solution set of x<7. What will it look like? (Answer: a half-line on the number line.) First I find the boundary point. I find that by replacing the "less than" symbol with an "equal sign" to get the **boundary equation** x = 7. I find x=7 on the number line. (I draw a circle at x=7.) Do I fill the circle in? No. Why not? Because "<" does NOT include "=." The inequality symbol of the original inequality x<7 tells us if the boundary is included or not. If it is not included, we do not fill the circle in. Now what do I need to do? Shade one side of the boundary. How can I decide which side of the boundary to shade? **Check a point but not the boundary!** Good. I'll check x=0. I find x=0 on the number line. I label it. I test this point. That is, I check it to see if it makes the original inequality true. I check 0<7…This is TRUE! I shade the side of the boundary that x=0 is on because all the true points are on that side and all the false points are on the other side! The equation breaks the number line into three parts: the boundary point is where x=7, one side is where x<7 (true points, in this case), the other side is the set of points for which x>7 (false points in this case).

Inequalities in 2 variables
~20 minutes

Only three more to go!
- Okay, to graph x≥7, I find the boundary equation x=7. I locate the graph of the boundary point x=7 on the line. I decide that the boundary point is included. (The greater than or equal to sign means equality is included in the solution set!) So, I fill in the circle. Now, I need to check a point to decide which side to shade. I check a point that is not x=7. Why? I already know x=7 IS included because of the inequality symbol ≥. Now I want to know what other

values make the original inequality true. So, I pick a check point and substitute the value into the original inequality. I'll pick x=0. Is $0 \geq 7$ a true or false statement? $0 \geq 7$ is a false statement. This tells me that I should NOT shade the side of the boundary that x=0 is on. I should shade the OTHER side of the boundary.

- Now, I graph x>7. I find the boundary equation x=7. I locate x=7 on the numberline. I draw a circle but do not fill it in because ">" means the boundary is NOT included in the solution set. Next I pick a check point not on the boundary. I pick x=12, 12>7 makes the inequality true!!! So, I shade the side of the boundary on which the point x=12 is found. Done!

- For x≠7, I can rewrite the inequality as "$x \leq 7$ or $x \geq 7$." I find the boundary x=7. I do not fill in the circle. I now shade both sides of the boundary because x≠7 is equivalent to "$x \leq 7$ or $x \geq 7$." When we use OR to combine the two inequalities, we get everything on the number line EXCEPT the boundary point "x=7." We haven't seen this inequality "x≠7" much when graphing. It is possible, but we won't be emphasizing it as we move into linear inequalities in two dimensions!

I will use the overhead projector to preview a graph in two variables. This one will be erased soon. I write the inequality x<7 on the board. I say, what if this had been an inequality in two variables and there just happened to be zero y's? As a sneak preview, I would create the Cartesian Plane by putting a second number line perpendicular to the first (see picture below). Then, I would find the boundary x=7, I would extend that shaded region on the x-axis to go up and down for any values of y that we want because the y-value is not limited at all by the inequality, it can be anything.

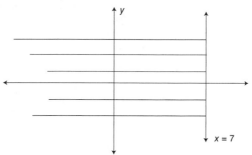

Whew! Now that we've done a thorough review of material we already know, let's put this information together to build new concepts. Today we'd like to find solutions of linear inequalities

(continued)

Table A.3.4 Continued

in two variables AND we'd like to graph the solution sets.

Here are examples of linear inequalities in two variables:

$$3x + 2y > 18 \qquad y \geq 2x + 7 \qquad x - 5y < 10 \qquad -8x + 5y \leq 40$$

Let's look at them. Why do we say inequalities? (Each expression has an inequality in it instead of an equal sign.) Why do we say linear? (The largest degree of any term in the each inequality is one. Explain that there is no xy term, no x^2 or x^3 or y^2 or y^3 or other higher order terms!) Why do we say "in two variables?" (Answer: Now we have two variables, x and y not just one variable x.)

Now write the following steps on the board in preparation for actually graphing the solution set of a linear inequality in two variables.

Each time I work with one of these problems, I perform the following steps by asking myself and answering the indicated questions.

IDENTIFY: What type of problem is this?	It is a linear inequality in two variables.
ANTICIPATE: What will the graph of the solution set look like?	The solution set will be a half-plane. [Draw a few half-planes here!]
What is the BOUNDARY equation? What will the graph of the boundary equation look like?	The boundary equation is the equation I get when I write the original inequality and replace the inequality symbol with an equal sign.
Is the BOUNDARY included in the solution set? How do I know? How do I indicate this on a graph?	If the inequality symbol is < or > the boundary line is NOT included in the solution set. We can't make an empty circle for a whole line, so we indicate that the boundary line is not included by making the line with dashes and calling it a dotted line. If the inequality symbol in the original inequality is an $\leq$ or $\geq$ the boundary line IS included in the solution set. We indicate this

	with a SOLID line. [Note: I say all of the above, but I write only the following to save space: < or > → NO boundary NOT included → DOTTED LINE! < or > → YES boundary IS included → SOLID LINE!
GRAPH THE BOUNDARY EQUATION (See the steps in Review Part I.)	Graph the line. Label two points with their coordinates. Label the boundary line with the boundary equation. Make the boundary line either dotted or solid based on whether the boundary is included in the solution set of the original inequality.
What side of the boundary line should I shade? How do I decide! CHECK A POINT THAT IS <u>NOT</u> ON THE BOUNDARY!	The boundary breaks the PLANE up into three parts. A check point NOT ON THE BOUNDARY will determine what side of the boundary to shade. Shade the part of the graph that makes the original inequality true. [I emphasize that we already know all about the boundary's inclusion or not by looking at the original inequality symbol. We need a point that is NOT on the boundary to learn NEW information: which side we shade!]

The above is the THIRD part that I write, intending to leave it visible throughout the lecture as mentioned in the opening paragraph.

Now, I turn on the overhead projector. The change provides a change of pace without losing time. The screen is already down. I pick one of the inequalities and go through the steps just outlined. I tell students to copy the example down exactly as I do it AND to be very careful to copy the exact location on the page. They should begin a new sheet of paper

(continued)

Table A.3.4 Continued

now. I bring enough graph paper to give each student a piece of paper to emphasize the importance of using graph paper. I will actually give each student two different pieces of graph paper—one dark and one light. [Note: if the students are not likely to buy graph paper, then I pass out a piece of graph paper with dark lines and recommend that they put a regular piece of paper over it. Then, they can turn regular paper into graph paper and reuse the piece I give them until they buy a pack of their own graph paper.] I also pass out a piece of graph paper with faint ink so that they can see a preferred type of graph paper when they go buy graph paper. I probably already gave this talk earlier in the week, but I plan to do it again on this day!]

Let's work with the linear inequality in two variables.

$$3x + 2y > 18$$

Identify. What type of problem is it? (Answer: A linear inequality in two variables.)

Anticipate. What will the graph of the solution set be? (Answer: a half-plane)

What is the boundary equation? (Answer: $3x + 2y = 18$)

What will the graph of this boundary be? (Answer: a line!)

Is the boundary line included in the graph of the solution set? (Answer: NO!)

How do I indicate this? (Draw a dotted line!)

What form of a line is the equation 3x+2y=18 ? (Answer: Standard Form!)

What is the easiest way to graph an equation of a line in standard form? (Answer: Find the intercepts!)

OKAY! Let's do all this work dealing with the boundary line. When I do my problem, I write the problem like this:

Example 1

$$3x + 2y > 18$$

BOUNDARY (dotted)

$$3x + 2y = 18$$

y-int. ➜ x = 0

$$3(0) + 2y = 18$$
$$0 + 2y = 18$$
$$2y = 18$$
$$y = 9$$

Summarize! (0,9) is the y-int.

x-int. ➜ y = 0

$$3x + 2(0) = 18$$
$$3x + 0 = 18$$
$$3x = 18$$
$$= 6$$

Summarize! (6,0) is the x-intercept

Graph the boundary line! Remember it is dotted!

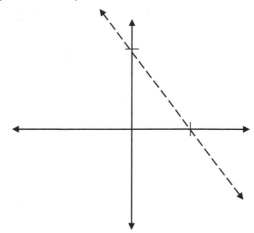

After we graph the boundary line, we ask: "Which side do we shade?"

How do we decide which side to shade? (Answer: We choose a check point or test point that is NOT on the boundary line.) How many points do we have to check? (Answer: One!)

Why? Because the boundary line breaks the plane up into three parts: 1. the line itself which is true for = only, 2. the part of the plane that makes the original inequality true, and 3. the part of the plane that makes the original inequality false!) Let's try (10, 0). We need to substitute the values x=10 and y=0 (pointing at the coordinates) into the original inequality 3x+2y=18. Let's do it!

I talk a lot, but I only write:

CHECK POINT (10, 0)

$$3(10) + 2(0) < 18$$
$$30 + 0 < 18$$
$$30 < 18$$

Is this a true statement or a false statement?
Answer: FALSE!

Therefore, we shade the OTHER side of the boundary. When we are sitting on a fence deciding whether to go play with friends who tell us the truth or hang out with people who tell us lies and false information, we should always run AWAY FROM FALSE (bad guys) and run TOWARD TRUTH (the good guys)! *(AL: example of personalizing!)*

Once I decide which side to shade, I draw little arrows. These are very important later when we have two or three or more lines on one graph! We don't want the graph to get

(continued)

Table A.3.4 Continued

	too messy! I'll explain that more later. But, I draw the little arrow and then when I'm ready, I sketch a few parallel lines to indicate the whole side is shaded. In this country, we shade the side of TRUTH! I have a friend from Lebanon. They shaded the false side in Lebanon, but in the US, we shade the final solution set. And, what is that solution set? It is the set of all the points that make the original inequality true!
Homework	So we shade the TRUE side (not the side that the false (10,0) is found on, but the other side!)
DAY 2: Review and Quiz	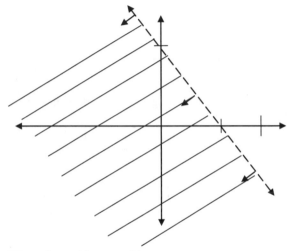
	We are done with one problem.
	[Note to teachers: The problem fits completely on one overhead projection slide.
	The entire problem would look like the following. But, all of the vocabulary is practiced at each stage of doing the problem. I ask all the questions. Then I summarize the answers as I repeat the questions.]

Example 1
Graph the solution set of the linear inequality:

   $3x + 2y > 18$

BOUNDARY (dotted)
   $3x + 2y = 18$
      y-int. ➔ $x = 0$
         $3(0) + 2y = 18$
         $0 + 2y = 18$
            $2y = 18$
             $y = 9$
   Summarize! (0,9) is the y-intercept

x-int. ➔ y = 0

$$3x + 2(0) = 18$$
$$3x + 0 = 18$$
$$3x = 18$$
$$x = 6$$

Summarize! (6,0) is the x-intercept

CHECK POINT (10, 0)

$$3(10) + 2(0) < 18$$
$$30 + 0 < 18$$
$$30 < 18$$
FALSE!!!

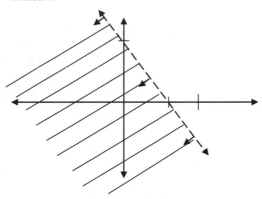

New equation form

I want to point out a few things. Notice that I have written neatly. I use indentation to tell someone ELSE reading my work where the important ideas are located. IF graphing the solution to one inequality is like a whole book, then the BOUNDARY and CHECK POINT sections are like Chapter Headings. If the problem is worth 15 points, I would give 5 points for the boundary section, 5 points for the check point section, and 5 points for the final graph. As you do your homework, do all the parts I have done on the board. Show your work. Take pride in your work. Pretend that you are planning to have me copy your work to give to all of your classmates as an example to follow! Pretend that I am the big boss for your dream job and you have to impress me by doing beautiful work in order to get that job of your dreams! Plan to do one or two problems per page. Do not squish more than two problems on a page of paper.

I am giving you copies of the solution of two other problems. Before you leave, copy the board exactly! Study the vocabulary and the ideas tonight and do your homework just like the models I have done and I am giving to you. Learn the material well. We will practice more of these problems tomorrow. I will also give you a quiz on the lecture material tomorrow. Study hard tonight! Many ideas in algebra and decisions in real life

(*continued*)

businesses and society are made using concepts that we learned today. *Example of two other problems handed out as examples to follow.*

HOMEWORK *Assign appropriate homework problems from text.*
If time allows do this before sending them out the door! Let's run through all of the major ideas again! Review the three major parts of the lecture and run through the major steps of the problem on the overhead projector.

Note: On the second day, do another problem in standard form like the one above. Review all the vocabulary and answers to the quiz while doing the example. Then erase the board and give the quiz. After passing the quiz to all students, read the instructions and the quiz out loud. I would pause after each question to give students a chance to answer. (The reading out loud is to help any poor readers understand the questions.) IF there are a lot of Spanish speakers, I may consider translating the terms and questions into Spanish during the lecture of the prior day and during the quiz.

QUIZ (*with Answers included*)
Suppose you are presented with a problem to graph the solution set of the inequality

$$2x + y \leq 4$$

DO not graph the solution set. Instead, answer the following questions briefly for the specific ORIGINAL inequality provided above. I will read the questions and pause to give you time to answer the questions. Do not look at anyone else's paper while I read the questions. Look down at your own paper. After I read the quiz, I will give you two more minutes to finish. Remember, I am NOT asking you to graph the solution set.

1. What type of problem is this? *(It is a linear inequality in two variables.)*
2. What will the graph of the solution set look like? *(It will be a half-plane.)*
3. What is the boundary equation? *(It is 2x+y=4.)*
4. What will the graph of the boundary equation be? *(it will be a line)*
5. Will it be solid or dotted, and how do you know? (It will be dotted because "<" means the boundary is not included!)
6. Why do you need to pick a check point? *(I need to pick a check point in order to decide which side to shade!)*

7. What must you be sure of when picking a check point?
   (I need to make sure that the check point is NOT on the boundary line.)

8. Do you substitute the coordinates of the check point into the ORIGINAL inequality or into the BOUNDARY equation? *(I substitute the check point coordinates into the ORIGINAL inequality!)*

Note: the quiz will take about 6 minutes. It will reinforce the importance of building vocabulary and of building fluency and getting information from a problem. Too often, students do not pay attention to details that provide interesting and important information. Some students will whine and complain that they needed more time. I will be adamant that they must not have understood the intent of the question. We will review the quiz right away. After collecting the quiz, I review the questions and give the correct Note: Reviewing the quiz takes a little more than one minute! The six minutes should have been plenty of time to take it! Now is a good time to learn what questions might be asked on a test in addition to the "Graph the solution set of the given inequality."

On Day 2, after giving the quiz, I would do an example with an inequality whose boundary equation is an equation in Slope-Intercept Form. The problem given in Guided Practice #12 on page 600 is this type of problem. Here it is!

Example #12 (pg. 600) Graph the inequality $y \geq \frac{1}{2} x - 1$.

Here is a brief presentation to guide the classroom discussion.

Identify. What type of problem is it? (Answer: A linear inequality in two variables.)

Anticipate. What will the graph of the solution set be? (Answer: a half-plane)

What is the boundary equation? (Answer:) $y \geq \frac{1}{2} x - 1$

What will the graph of this boundary be? (Answer: a line!)

Is the boundary line included in the graph of the solution set? (Answer: NO!)

How do I indicate this? (Draw a dotted line!)

What form of a line is the equation $y \geq \frac{1}{2} x - 1$? (Answer: Slope-Intercept Form!)

What is the easiest way to graph an equation of a line in standard form? (Answer: Find the y-intercept and use information about the slope $m = \frac{1}{2}$ to find a second point and graph the line.)

OKAY! Let's do all this work dealing with the boundary line. Then we'll pick a CHECKPOINT that is NOT on the boundary to decide what side to shade!

(continued)

Table A.3.4 Continued

When I do my problem, I write the problem like this:

12) $y \geq \frac{1}{2} x - 1$

BOUNDARY (Solid)

$y \geq \frac{1}{2} x - 1$

y-intercept is $(0, -1)$

The slope is $m = \frac{1}{2}$

Use this information
to graph the boundary line.

CHECK POINT $(2,4)$ Sub. into original inequality!

$4 \geq \frac{1}{2}(2) - 1$

$4 \geq 1 - 1$

$4 \geq 0$

True!

Shade toward $(2,4)$

Also, on Day 2, I would discuss the questions on page 600 that discuss whether particular points are solutions of the inequality. To be a solution means that the coordinates (x-value and y-value of the ordered pair) make the original inequality a true statement when they are substituted in for the appropriate variable. I would also plan to do some of Exercises 32-40 on the board. The remaining problems would be assigned for homework.

Day 2 HOMEWORK: Page 600 Guided Practice #1-3, 8, 12, and Practice and Problem Solving: 16–19, 20–22, 23 (I think the x is missing by accident!), 24, 26, 27, and 32–40

Day 3: Finally, on the third day, I will give a quiz to graph one inequality in standard form and one in slope-intercept form.

After going over the quiz, we will graph solution sets of systems of equations and systems of inequalities in two variables! (Section 11.9 in the textbook.)

ASSESSMENT	The Quiz and homework described above can easily be used as assessment.
REFLECTION	This lesson would benefit from the inclusion of real-world examples that might be relevant to your students' lives. Linear equalities form the basis for optimization of profit in many business models (i.e. cost: benefit ratios), and can also be used in biology for decisions involving dietary choices and feeding strategies in animals. Examples that are more relevant to a student audience would be even better.

Contributed by Janet W. Tarjan, Ed.D.

Sample Lesson Plan 3.5: Introduction to Relations and Functions (Math)

Unit: Functions
Position within Unit: Introduction
Lesson Plan: Introduction to relations and functions
Title: Introduction to relations and functions (Janet W. Tarjan, Ed.D., Mathematics Professor, CALLI Grant)

Table A.3.5 Introduction to Relations and Functions

OBJECTIVE(S) PURPOSE	Students will learn the definition of a relation and a function. They will learn how to recognize functions when presented as ordered pairs, a table of values, and a graph.
	This will set the stage for graphing functions and for finding inverse functions. It will also help prepare a firm foundation for future study and success in algebra, trigonometry, pre-calculus, and calculus.
CA STANDARDS	Standard AF 1.1 Use variables and appropriate operations to write an equation that represents a verbal description. Standard AF 3.0. Interpret linear functions.
MATERIALS	Basketball Volleyball Soccer ball Earth
ACTIVITIES Introduction/ Anticipatory Set (~ 15 Minutes)	INTRODUCTION Students are asked to think about different relationships they have with family members. We will talk about a few so that we can understand the different "relations" that numbers and sets might have. There are lots of relationships: sibling, cousin, brother, sister, uncle, aunt, grandparents, nieces, nephews, friends, spouses, husband, wife, etc. Let's examine three "relationships between people" just in terms of keeping track of ordered pairs, inputs, and outputs. So, ask students for volunteers to give names of their cousins. Usually someone is willing to help. That breaks the ice and others jump in! If not, the teacher could ask someone if they'd be willing to name just a couple of cousins. Or, the teacher could name his/her own to get things started. The student is the input. The cousin name is the output: Student (Input) Cousin (Output) Maria Jose Maria Bobby Maria Lupe

(continued)

Table A.3.5 Continued

Maria	Susie
Juan	Amy
Juan	Miriam
Lisa	Robert
Lisa	Jocelyn
Lisa	Dylan
Jose	Daniel
Jose	Maria
Jose	Claudia

Give some example ordered pairs (Maria, Jose), (Maria, Bobby), (Lisa, Robert).

Have students point out things they notice about the list. Be sure to emphasize the fact that if you ask someone to name a cousin, the single input may have more than one output (i.e. one person can have more than 1 cousin).

Moving on! Let's look at bio-Mom (biological mother). Students will object, they may want step-Mom, Mom, Grandma, but I insist bio-Mom for a very particular reason which will probably become obvious. [Only once has a student not cooperated: "I don't know my bio-Mom's name!" Well, what a beautiful intro. to the idea of a domain. I don't make a big deal about that right away. I just respond, "Well, then, we can't use you as an input, then, because the output isn't defined" with a smile.] Very quickly we get a list. Students are asked to see patterns or differences between this list and the prior one. Someone probably will notice that each input had exactly one output. I ask for names of siblings to put in the list. We notice that different inputs might list the same output, but each input, once identified only gives ONE bio-Mom! VERY IMPORTANT concept for function save it!

Student (Input)	Bio-Mom (Output)
Maria	Julia
Gregory	Susan
Susie	Laura
Olga	Victoria
Becky	Betty
Jose	Rosa
Claudia	Rosa
Lupe	Rosa
Sarah	Bonnie

Finally, let's try spouse (in college classes, I can do this with the students, but in the HS class, I'd probably ask for names of friends or family and current spouse to try to avoid too much divorce discussion). I begin with mine.

Input Name	Output Name (Legal Spouse)
Janet	John
Etc.	

Now we talk about this list. Laws make it impossible for an input to have more than one legal spouse. So, each person in the input list has ONE AND ONLY ONE OUTPUT, just as for bio-mom…Even more strong…each person in the output list has only one possible input name associated with him/her. That is, if you ask me my spouse's name I say "John." AND, if you ask John his spouse's name, he says, "Janet."

Review the three relationships!

Cousin: One input, one or more than one output is possible

Bio-Mom: One input yields ONE AND ONLY ONE OUTPUT

Interesting that two different inputs might name the same Bio-Mom.

And, if you ask the Bio-Mom to name Bio-Child, she may have more than one name to give. That is a different relationship (Bio-Child) so we can't let ourselves get confused!

Important point about Bio-Mom:

ONE INPUT YIELDS ONE AND ONLY ONE OUTPUT!

Spouse: ONE INPUT YIELDS ONE AND ONLY ONE OUTPUT.

Defining terms

(~5 minutes)

(This relationship is so special, the output only has one input associated with it.)

Let's look at some math definitions:

A relation is a set of ordered pairs. All three "relationships" above would qualify as "relations."

A function is a rule that assigns to each number in a given set a number in another set. Starting with a number called an input, the function associates with it exactly one number called an output.

SO, the essential characteristic, indeed the definition of a function is that each input yields ONE AND ONLY ONE OUTPUT!

So, the relations Bio-Mom and Spouse are both FUNCTIONS! (if we deal with "number" concept a little more loosely than the book.)

So, Cousin is a relation

Bio-Mom is a function

Spouse is a function. But, it was a special function. Later in higher levels of math, we'll need to spend more time with this

(continued)

Table A.3.5 Continued

	type of function. It is a one-to-one function. For now, we just need to identify FUNCTION vs. NOT A FUNCTION
	IMPORTANT DEFINITION: A function is a rule for which each input yields EXACTLY ONE output!
	Explain why "exactly one" means the same thing as "one and only one."
	So, let's look for some functions and not functions:
Practice defining functions	Let's use tables of values that we can get from examples we've seen earlier.
(15minutes)	I would have examples of all of the items in the table below:

ITEM of interest	INPUT r = radius	OUTPUT volume of the sphere
Basketball	12 cm	2304 π cm³
Volleyball	10.5 cm	1543.5 π cm³
Soccerball	11 cm	1774.7 cm³
Earth	4000 mi	268,000,000,000 mi³

Is the volume of a sphere a FUNCTION of the radius? Yes or No (Answer: Yes!) Why? (Each input yields exactly one output!)

Can you describe the rule? Yes, in words, in table and as an equation!

In words: IF you give me the radius, I'd cube it. Then, I'd multiply the result by $\frac{4}{3}\pi$. That would give me the volume of the sphere.

In table form, see above! We did it!

As an equation: $V = \frac{4}{3}\pi r^3$.

Here's another
Words: When you are given a positive number as an input, find the numbers that have that number for a perfect square.

INPUT	OUTPUT
25	5
25	– 5
4	2
4	– 2
1	1
1	– 1
0	0

As an equation: $y = \sqrt{x}$

Is this a function? (Answer: No.)

Why not? (Answer: One input 4 gives two outputs 2 and – 2.) Notice that although we almost always talk about inputs and outputs (not outputs and inputs), equations usually place the output first. In the equation above, y is the output and x is the input. This reversing of the order of terms can cause trouble for students so be sure to make it explicit.

Here is another!

Words: We are discussing the figure with 4 equal sides known as a square. Tell me the length of a side and I will tell you the perimeter.

Input	Output
2 in.	8 in.
3 in.	12 in.
4 ft.	16 ft.
5 cm	
11 mm	

Can you find the rule as an equation? If I give you the input x=the length of one side, what would the output P (P=perimeter) be?

Answer: p = 4x

Is this a function?

YES!

Find the missing values in the table above.

| Conclusion (10 minutes) | Definition: |

Definition:
To figure out the value of a function if the input is given to you is "TO EVALUATE THE FUNCTION."

Look at the word

E-Value-ate the suffix "ate" means to do what comes before, value is the value, "e-" as a prefix means "out" as in exit, emerge.

Evaluate means to figure out the value that COMES OUT when you put a certain value in!

A rule that RELATES two values may be described in words, as ordered pairs, as a table of input and output values, or as an equation.

Our goals for today are:

To be able to tell when a given rule is a function or is not a function.

To be able to "evaluate" a function for given inputs

To be able to write a function rule from words or a table

(*continued*)

Table A.3.5 Continued

	Example: I went to the Ranch Market and bananas cost 19 cents each. Write a rule that tells how my total cost $C(x)$ for bananas if I buy x bananas. (Answer: $C(x)=19x$) Assign homework from the text following your usual practices for homework.
ASSESSMENT	Most textbooks will have a section on this, so homework from your text will generally be sufficient to assess students understanding. If you do not have a section in your text on defining functions, it should be fairly easy to adapt a problem set with equations and ask the students to not only evaluate the expressions, but identify whether each is a function or a relation. You could even just have them evaluate only the functions, which will put a premium on proper identification, since if they identify a relation properly, they will do less work!
REFLECTION	Other relations/functions that you could use to introduce the concept could involve popular musicians and their songs, local schools and team names, or clothing and body parts. Use whatever subjects are likely to spark interest from your students.

Contributed by Janet W. Tarjan, Ed.D.

Sample Writing Rubric

See chapter 6 for details on this sample rubric.

Table A.4.1 Sample Writing Rubric

	Organization	Mechanics (Spelling, grammar, etc.)	Evidence (Content)	Sentence Structure (Vocabulary, combined sentences, etc.)
0: **No** **Evidence**	Only a few words or phrases are written, there is no beginning or end	Student writing is not comprehensible— little or no punctuation is used and nearly all words are misspelled	Student writing does not relate to assigned topic	Student vocabulary is mostly incomprehensible, with few or no complete sentences
1: **Little** **Evidence**	Student writes words/ phrases which demonstrate a beginning & some related concepts	Student writing includes some mechanics (subject/verb agreement), but still demonstrates little punctuation and uses invented spelling	Student writing addresses the content of the topic 2–3 times, but the writing mostly relates to something else	Student vocabulary is somewhat comprehensible— it is sometimes used appropriately as related to the syntax; very few complete sentences

(*continued*)

Table A.4.1 Continued

	Organization	Mechanics (Spelling, grammar, etc.)	Evidence (Content)	Sentence Structure (Vocabulary, combined sentences, etc.)
2: Some Evidence	Student writes sentences or paragraphs which introduce and summarize the topic	Student writing includes invented spelling, but demonstrates correct ending punctuation, capital letters, and subject/verb agreement, etc.	Student has some information on the topic which is coherent, but frequently strays and is not totally coherent	Student vocabulary is still primary level, but does relate to the syntax; most sentences are complete, but very simple
3: Somewhat Adequate Evidence	Student writes sentences or paragraphs which introduce and summarize the topic using a few transition words (first, next, then)	Student writing still includes spelling errors, but now demonstrates correct use of adjectives, adverbs and descriptive phrases, with appropriate middle (commas, quotation marks) and ending punctuation	Student is more coherent, demonstrates more knowledge of the topic but is not yet able to make the writing completely understandable	Student vocabulary is several grade levels below expectancy, but clear; almost all sentences are complete with some complex sentences used
4: Adequate Evidence	Student writes sentences or paragraphs which introduce and summarize the topic with appropriate transitions and few errors	Student writing is nearly free of spelling errors, most grammar is correct with some, but few, errors still evident—exhibits correct use of most parts of speech (including prepositional phrases and remaining punctuations marks)	The writing is coherent and knowledgeable and sticks to the topic, but there is room for embellishment and more interesting reading	Student vocabulary is near grade level, precise, memorable and not redundant; sentences are complete and vary in length and structure

	Organization	Mechanics (Spelling, grammar, etc.)	Evidence (Content)	Sentence Structure (Vocabulary, combined sentences, etc.)
5 Proficient	Student demonstrates clear sequencing and proficiency appropriate for their grade level state standards	Student demonstrates clear and concise knowledge of mechanics and makes few to no errors, according to state standards, including correct use of apostrophes, colons and semicolons	Student is clear, concise and entertaining— they capture the reader's interest while focusing on the topic	Student vocabulary is rich with strong verbs and communicated ideas; sentence structure is effectively used to communicate precise ideas

Writing Rubric (© D. Cook Hirai, 2005)

List of Useful Web Sites for Math and Science

In this appendix you will find a list of Web sites with a variety of information. These sites were provided by a group of extremely active high school math and science teachers with whom the authors have been working for over 2 years. We have tried to group the Web sites by subject matter, but several sites defy easy categorization. Some of the sites include lesson plans, others general information, and still others have excellent images, demos, and examples for building anticipatory sets. The authors provide this information to give you some ideas of ways to use the Web to help with your instruction, but we do not endorse, implicitly or explicitly, any lessons or products you may find on these Web sites. Explore and enjoy.

Science Web Sites

Lesson Ideas, Lesson Plans, and Other Resources

www.merlot.com — Multimedia educational resource for learning and online teaching lessons
www.sciencespot.net — A resource for middle and high school teachers

Science Literacy Issues

www.teachinginterchange.org/Projectinfo.html — Teaching and Learning Interchange Project
www.sln.org — *Science Learning Network: Resources for Inquiry-Based Science Education*

www.project2061.org —science education project of the American Association for the Advancement of Science. Several publications available free online including textbook reviews, unit plans, and "Science for all Americans"

General Science

www.scilinks.org — National Science Teachers Association

www.pathfinderscience.net — physical science, earth and space, biology, and technology resources

www.nationalgeographic.com/science — science and space program information

www.pbs.org/teachers/sciencetech — Public Broadcasting System resources for preK-12 educators

www.nsta.org — National Science Teachers Association

Biology

www.birdsource.org — Cornell Lab of ornithology

www.cellsalive.com — images and resources for cell biology, microbiology, immunology, and microscopy

www.dnaftb.org — DNA science from the Cold Spring Harbor Laboratories

Chemistry

www.chem.leeds.ac.uk/delights/texts — Leeds chemistry lecture demonstrations

www.chemicool.com — tables and chemical data information

Environmental Science

www.earthweek.com — a diary of a planet resource; current news stories on environmental issues

www.frogweb.gov — information on amphibian extinctions from the national biological information infrastructure

www.education.noaa.gov — education-oriented information from the National Oceanic and Atmospheric Administration

www.nature.nps.gov — topics related to air, biology, geology, natural sounds and water science from the National Parks Service.

www.climatechangeeducation.org — climate change education/global warming and Science from UC Berkeley.

Geology

www.ucmp.berkeley.edu — University of California Museum of Paleontology: information on plate tectonics, earth history

Physics and Astronomy

www.nasa.gov — National Aeronautics and Space Administration
http://pumas.jpl.nasa.gov — NASA practical uses of math and science

Math Web Sites

General Math

www.aaamath.com — study of basic math skills, also available in Spanish.
www.pbs.org/teachers/math—Public Broadcasting System resources for preK-12 educators
www.nctm.org — National Council of Teachers of Mathematics
www.coolmath.com — math games, puzzles, and lessons
www.math.com/homeworkhelp/algebra.html — the world of math online resource
www.aplusmath.com—interactive math help for students
www.edhelper.com — math worksheets include algebra, trigonometry, and daily math skill problems

Algebra

http://www.webmath.com/ — Got a problem that needs solving? Resource to assist in problem solving
http://www.cs.cmu.edu/~neil/ — "Ms. Linquist": an interactive, Web-based tutoring program from Carnegie Mellon University.

Geometry

http://www.gogeometry.com/ — geometry related to Inca civilization and other geometry examples

Other

www.edhelper.com — math help and assistance for teachers, students, and parents
www2.edc.org/mcc — The K-12 Mathematics Curriculum Center. Administrative Resources

www.illuminations@nctm.org — National Council for Teachers of Mathematics official Web site. Principles, standards, and activities for school mathematics

www.mathforum.org — information on math resources from Drexel University

http://puzzlemaker.disoveryeducation.com — math resource by discovery

www.learningpage.com — instructional materials and resource ideas

All Subjects

http://babelfish.altavista.com/tr — assists teachers in translation of subject matter key words to other languages for use with lesson delivery.

Common Cognates

Science Cognates

abdomen	Abdomen	circulation	circulación
absorb	Absorbar	classify	Clasificar
adaptation	Adaptación	climate	Clima
algae	Algas	community	comunidad
amoeba	Ameba	compound	compuesto
amphibian	Anfibio	concave	Cóncavo
astronaut	Astronauta	condense	condensar
astronomer	astrónomo	conductor	conductor
atmosphere	atmósfera	constant	Constante
atom	átomo	constellation	constelación
bacteria	bacteria	continent	continente
barometer	barómetro	contract	contrato
battery	batería	control	control
bilologist	biólogo	convex	convexo
calcium	calcio	current	corriente
capillary	capilar	decompose	descomponerse
cartilage	Cartílago	desert	desierto
cell	Célula	diaphragm	diafragma
centimeter	centímctro	digestion	digestión
chemical	Químico	dinosaur	dinosauro
chlorine	Cloro	dissolve	disolver
circuit	Circuito	eclipse	eclipse

Science Cognates, continued

electricity	electricidad	organic	orgánico
embryo	embrión	ozone	ozono
energy	energía	particle	partícula
equator	equador	pasteurization	pasteurización
erosion	erosión	primate	primate
esophagus	esófago	proton	protón
evaporate	evaporar	protoplasm	protoplasma
evidence	evidencia	radar	radar
extinct	Extinto	radiation	radiación
fertile	Fértil	resonance	resonancia
force	Fuerza	respiration	respiración
fossil	Fósil	retina	retina
friction	Fricción	solar	solar
geyser	Géiser	solid	sólido
glacier	Glacier	suspension	suspensión
gravity	Gravedad	temperature	temperatura
habitat	Hábitat	theory	Teoría
hemisphere	hemisferio	thermostat	termostato
hibernate	Hibernar	tranpiration	transpiracíon
horizon	Horizonte	transfusion	transfusión
human	Humano	tumor	Tumor
hurricane	Huracán	vaccine	Vacuna
iceberg	Iceberg	valve	Válvula
image	Imagen	vapor	Vapor
liquid	Líquido	velocity	velocidad
luster	Lustre	virus	Virus
lymph	Linfa	vitamin	Vitamina
microorganism	microorganismo	voltage	Voltaje
molecule	molécula	volume	Volumen
neutron	neutrón	zoology	Zoología
omnivore	omnivero		

Math Cognates

algebra	álgebra	isosceles	Isósceles
angle	ángulo	kilometer	Kilometro
approximate	aproximado	line	Línea
associative	asociativa	longitude	Longitud
bills	billetes	mark	Marca
centimeter	centímetro	mean	medio
circle	circulo	measure	medir/medida
circumference	circunferencia	median	mediano
communitive	conmutativa	meter	metro
congruent	congruente	metric	métrico
conversion	conversión(es)	mixed number	numero mixto
coordinates	coordenadas de un punto	mode	modo
		multiples	múltiplos
correct	correcto	multiply	multiplicar
decagon	decágono	number represented	numero representado
decimals	decimales		
denominator	denominador	numerator	numerador
diameter	diámetro	obtuse	obtuso
difference	diferencia	octagon	octágono
discount	descuento	operation	operación
distributive	distributiva	parallel	paralelas
divide	Dividir	pattern	patrones
dodecagon	dodecágono	pentagon	pentágono
equation	Ecuación	per cent	por ciento/ porcentaje
equilateral	equilátero		
estimate	estimación	percentage	porcentaje
exponent	exponente	perimeter	Perímetro
factor	factor(es)	perpendicular	perpendicular(es)
figures	Figuras	polygon	polígonos
fraction	fracción/quebrado	prime	Primo
geometry	geometría	probability	probabilidad
hexagon	hexágono	problem	Problema
horizontal	horizontal	property	Propiedad
integers	Integres	proportion	Proporción
intersect	intersecten	quadrilateral	cuadrilátero

Math Cognates, continued

reduce	reducir/reduce	symbol	Símbolo
regroup	Reagrupar	triangle	Triángulo
round	Redondear	value	Valor
similar	Similares	velocity	Velocidad
substitute	Substituye	volumen	Volumen
subtract	sustrae/restar	yard	Yarda

Social Studies Cognates

Administration	administración	Governor	Gobernador
Area	area	History	Historia
Assembly	asemblea	Immigrant	Inmigrante
Authority	autoridad	Independence	independencia
Balance	balanza	Invention	Invención
Candidate	candidate	Judicial	Judicial
Capital	capital	Justice	Justicia
Civil	civil	Legal	Legal
Civilization	civilizacion	Legislative	Legislativo
Colony	colonia	Map	Mapa
Communist	conumista	Minority	Minoria
Community	comunidad	Monarch	Monarca
Compromise	compromiso	Monarchy	Monarquia
Congress	congreso	Mountain	Montaña
Constitution	constitución	National	Nacional
Continent	continente	Native	Natal
Culture	cultura	Ocean	Océano
Declaration	declaración	Patriot	Patriota
Democracy	democracia	Political	Político
Democrat	demócrata	Posesión	posesion
Direction	Dirección	President	presidente
Distance	Distancia	Primary	Primario
Election	Elección	Prohibit	prohibir
Expedition	Expedición	Puritan	puritano
Federal	Federal	Represent	representar
Geography	Geografia	Republic	republica

Social Studies Cognates, continued

Republican	republicano	Altitude	Altitud
Society	sociedad	Archipelago	Archipiélago
State	estado	Autonomy	autonomia
Astronaut	astronauta	Canal	Canal
Ancient	antiguo	Canyons	Canon
Armmada	armada	Census	Censo
Bill	billete	Coast	Costa
Citizen	cuidadano	Comercial	comercial
City	ciudad	Community	comunidad
Conquer	conquistar	Condensation	condensación
Convert	convertir	Coniferous	conífiero
Discover	descubrir	Crater	Cráter
Document	Documento	Current	corriente
Government	Govierno	Data	Datos
Illegal	Illegal	Density	densidad
Labor	Labor	Diversity	diversidad
Law	Ley	Domestic	domestico
Majority	Mayoria	Eclipse	eclipse
Museum	Museo	Ecology	Ecología
Official	Oficial	Economy	Economia
Opinión	Opinión	Elevation	Elevación
Opposed	Opuesto	Equinos	Equinoccio
Organization	Organización	Evaporation	Evaporación
Passage	Pasaje	Export	Exportacion
Peon	Peon	Fertile	Fertil
Property	Propiedad	Nationality	nacionalidad
Religión	Religión	Pasture	Pasto
Rural	Rural	Peninsula	Peninsula
Senate	Senado	Region	Region
Territory	Territorio	Temperate	Templado
Violence	Violencia	Temperature	Temperatura
Agriculture	Agricultura	Universal	Universal
Alluvial	Aluvial	Vegetation	Vegetación

Literary Genre Cognates

Activate	Activar	inspirational	inspiracional
Action	Acción	juvenile	juvenil
Adventure	Aventura	letter	letra
Animals	Animales	mystery	misterio
Autobiography	autobiografía	novel	novela
Ballad	Balada	occult	ocultismo
Biography	Biografia	Ode	Oda
Comedy	Comedia	poetry	poesia
Diary	Diario	prose	prosa
Drama	Drama	reference	referencia
Editorial	editorial	religious	religioso
Epic	epopeya	romance	romántico
essay	Ensayo	satire	Satira
ethnic	Étnico	serial	Serie
fable	Fabula	sermón	Sermón
fantasy	fantasia	technical	Técnico
fiction	ficción	tragedy	Tragedia
futuristic	futurista	verse	versos, poesia
humor	humour	western	oeste, occidental
horror	horror		

Grammar Handbook

As noted in chapter 6, grammar can be one of the more difficult areas of language for content teachers when they need to help their students. In order to provide teachers with a resource for help with grammar, we include the following grammar guide, contributed by Deborrah Wakelee and Vicki Murray. This guide can be used as a quick reference to answer questions about specific grammatical issues while designing rubrics for targeting specific issues.

Grammar Handbook Contents

> **Parts of Speech**
>> Nouns
>> Pronouns
>> Verbs
>> Adjectives
>> Adverbs
>> Prepositions
>> Articles
>> Interjections
>> Conjunctions
>
> **Sentence Parts**
>> A Complete Sentence
>> Subjects
>> Complete Predicate
>> Phrases
>> Coordination (**two** or more independent clauses)
>> Subordination (independent **and** dependent clauses)
>> Using a Relative Pronoun to Create a Complex Sentence

Parts of Speech

Nouns

> *Noun:* **A word that names persons, places, things, or ideas.**

Noun check—ask the following questions:
1. Can I make it plural?
2. Can I put the article *the* in front of the word?
3. Is the word used as the subject or object of the sentence?

Common Nouns

Most nouns in English are common nouns. They are not capitalized.
- boy
- island
- pen

Proper Nouns

Proper nouns name particular persons, places, or things. These words are capitalized.
- President Lincoln
- Hawaii
- Statue of Liberty

Concrete Noun

Names things that we can see or touch.
- hand
- family
- water

Abstract Noun

Names things we cannot see or touch.
- courage
- patriotism
- character

Forming the Plurals of Nouns

Most nouns form plurals by simply adding -s to the singular form.
- girl > girls
- dinner > dinners

Words Ending In -ch, -sh, -s, -x, and -z

Words ending in -ch, -sh, -s, -x, and -z require adding -es to form the plurals
- di<u>sh</u>es
- dit<u>ch</u>es
- dre<u>ss</u>es
- fo<u>x</u>es
- bu<u>zz</u>es

Words Ending In -fe or -f

Some words ending in -fe or -f change the f to v and add -es
- wife > wives
- leaf > leaves

Some words ending in -fe or -f keep the f and just add -s
- sheriff > sheriffs
- belief > beliefs

Words Ending In -o

Most words ending in -o preceded by a consonant add -es to form the plural
- hero > heroes
- potato > potatoes
- echo > echoes

Words Ending In -o Preceded By a Vowel

Words ending in –o preceded by a vowel, add -s
- patio > patios
- radio > radios
- rodeo > rodeos

Words Ending In -o Exceptions

Some words ending in -o may form their plural with -s or -es
- pinto > pintos > pintoes
- Zero > zeros > zeroes

Words Ending In -y Preceded by Consonant

In words ending in -y preceded by a consonant, change the -y to -i and add -es
- lady > ladies
- ceremony > ceremonies

Words Ending In -y Preceded by Vowel

Words ending in -y preceded by a vowel form their plurals in the regular way—just add -s

- day > days
- donkey > donkeys
- valley > valleys

Compound Nouns

Compound nouns form their plurals by putting the -s on the end of the main word.

- brother-in-law > brothers-in-law
- passer-by > passers-by

Foreign Words

Some words borrowed from other languages keep the plurals from those other languages to form the plural in English.

- crisis > crises
- phenomenon > phenomena
- alumnus (masc.) > alumni
- alumna (fem.) > alumnae
- alga > algae

Irregular Plurals

Some nouns in English have irregular plurals:

- child > children
- deer > deer
- foot > feet
- goose > geese
- man, woman > men, women
- moose > moose
- mouse > mice
- ox > oxen
- sheep > sheep
- tooth > teeth

4 Musical Terms

However, musical terms or names of musical instruments add only -s.

- piano > pianos
- solo > solos

Pronouns

Pronoun: A word that takes the place of the noun.

Personal Pronouns

Personal pronoun: a pronoun designating the person speaking (I, me, we, us), the person spoken to (you), or the person or thing spoken about (he, she, it, they, him, her, them).

	First Person	Second Person	Third Person
Subjective			
Singular	I	you	he, she, it
Plural	we	you	they
Objective			

Singular	me	you	him, her, it
Plural	you	you	them
Possessive			
Singular	my/mine	your(s)	his, her(s), it(s)
Plural	our(s)	your(s)	their(s)

Personal pronouns are characterized in three different ways:

1. Case

    Pronoun case: refers to the way some pronouns change their form depending on how they are used in a sentence

    a. subjective/objective

    b. possessive/reflective

2. Person

    a. First

    b. Second

    c. Third

3. Number

    a. singular

    b. plural

Intensive/Reflexive Pronouns

Intensive/reflexive pronouns: A pronoun that ends in -self or -selves.

An intensive or reflexive pronoun always refers to another noun or pronoun in the same sentence that denotes the same individual or individuals.

- Himself
- Myself
- Herself
- Themselves

Relative Pronouns

Relative pronoun: A pronoun that introduces a relative clause and has reference to an antecedent.

The relative pronoun and its clause must immediately follow the work to which it is related.

- Who
- Whose
- That
- Whichever
- Whom
- Which
- Whoever
- Whatever

Examples:
The researcher had a breakthrough. He was studying diabetes." becomes "The researcher <u>who</u> was studying diabetes had a breakthrough.
<u>Who</u> in…the child <u>who</u> is wearing a hat.
<u>That</u> in…in the house <u>that</u> you live in.

Demonstrative Pronouns

> **Demonstrative pronouns: A pronoun specifying or singling out the person or thing referred to.**

- this, that (singular)
- these, those (plural)

The words *this* and *these* refer to things that are near in proximity; while the words *that* and *those* refer to things that are far away. A demonstrative pronoun can point out the antecedent.
Example: That dog is very slow and fat.

Indefinite Pronouns

> **Indefinite pronoun: A pronoun that does not specify the identity of its object.**

Because it is an indefinite pronoun, there is not a direct object or an exact number. The plural is now standard usage in all speech and most writing (they vs. he/she).

Common or Standard English generally ignores the question of singular or plural for the verb form following, especially in view of the campaign for inclusive language, which objects to the use of the generic masculine singular pronoun as sexist language.

For formal edited English, indefinite pronouns are separated by singular or plural and the verb form following must match:

Singular

- someone
- anyone
- no one
- nobody
- everyone
- somebody
- anybody
- nothing
- everything
- something
- anything
- neither
- each
- another
- either

Singular or Plural (Dependent on Meaning)

- all
- none
- any
- some
- more
- most

Plural

- both
- few
- many
- several

Verbs

Verbs: Words that show action or express being; can also change form in order to show the time (past, present, or future) of that action or being.

Intransitive verb: Designates a verb or verb construction that does not require or cannot take a direct object; may take an adverb descriptor.

Transitive Verb: Verbs that take direct objects to complete meaning.

Examples:
- I grew weary. (linking)
- I grew roses. (transitive)
- I grew slowly. (intransitive)

Three Classes of Verbs

Action Verbs

Action verbs: Verbs that tell what the subject is doing and when the subject does that action.

Example: The boy jumped over the log.

Linking Verbs

Linking verbs: Verbs that show state of being; link subject to the other parts of the sentence.

Example: He was an actor at the theater.

Common Linking Verbs
In almost all uses the following are linking verbs:
- be (am, is, are, was, were, have been)
- seem   • become

The following can serve as linking verbs or transitive verbs or intransitive verbs:
- come   • feel   • get
- go   • grow   • lie
- look   • prove   • remain
- sound   • stay   • turn

Examples:
- **Linking:**   • I grew weary.
- **Transitive:** • I grew roses.

Intransitive: I grew slowly.

Historically, adverbs used to appear regularly after linking verbs too.

Helping Verbs

> *Helping verbs:* These are auxiliary verbs that cannot stand alone—always used just before the main verb.

Example: She may be singing here tonight.

The complete verb is the main verb and all of its helpers.

Common Helping Verbs
- can, could
- will, would
- may, might, must, shall, should

Forms of the irregular verbs *be, have,* and *do*

Adverbs sometimes come in verb phrases:

Example: Dreams <u>can</u> <u>often</u> <u>frighten</u> younger children.

Regular and Irregular Verbs

> *Regular verbs:* Verbs that form their past tenses and past participles by -d or -ed.

Examples:
- walked
- wanted
- hoped
- stared

> *Irregular verbs:* Verbs form their past tense and past participle by usually changing the base word.

Examples: blow blew blown   drink drank drunk

Some irregular verbs do not change their forms (notice they all end in *-t* or *-d*).

Simple Form	Past	Past Participle
bet	bet	bet
cost	cost	cost
fit	fit	fit
hit	hit	hit
hurt	hurt	hurt
quit	quit	quit
spread	spread	spread

Some irregular verbs use the same word form for the past and past participle.

Simple form	Past	Past Participle
creep	crept	crept
teach	taught	taught

The Six English Verb Tenses

Simple Tenses	*Perfect Tenses*
Present	**Present Perfect**
↦ you walk	↦ you have walked
Present continuous form	*Present perfect continuous form*
↦ you are walking	↦ you have been walking
Past	**Past Perfect**
↦ you walked	↦ you had walked
Past continuous form	*Past perfect continuous form*
↦ you were walking	↦ you had been walking
Future	**Future Perfect**
↦ you will walk	↦ you will have walked
Future continuous form	*Future perfect continuous form*
↦ you will be walking	↦ you will have been walking

Adjectives

Adjective: **Word that modifies nouns or pronouns; typically show which one, what kind or how many.** Adjectives usually come before the nouns they modify, but they may also modify their nouns from the predicate of the sentence.

Adjective Endings

- -able, -ible
- -ful
- -ish
- -ous, -eous, -ious
- -al, -ial
- -ic
- -ive, -ative
- -y
- -ed
- -ical
- -less

Adjective Gradability

Most adjectives function on a scale. Intensifiers are used to indicate where on the scale the adjective falls. The most common intensifier is the adverb *very*.

Examples:
- a bit hot
- very hot
- somewhat hot
- extremely hot
- quite hot

Comparisons

Comparisons are gradable. There are three phases:

Positive (or Absolute)

Example: polite

Comparative—Comparing Two Items

Example: politer/more polite

Superlative—Comparing Three or More Items

Example: politest/ most polite
The phases conform to three degrees of comparison

Higher
Examples:
- She is politer than he is. (comparative)
- She is the politest child in the family. (superlative)

Same
Example: She is as happy as he is.

Lower
Example:
- She is less friendly than he is. (comparative)
- She is the least friendly child in the family. (superlative)

Neat Adjective Rule

One-syllable words typically use a suffix for comparisons:
- old, older, oldest

Two syllable words typically take either form:
- polite, politer, politest/polite, more polite, most polite

Words longer than two syllables typically use more and most:
- impolite, more impolite, most impolite.

Adverbs

Adverbs: Words that modify verbs, adjectives, or other adverbs; typically show how, when, where, why, how often, to what degree or under what conditions.

Examples:
- *Adverb modifies the verb:* The student walked happily into the room.
- *Adverb modifies an adjective:* It will be very cold tomorrow.
- *Adverb modifies another adverb:* Winter has come too early.

Common Adverbs

Adverbs of Frequency
- often
- seldom
- never
- always
- sometimes
- ever

Adverbs of Degree
- even
- more
- quite
- very
- extremely
- much
- surely
- just
- only
- too

Prepositions

Preposition: **A word used to relate a noun or pronoun to some other word in the sentence.**

The preposition with its noun or pronoun is called a prepositional phrase.

Examples:
- The letter is <u>from my father</u>.
- The envelope is addressed <u>to my sister</u>.

Common Prepositions

- about
- against
- at
- beneath
- by
- for
- into
- off
- past
- toward
- upon
- above
- along
- before
- beside
- down
- from
- like
- on
- since
- under
- with
- across
- among
- behind
- between
- during
- in
- near
- outside
- through
- until
- within
- after
- around
- below
- beyond
- except
- inside
- of
- over
- to
- up
- without

Articles

 Articles: **Words used to identify nouns.**

There are two types of articles in the English language: definite (*the*) and indefinite (*a, an*). The use of these articles depends mainly on whether you are referring to any member of a group, or to a specific member of a group.

Examples:

	Indefinite (a or an)	**Definite** (the)
Singular	a dog (any dog) an apple (any apple)	the dog (that specific dog) the apple (that specific apple)
Plural	some dogs (any dogs) some apples (any apples)	the dogs (those specific dogs) the apples (those specific apples)

Indefinite Articles: "A" and "An"

A and an signal that the noun modified is indefinite, referring to any member of a group. The indefinite articles are used with singular nouns when the noun is general; the corresponding indefinite quantity word some is used for plural general nouns.

The "A"/"An" Rule

For a singular noun beginning with a consonant or consonant sound, use *a*:

Examples:
- a boy   • a user   • a year

For a singular noun beginning with a vowel or vowel sound, use *an*:

Examples:
- an elephant   • an honorable   • an hour

Noun Modified By an Adjective

The choice between *a* and *an* depends on the initial sound of the adjective that immediately follows the article:

Examples:
- a **b**roken egg   • an **u**nusual problem • a **Eur**opean country

Definite Article: "The"

The definite article *the* is used before singular and plural nouns when the noun is particular or specific. *The* signals the noun is definite, that it refers to a particular member of a group.

Interjections

Interjection: A word that expresses a strong feeling and is not connected grammatically to any other part of the sentence; sometimes followed by an exclamation mark when written.

Examples:
- Oh, I lost the key.
- Well, that means I'll have to sit here all day.
- Wow! You did a great job!
- Ouch! That hurt!

Conjunctions

Conjunction: A word that joins or connects words, phrases, or clauses.

Examples:
- *Connecting two words:* Sooner or later, you will have to come home
- *Connecting two phrases:* The story was on the radio and in the newspaper.
- *Connecting two clauses:* Dinner was late because I had to work late.

Coordinating Conjunctions

Coordinating conjunction: A conjunction that links items of equal weight.

- and
- or
- nor
- so
- but
- for (meaning because)
- yet

Subordinating Conjunctions

Subordinating conjunction: A conjunction that links items of unequal weight.

- after
- because
- provided that
- when/whenever
- while
- although
- before
- since
- as, as if, as though
- how
- unless
- where/wherever
- if, even if
- until

Correlative Conjunctions

Correlative conjunctions: A conjunction that links items when there is an inseparable relationship between them.

- either…or
- both…and
- neither…nor
- not only…but also

Adverb Conjunctions (Also Known As Conjunctive Adverbs)

Adverb conjunction: A conjunction that links items to add an idea, to contrast, to show results or to show an alternative.

To Add an Idea
- furthermore
- moreover
- likewise

To Contrast
- however
- nevertheless

To Show Results
- consequently
- therefore

To Show an Alternative
- otherwise

Sentence Parts

A Complete Sentence

A complete sentence must be a complete thought that has complete subject phrase.

Complete subject: The noun or pronoun the sentence is about and all of its modifiers.

Complete Predicate Phrase

Complete predicate: The verb and all of its modifiers.

- Verb
- Direct object (part of predicate)
- Indirect object (part of predicate)
  - Subject complement (part of predicate)
- Object complement (part of the predicate)
- Direct objects (part of the predicate)

Subjects

> **Subject:** The noun or pronoun the sentence is about.

- In a sentence the subject usually answers the question "who" or "what" the sentence is about.
- The subject usually occurs early in the sentence.
- The subject of a sentence is usually a noun or a pronoun.
- Noun or pronoun subjects in a sentence can be modified by adjectives.
- The subject of the sentence can be compound.

Example: Jane and Mary walk to school.

Identifying Subjects

Take out prepositional phrases (see prepositional phrases).

The nouns or pronouns in a prepositional phrase can never be the subject. Ignore all nouns and pronouns in prepositional phrases.

Question words are never the subject.

Sometimes question words such as *why, how*, or *what* begin a sentence. These are never the subjects. Change a question to a statement to find the subject.

Commands and requests have an understood subject. The understood subject is *you*.

Example: Go home!

Appositive phrases are not the subject.

> **Appositive phrase:** Phrase that gives more information or renames the subject.

Example:
- Joe, the player on second base, ran 10 miles before practice.
- (The appositive phrase the player on second base refers to Joe.)

Complete Predicate

The complete predicate includes the verb and all of its modifiers; the predicate contains (and may consist solely of) a finite verb, and it may also contain direct or indirect objects, object complements, or modifiers of the verb or its complements.

Examples: In the following sentences, the underlined words form the *predicates:*

- She <u>smiled</u>.
- I <u>went</u> home.
- They <u>planned</u> a long vacation.
- They gladly <u>gave</u> me the keys to the car.
- She <u>told</u> me that my book was overdue.
- The black and white dogs <u>walk</u> hurriedly near the park each day of the week.

Verbs

(see "Verbs and Transitive Verbs")

Identifying Verbs

Verbs tell time.

    Test verb by finding its past, present, or future tense (see verb tenses).

Example: The ballerina <u>danced</u> all night. (<u>dance</u>, <u>will dance</u>)

    Verbs can never be in a prepositional phrase.

Objects

Like objects of prepositions, the direct and indirect objects are always in objective case.

Direct Objects

    ***Direct object:* What the verb is acting on.**

In order to determine the direct object of a sentence ask "who" or "what" about the verb.

Examples:
- He bought (what) flowers.
- He lifted (what) weights.

Indirect Objects

    ***Indirect object:* The receiver of the direct object.**

    An indirect object is only possible if there is a direct object.

Example: She gave <u>him</u> the car. (<u>him</u> is the indirect object)

Subject Complement

Subject complements occur only with a linking verb. It renames the subject of the sentence and can be either a noun or an adjective.

Examples:
- The man is happy.
- The man is a firefighter.

Object Complement

The object complement tends to go with transitive verbs and complement direct objects. These complements say /rename something about the direct object.

Example: Love makes all hard hearts soft.

Phrases

> *Phrase:* A group of words belonging together but lacking one or more of the three elements necessary for a sentence: a subject, a predicate, or a complete thought.

Noun Phrase

> *Noun phrase:* A noun plus its modifiers.

Example: small round stones

Prepositional Phrase

> *Prepositional phrase:* A preposition plus its object and modifiers.

Example: above the trees (see Prepositions)

Verb Phrase

> *Verb phrase:* The main verb plus its helping verbs.

Examples:
- is running
- could have run
- should have been running

Participial Phrase

> *Participle:* A form of a verb that can function independently as an adjective.

Example:
- the past participle <u>baked</u> in
- We had some <u>baked</u> beans

> *Participial phrase:* A form of verb phrase that functions as an adjective in a sentence.

Participial phrases are commonly used in English to modify nouns or pronouns.

Care must be taken when incorporating such phrases into sentences to ensure it is clear to the reader or listener what is being modified (see "Dangling Participles").

Examples:
- Walking down the street
- Having finished her homework
- Running home, the worker lost her wallet.
- Looking very unhappy, she retraced her steps.
- Greatly disappointed, she could not find it.
- Told tearfully, her story saddened her friends.

How is the participial phrase formed? A participial phrase can be formed from the present form of a verb ending in -ing and any other words necessary to complete the phrase.

Examples:
- running home
- looking very happy

It can be formed from the past form of a verb ending in -d or -ed if it is a regular verb and any other words necessary to complete the phrase. (Note: the past participles for irregular verbs must be memorized.)

Examples: greatly amazed   told cheerfully

Gerund Phrase

Gerund: A verb ending in -ing when used as a noun.

Example: <u>Swimming</u> is my best sport.

Gerund phrase: The present form of a verb ending in -ing and any other words necessary to complete the phrase that functions as a noun.

Example: "the choir's singing" in "We admired the choir's singing."

Gerund phrases can function as the subject of a sentence.
Example: Running in a race is strenuous exercise.

Gerund phrases can function as the direct object of a sentence.
Example: I like running in a marathon.

Infinitive Phrase

Infinitive phrase: To add the base form of the verb and any other words necessary to complete the phrase.

Example: to run the race

Coordination (two or more independent clauses)

Clause: A clause that has a subject and a verb; can have a complete thought; can be a complete sentence.

Independent clause: Clause that presents the more important idea; can stand alone as a simple sentence.

Example: He spoke.

Dependent clause: Clause that presents the less important idea; cannot stand alone as a complete sentence.

Example: When she spoke

Coordination: A combination of two or more independent clauses that are related and contain ideas of equal importance; the result is a compound sentence.

Three Methods of Coordination

Comma and Coordinating Conjunction
Sentence Structure: Independent clause plus comma and coordinating conjunction plus independent clause.

Example: He spoke forcefully, and I felt compelled to listen.

Connectors: Coordinating Conjunctions
Used independently:
- and   to add an idea
- but   to contrast two opposing ideas
- or   to show a choice
- nor   to add an idea when the first clause is in the negative
- for   meaning "because"; to introduce a reason
- yet   to contrast two opposing ideas
- so   to introduce a result

Used in pairs
- either…or
- neither…nor
- not only…but also

Semicolon and Adverbial Conjunction and Comma
Sentence Structure: Independent clause plus semicolon and adverbial conjunction and comma plus independent clause.

Example: I had worked hard; therefore, I expected results.

Connectors: Frequently Used Adverbial Conjunctions

Addition (and)
- in addition
- moreover
- also
- furthermore
- besides

Contrast (but)
- however
- nevertheless
- nonetheless

Likeness
- likewise
- similarly

Emphasis
- indeed
- in fact

Alternative (or)
- instead
- on the other hand
- otherwise

Result (so)
- accordingly
- thus
- hence
- therefore

To show time
- meanwhile

Use of a Semicolon

Sentence structure: Independent clause plus semicolon plus independent clause.

Example: He arrived at 10; he left at midnight.
   Choose a semicolon if:
1. The grammatical structure of each independent clause is similar.
   Example: The women pitched the tents; the men cooked the dinner.
2. The ideas of both independent clauses are closely related.
   Example: The women pitched the tents; they were happy to set up camp before dark.

Subordination (independent and dependent clauses)

Subordination: The method of combining two clauses that contain ideas not equally important. (also see "Independent clause," "Dependent clause")

Complex sentence: A sentence composed of one dependent clause and one independent clause and a subordinating conjunction (subordination).

Example: When I drank the water, I got sick.
Sentence Structure: There are two ways to write a complex sentence:
1. Independent clause plus dependent clause
   Example: We can finish our homework if Barbara leaves.
2. Dependent clause plus comma plus independent clause
   Example: If Barbara leaves, we can finish our homework.

Using Subordinating Conjunctions

Keep in mind that these words usually begin a dependent clause.
Some of the words such as after or before could also be used as a preposition
to begin a prepositional phrase.

Examples:
> *Prepositional phrase:* After the game, we all went out for pizza.
> *Subject and verb present in the clause:* After the game was over, we all
> went out for pizza.

Connectors: Frequently Used Subordinating Conjunctions

- after
- because
- if, even if
- unless
- where, wherever
- although
- before
- provided that
- until
- while
- as, as if, as though
- how
- since
- when, whenever

Functions of Subordinating Conjunctions

> *To introduce a condition:* if, even if, as long as, provided that, unless
> (after a negative clause).

Examples:
I will go as long as you go with me.
I won't go unless you go with me.
- To introduce a contrast: although, even though, though
- Example: I will go even though you won't go with me.
- To introduce a cause: because, since
- Example: I will go because the meeting is very important.
- To show time: after, before, when, whenever, while, until (independent
  clause is negative)

Examples:
I will go whenever you say.
I won't go until you say it is time.
- To show place: where, wherever
- Example: I will go wherever you send me.
- To show purpose: in order that, so that
- Example: I will go so that I can hear the candidate for myself.

Using a Relative Pronoun to Create a Complex Sentence

Sentences can often be combined with a relative pronoun.

Relative Pronouns

- who   refers to people
- whose   refers to people
- whom   refers to people
- which   refers to things
- that   refers to people   and/or things

The relative pronoun and its clause must immediately follow the word to which it is related.

Examples:
- The teacher had a breakdown.
- She was teaching grammar.
- The teacher, who was teaching grammar, had a breakdown.

Restrictive Relative Clause

> **Restrictive relative clause: A relative clause is said to be a restrictive clause if it is essential to the meaning of the sentence.**

A restrictive relative clause does not require commas; the pronoun that is often used.

Example: You should never eat meat that is not thoroughly cooked.

Nonrestrictive Clauses

> **Nonrestrictive clause: A relative clause is said to be nonrestrictive clause if it is not essential to the meaning of the sentence.**

A nonrestrictive clause does require comma to set it off; the pronoun which is often used.

Example: The dog's dish, which was in the garage, was empty.

Four Sentence Structures

Simple Sentence

> **Simple sentence: Subject + verb (one independent clause).**

Example: Bob ran into the street.

Compound Sentence

> *Compound sentence:* **A sentence that uses coordination (two independent clauses with coordination).**

Examples:

Two independent clauses: Bob ran to the car. Bob kicked the bumper.

Comma and a coordinating conjunction: Bob ran to the car, and he kicked the bumper.

Semicolon and adverbial conjunction and comma: Bob ran to the car; in fact, he kicked the bumper.

Semicolon in between two independent clauses: Bob ran to the car; he kicked the bumper.

Complex Sentences

(also see "Complex sentence" and "Subordinating conjunctions")

Examples:

<u>After</u> Bob ran to the car, he kicked the bumper.

Bob kicked the bumper, <u>after</u> he ran to the car.

Relative Pronouns

- *Nonrestrictive* (two sentences joined with commas and which)

Example: The bumper, which is chrome and covered with stickers, was kicked by Bob.

- *Restrictive* (clause essential to meaning of sentence; no comma is needed; the word that is commonly used)

Example: Bob ran into the street and kicked the bumper of the car that hit his child.

Compound-Complex Sentence

> *Compound-complex sentence:* **A sentence with at least two independent clauses and one dependent clause.**

Example: Since John likes ice cream, he eats it all the time; but, it can give him a toothache.

Four Sentence Purposes

Declarative Sentence

> *Declarative sentence:* **A sentence used to make a statement.**

Example: The boy in the red hat is mean.

Imperative Sentence

Imperative sentence: A sentence used to issue requests or commands (subject <u>you</u> is understood).

Example: Don't stay out too late.

Interrogative Sentence

Interrogative sentence: A sentence used to ask a questions

Example: Are you finished with the newspaper?

Exclamatory Sentence

Exclamatory sentence: A sentence used to make exclamations.

Example: I'm trying to cool the house, not the whole neighborhood!

Problems with Sentences

Sentence Fragments

Sentence fragment: An incomplete sentence.

A group of words may look like a sentence but the sentence is incomplete and only makes a fragment if one of the following is true:

1. The subject is missing.
2. The verb is missing.
3. Both the subject and verb are missing.
4. The subject and verb are present but the words do not express a complete thought.
   - A fragment could be a phrase.
   - A fragment could be a dependent clause.
   - A fragment could be a combination of phrases and dependent clauses.

Strategies for Correcting Fragments
- Connect fragment to sentence before or after it.
- Supply what the fragment needs to be a complete sentence.

Run-On Sentences

Run-on sentences: Independent clauses that have been combined incorrectly.

There are two kinds of run-on sentences:

The Fused Run-On Sentence

> *Fused run-on sentence:* **Two or more independent clauses, run together without any punctuation.**

Example: I met Charles we soon became friends.

The Comma Splice

> *Comma splice:* **Two or more independent clauses, run together with only a comma.**

Example: I met Charles, we soon became friends.

Guide for Correcting Run-Ons

- Make two sentences with end punctuation.
- Make a compound sentence using one of the two methods of coordination.
- Make a complex sentence using subordination.

Making Sentence Parts Work Together

Subject–Verb Agreement

A verb must agree with its subject in number (singular or plural).
  When the <u>subject</u> is a singular noun, the verb takes an *-s* (or *-es*) in the present tense.
  Example: The <u>baby</u> sleeps. The <u>baby</u> cries.

  When the <u>subject</u> is a plural noun, the verb does **not** take an *-s* (or *-es*) in the present tense.
  Example: The <u>babies</u> cry. The <u>babies</u> sleep.

Personal Pronouns

- I *sleep*
- you *sleep*
- he, she, it *sleeps*

- we *sleep*
- you *sleep*
- they *sleep*

Pay special attention to the verbs Do and Be
The verb **To Do**

- I *do*
- You *do*
- He, she, it *does*

- we *do*
- you *do*
- they *do*

Never use *he don't* or *she don't* or *it don't*.

The verb *To Be*
- I *am*
- you are
- he, she, it *is*

- we *are*
- you *are*
- they *are*

- I *was*
- you *were*
- he, she, it *was*

- we *were*
- you *were*
- they *were*

Never use *we was* or *you was* or *they was.*

Special Problems with Subject–Verb Agreement

Subject–Verb Agreement with Collective (Or Group) Nouns

Collective noun: **A noun that names a group of people or things.**

Frequently Used Collective Nouns
- assembly
- clergy
- council
- family
- herd
- senate

- audience
- club
- crowd
- flock
- jury
- team

- board
- committee
- enemy
- government
- panel
- tribe

- class
- company
- faculty
- group
- public

Usually, a collective noun takes a singular verb or requires a singular pronoun to refer to that noun. That is because the group acts as a single unit.

Example: The <u>class</u> is waiting for its turn to use the gym.

Sometimes a collective noun takes a plural verb or requires a plural pronoun to refer to that noun.

This applies when the members of a group are acting as individuals, with separate actions as a result.

Example: The <u>class</u> are putting on their coats.

"Number" as a Collective Noun

As a collective noun, number may take either a singular or a plural verb. It takes a singular verb when it is preceded by the definite article *the.*

Example: The number of skilled workers is increasing.

Number takes a plural verb when preceded by the indefinite article *a.*

Example: A number of the workers have learned new skills.

Subject–Verb Agreement with Indefinite Pronouns

Indefinite pronouns taking a singular verb:
- another
- each
- everything
- nothing

- anybody
- either
- neither
- somebody

- anyone
- everybody
- no one
- someone

- anything
- everyone
- nobody
- something

Indefinite pronouns taking a plural verb:

- both
- few
- many
- several

Indefinite pronouns taking a singular or plural verb depending on the meaning in the sentence:

- any
- all
- more
- most
- none
- some

Example:

- The <u>books</u> are gone. All were very popular.
- The <u>sugar</u> is gone. All of it was spilled.

Subject–Verb Agreement with Compound Subjects
If the conjunction used to connect the compound subjects is and, the verb is usually plural.

Example: Mary and Steve are my good friends.

The exception to this is if the two subjects are thought of as a single unit.

Example: Peanut butter and jelly is my favorite sandwich.

If the conjunction used to connect the compound subjects is or, nor, either, either/or, neither, neither/nor, not only/but also, you need to be particularly careful.

Example: Mary or Steve <u>is</u> going to help me.
The verb is plural if both subjects are plural.

Example: My <u>friends</u> or my two <u>brothers</u> *are* going to help me.

The verb agrees with the subject closest to the verb if one subject is singular and one subject is plural.

Example: My friends or my <u>brother</u> *is* going to help me.

Subject–Verb Agreement with Unusual Nouns
Don't assume that every noun ending in -s is plural, or that all nouns that do end in -s are singular. There are some exceptions. Here are a few of the most common exceptions:

Some nouns are always singular in meaning, but end in -s.

- diabetes
- economics
- Kansas
- mathematics
- measles
- United States

Some nouns are always plural in meaning.

- clothes
- fireworks
- headquarters
- pants
- scissors
- tweezers

Some nouns have unusual plural forms.

Some foreign words used in English use rules of their own languages to make words plural.

Latin Rule for Plurals

> **Latin rule for plurals:** Latin words ending in -um change to -a to form the plural.

Examples:
- bacterium > bacteria
- medium > media
- datum > data
- stratum > strata

Some Words Change Internally Rather Than Add -S at the End
Examples:
- foot > feet
- child > children
- woman > women
- ox > oxen
- tooth > teeth
- man > men
- mouse > mice
- goose > geese

Some Words Remain the Same Whether Singular or Plural
Examples:
- deer > deer
- fish > fish
- elk > elk
- moose > moose

Pronoun-Antecedent Agreement

> **Antecedent:** A word(s) replaced by a pronoun later in a piece of writing.

Example: The pool was crowded. <u>It</u> was a popular place on a hot summer day.

A pronoun must agree in number (singular or plural) with any other word to which it refers.
> **Example:** <u>Everyone</u> worked on <u>his</u> or <u>her</u> final draft.
> **or** All the <u>students</u> worked on <u>their</u> final draft.

Pronouns must also agree with their antecedents in person.
> **Example:** When mountain climbing, <u>you</u> must maintain <u>*your*</u> concentration at all times.

The antecedent of a pronoun should not be missing, ambiguous, or repetitious.
> **Example:**
> - *Incorrect:* In Florida, they have many beautifully developed retirement areas.
> - *Correct:* Florida has many beautifully developed retirement areas.
> - *Incorrect:* Margaret told Lin that <u>she</u> needed to earn one thousand dollars during the summer.

- *Correct:* Margaret said that Lin needed to earn one thousand dollars during the summer.
- *Incorrect:* The newspaper article, <u>it</u> said that Earth Day, 1990, reestablished people's commitment to the earth.
- *Correct:* The newspaper article said that Earth Day, 1990, reestablished people's commitment to the earth.

Parallel Structure

Balance within the Sentence Structure
Words in a series should be the same part of speech.
   Example: The town was small, quiet, and peaceful.

Phrases in a series should be the same kind of phrase (infinitive, prepositional, verb, noun, or participial phrases).
   Example: Her lost assignment is in her closet, on the floor, and under a pile of clothes.

Clauses in a series should not be mixed with phrases.
   Example: The street was narrow, the shops were charming, and the café was crowded. (The series is composed of three clauses.)

Misplaced and Dangling Modifiers

Modifiers: **Words or groups of words in a sentence that function as adjectives or adverbs.**

Example: My <u>only</u> brother **or** the marine <u>who is my brother</u> **or** <u>just</u> yesterday

Misplaced modifier: **A modifier that has been placed in a wrong, awkward, or ambiguous position in a sentence.**

Modifiers Often Misplaced

• almost	• barely	• even	• exactly
• hardly	• just	• merely	• nearly
• only	• scarcely	• simply	

Examples:
- *Wrong placement:* The salesperson sold the used car to the customer <u>that needed extensive body work.</u>
- *Correct placement:* The salesperson sold the customer a used <u>car that needed extensive body work.</u>
- *Awkward placement:* Alex planned to <u>exactly</u> arrive on time.
- *Revised placement:* Alex planned to arrive <u>exactly</u> on time.

- *Ambiguous placement:* Ms. Douglas having arranged other parties secretly planned the surprise party for her friend.
- *Revised sentence:* Having arranged other parties, Ms. Douglas secretly planned the surprise party for her friend.

Dangling Modifiers

Dangling modifier: A modifier without a word, phrase, or clause that the modifier can describe.

Examples:
- *Dangling modifier:* Working on the car's engine, the dog barked all afternoon. (Who worked on the engine?)
- *Revised sentence:* Working on the car's engine, I heard the dog barking all afternoon.

Capitalization and Punctuation

Italics and Underlining

Italics in a Title
Italicize the title of a full-length work such as a book, a play of several acts, a magazine, or a newspaper.

The title of a full-length work is *italicized in print* and <u>underlined when hand written</u>.

Basic Rules for Capitalization

Capitalize the first word of every sentence.

Example: My dog is black and white.

Capitalize the names of specific things and places (see proper nouns).
Examples:
- *Specific buildings:* Oklahoma City Civic Center
- *Specific streets, cities, states, and countries:* Main Street, Bakersfield, California, United States
- *Specific organizations:* Girl Scouts
- *Specific institutions:* Union Bank of Colorado
- *Specific bodies of water:* Ohio River

Capitalize days of the week, months of the year, and holidays. Do not capitalize the names of seasons.

Example: Thursday, November, Christmas, summer, spring, winter, autumn

Capitalize the names of all languages, nationalities, races, religions, deities, and sacred terms.
Example: English, American, Asian, Protestant, Bible

Capitalize the first word and every important word in a title. Do not capitalize articles, prepositions, or short connecting words in a title.
Example: The Cat in the Hat

Capitalize the first word of a direct quotation.
Example: The President said, "The No Child Left Behind Act is successful."

Capitalize historical events, periods, and documents.
Example: the Reformation, the Colonial Period, the Bill of Rights

Capitalize the words north, south, east, and west when they are used as places rather than as directions.
Example: We live in the North.

Capitalize people's names.
Example: John Doe, Professor Wakelee

Capitalize brand names.
Example: Campbell's Soup, Kraft Cheese

Apostrophe

Apostrophe: A punctuation mark used to form a possessive; used to replace letters in a contraction.

Apostrophe to Form Possessive
Use 's to form the possessive
- Add an 's to any singular noun
- **Example:** teacher's desk
- Hyphenated words
- **Example:** mother-in-law's visit (Joint possession)
- **Example:** Lucy and George's children (Individual possession)
- **Example:** Mary's and Helen's ideas
- Add an 's to any irregular plural noun that does not end in –s:
- **Example:** the coats of the children = the children's coats
- Add an 's to any indefinite pronouns:
- **Example:** everyone's responsibility nobody's fault

Never use an apostrophe in front of the -s ending that forms a plural noun.

Examples:
- *Incorrect:* teacher's lounge (the lounge does not belong to one teacher)
- *Correct:* teachers' lounge

Do not use an apostrophe in front of the -*s* that forms a third-person singular present tense verb.

Examples:
- *Incorrect:* The accused plead's insanity.
- *Correct:* The accused pleads insanity.

A possessive pronoun (*his, hers, its, ours, your, theirs, whose*) never uses an apostrophe

Examples:
- *Incorrect:* This hat is her's.
- *Correct:* This hat is hers.
- *Incorrect:* The groundhog saw it's shadow.
- (*it's* is a contraction meaning *it is*)
- *Correct:* The groundhog saw its shadow.

Watch the position of an apostrophe for clarity in written text. You cannot tell the difference in the following examples in speech, but the apostrophe clarifies the meaning.

Examples:
- boy's = belonging to one boy
- boys' = belonging to more than one boy
- boys = more than one boy

Apostrophe to Form a Contraction

Contraction: The result of compressing two or more words; the apostrophe replaces the omitted letters.

Examples:
- *he is > he's*
- *they are > they're*
- should not > shouldn't
- is not > isn't
- Madam > ma'am
- I have > I've
- *I am > I'm*
- *will not > won't*
- can not > can't
- it is > it's
- of the clock > o'clock
- you all > y'all

Contractions are conversational. Standard English employs them, usually in informal writing. Standard use employs contractions sparingly in semiformal and rarely or never in formal writing. Use them with care.

Apostrophe for Plural Numbers and Letters

An apostrophe is sometimes used to mark plural numbers and letters.
Examples: three 6's   two A's

Brackets

> **Brackets:** punctuation marks ([ ]), also called square brackets, used within quotations; used within parentheses; used in a mathematical equation.

Brackets in Quotations

In quotations brackets distinguish material added to a quotation.
  • Brackets may be used as a disclaimer of responsibility
Example: identifying a misspelling in the original text within a quote
  • "it was a separate [sic] meeting"
  • Brackets may present information to further explain quoted matter
Example: He said, "I read my favorite novel [War and Peace] every year."

Brackets within Parentheses

Brackets may serve as parentheses within parenthetical text.

Brackets in a Mathematical Equation

Brackets may be used in a complex math equation to enclose a calculation within parentheses.
Example: $[(x*6)+(5*y)]*2$
  (see "Parentheses—Conventions of Use")

Colon

> **Colon:** A punctuation mark (:) used before a list; used before an explanation that is preceded by an independent clause.

Colon to Signal a List

Use a colon in a sentence preceding a list.
Example: Please bring the following: tape, scissors, paper, and crayons.

A colon is not needed if the sentence does not contain a complete sentence before the colon.

Colon as a Summary

A colon can used to set off a summary of previous text.
Example: She finally had her heart's desire: a home and family.

Colon to Identify an Explanation

A colon can set off two clauses when the second one explains the first.
    Example: She was late for work again: her car broke down.

Colon as a Separator of Information

Time
    Examples: 12:05 a.m. 7:00

Biblical References—Chapter and Verse
    Example: *John* 3:16

Sections in a Play
    Example: *Henry IV*, Pt. I, II: iv: 122

Sections in a Bibliography
    Example: New York: Longman, 2008

Leading into an Extended Quotation
    Example: Jefferson wrote: When in the course of human events,...

Colon in a Business Letter Salutation

Use a colon for the salutation of a business letter.
    Examples: Dear Sir: To whom it may concern:

Colon in a Book Title

Use a colon between the title and subtitle of a book.
    Example: Grammar Handbook: A Digital Quick Reference

Comma

Comma: A punctuation mark used to represent a slight pause in a sentence; separate items in a series.

Comma in a Series

Use a comma to separate items in a series (more than two items).
    Example: I had eggs, bacon, and toast for breakfast.

Comma with Multiple Adjectives

Use a comma to separate a series of adjectives modifying a noun
   Example: It was a dark, windy, stormy night.

Comma in a Compound Sentence

Use a comma along with a coordination conjunction to combine two simple sentences (also called independent clauses) into a single compound sentence.
   Example: The house was chilly, so I put on a sweater to stay warm.

Comma with Introductory Items

Use a comma after introductory words, expressions, phrases, or clauses.

Examples:

- *Introductory words:* yes, no, oh, well
- *Introductory expressions:* as a matter of fact, finally, second, furthermore, consequently
- *Long prepositional phrases:* In the beginning, I thought this class would be too difficult.
- *Participial phrases:* Giving me directions, the man pointed down the street.
- *Infinitive phrases:* To be quite honest, I hadn't thought of that.
- *Introductory dependent clauses beginning with a subordinating conjunction:* When the guests arrived, we greeted them at the door.

Comma Surrounding a Secondary Idea

Use commas surrounding a word, nonrestrictive modifier, phrase, or clause when the word or group of words interrupts the main idea and contains parenthetical/secondary information.

Examples:

- *Interrupting word:* We will, however, be home soon.
- *Interrupting phrase:* We saw, despite the dim light, that she was injured.
- *Prepositional phrase:* I wanted, of course, to leave.
- *Appositive phrase:* Bill, the good-looking man, gives advice to everyone.
- *Interrupting clause:* Vicki and Debbie, who wrote this chapter, have an opinion about everything.
- *Parenthetical information:* His humor is, I think, bizarre.
- *Rhetorical question:* He's a fool, isn't he?

Comma in a Direct Address

> **Direct address:** **A noun that is the name or title of the person to whom statement is directed.**

Use a comma around nouns in a direct address.
    Example: George, I thought you understood.

Comma in Numbers of One Thousand or More

Use a comma in numbers of one thousand or larger.
    Examples: 1,999   1,889,876,597

Comma in Spoken Dialogue

Use a comma to introduce, enclose, and end direct quotations. Commas come **inside** the quotation mark.

Examples:
  • "Go home," I said. I said, "Go home."
  • I said, "Go home," and I threw him out.

Comma for Clarity

A comma can make clear that a word or words have been omitted in an otherwise repetitive locution.
    Example: Some like it hot; others, cold.

Use a comma where it is necessary to prevent a misunderstanding.
    Example: Before eating, the cat prowled through the alley.

Comma in Written Style

Use a comma before *and after* the year in a written date.
    Example: Please attend the meeting on February 7, 2008, from 1 to 4 p.m.

Use a comma to separate city from state.
    Example: Chicago, Illinois

Use a comma to separate day from date.
    Example: Monday, April 10

Use a comma to separate a name from a title in an appositive phrase.
    Example: David Hankins, Building Monitor, was in charge.

A comma is used to separate the last name from the first, when they are presented in reverse order.
    Example: O'Hara, James D.

In each of these cases, a comma may (and sometimes must) follow the second element as well.

Dashes

> **Dash:** Punctuation mark used to interrupt the main idea of a sentence; used in informal writing; usually an em dash.

> **Em dash:** Punctuation mark, usually referred to as a "dash," used to interrupt the main idea of a sentence; the width of a letter M.

>> An em dash typed on a standard keyboard (not a laptop): If your software does not automatically replace a double hyphen with an em dash, type it manually—hold the <Alt> key and using the 10-key pad, type 0151, release the <Alt> key; your software may automatically replace double hyphens with an em dash.

> **En dash:** Punctuation mark used in place of a hyphen to separate compound words used adjectively; width of the letter N, about 1/2 to 2/3 the width of M.

>> An en dash typed on a standard keyboard (not a laptop): Hold the <Alt> key and using the 10-key pad, type 0150, release the <Alt> key.

> **Hyphen:** punctuation mark used to (1) break a word at the end of a typographical line; or (2) to join elements of a compound word or phrase; approximate 1/4 the width of M.

Use the dash for a less formal and more emphatic interruption of the main idea. Dashes were once seldom used in formal writing. Today, however, they are now being more often incorporated into formal writing.
Example: He came—I thought—by ship.

The dash (—) is a mark of punctuation similar to, but physically longer than a hyphen, and used for other purposes. A dash is usually typed as two hyphens (common word processing programs translate the double hyphen to an em dash); in printed matter, it is usually an em dash.

Dashes do not have spaces around them. In writing, do not use a hyphen, use an em dash (—) (see also "Hyphens, Prefixes, Suffixes and Compound Words").

Em Dash to Interrupt Syntax

Em Dash to Clearly Interrupt the Sentence Idea
Example: When the governor understood how—did you hear the phone?

Em Dash to Interject a Question or Exclamation
Example: The need now—urgent, is it not?—is for more funding.

Em Dash to Replace Other Punctuation Marks

Em Dash Replacing a Colon
A dash can be used as a colon might be used to introduce a summary phrase after a list of details.
Example: The degree program included math, English, chemistry, philosophy, history—the whole liberal arts curriculum.

Em Dash Replacing a Comma or Set of Parentheses
A dash can replace commas or parentheses that enclose grammatically parenthetical clauses or phrases.
Example: They took every precaution—it seemed to take forever—to ensure our safe arrival.

Em Dash to Identify Source of a Quote
Example: Water, water, every where, nor any drop to drink.—Coleridge.

Em Dash in Informal Writing
The dash is frequently used in informal writing—especially in personal letters—to suggest the spontaneity, breeziness, and relaxed structure we usually find in conversation.

> **Using dashes can be effective for a relaxed style; however, overuse to avoid other punctuation and to evade the requirements of more conventional syntax can be confusing to the reader.**

En Dash with Numbers to Mean "Up to and Including"
When two numbers or dates are separated by an en dash, it means "up to and including."
Examples:
50–59 (includes 50 and 59)
The conference is February 3–5 (begins on the 3rd and ends on the 5th).
In printed text an en dash is used to separate numbers and dates inclusively.

Exclamation Mark

> *Exclamation mark:* **Punctuation mark (!) used to show emphasis or surprise.**

An exclamation mark (!) gives emphasis to a word, phrase, or sentence that suggests surprise or loud, attention-getting delivery. The exclamation mark goes at the end of the sentence or phrase being emphasized.
> **Example:** Never! Free at last! Never darken my door again!

Just as overuse of loud or excited delivery in speech is discouraged, take care not to overuse the exclamation mark in written material. Your words, not your punctuation, should deliver your passion.

Hyphens, Prefixes, Suffixes, and Compound Words

A root word plus a prefix or suffix is not usually considered to be a compound word; however, compound words are included in this section because they are sometimes created using a hyphen.

Prefixes and Suffixes

> *Affix:* **A word element, such as a prefix or suffix, that can only occur attached to a base form.**

> *Prefix:* **An affix put before a word to alter its meaning.**

> *Suffix:* **An affix put at the end of a word to alter its meaning (new word) or to serve as an inflectional ending.**

> *Inflection:* **A change in a word that expresses a grammatical relationship (case, gender, number, person, tense, or mood); the word form or element that is involved in this change—most inflections are affixes, such as -s (plural), or -ed (past tense); some inflections change the base form of the word (irregular verbs).**

Currently, the trend is to avoid using hyphens; therefore, a root word joined with a prefix or suffix is not usually hyphenated.
Examples:
- noncompliance • semiconscious • antiwar • childlike

The following are general rules but there are always exceptions!
- Hyphenate prefixes ending in an -a or -i only when the root word begins **with the same letter.**
- **Examples:** ultra-ambitious   semi-invalid
- Prefixes and root words that result in double -e and double -o are usually combined to form one word.

Examples: reenter coordinate
- **Exceptions:** de-emphasize co-owner
- When a prefix ends in one vowel and a root word begins with a different vowel, generally attach them without a hyphen.

Examples: antiaircraft proactive
- Some prefixes, through common usage, are added without a hyphen although a double vowel is the result.

Examples:
- **co-** cooperate coedit
- **de-** deactivate decompress
- **pre-** preexisting preempt
- **pro-** proactive
- **re-** reengage reenlist

- These same prefixes are often accepted in either form

Examples:
- coordinate/co-ordinate
- preempt/pre-empt
- reenact/re-enact
- preemployment/pre-employment
- preeminent/pre-eminent
- reenter/re-enter
- copayment/co-payment

- When the root word is a proper noun (capitalized), a hyphen should follow a prefix or precede a suffix.

Example: anti-American
- Often words that begin with all-, ex- ("former"), half-, quasi- (with an adjective), and *self*– use a hyphen.

Examples:
- all-around
- self-respect
- self-defense
- all-inclusive
- half-life
- self-assured
- ex-governor
- quasi-scientific

Exceptions:
- halfhearted
- halfway
- selfish
- halfpenny
- quasi success
- selfless
- halftone
- selfhood
- selfsame

- In general a hyphen is not used following the *re-* prefix; the exception is when the *re*– means *again* and omitting the hyphen would cause confusion with another word.

Examples:
- *Re-* **does not mean** *again*: Will she recover from her illness?
- *Re-* **means** *again* **but confusion with another word:** I want to re-cover the sofa.
- *Re-* **means** *again* **and does not cause confusion:** The stamps have been reissued.
- *Re-* **means** *again* **but causes confusion without a hyphen:** I must re-press the shirt.

Compound Words

> **Compound word:** A word made up of two or more words that together express a single idea.

Three Types of Compounds

Open Compound

> **Open compound:** Two or more words written separately that together convey one meaning.

Examples:
- salad dressing
- wine cellar
- Boston terrier
- broom closet
- April Fools' Day
- house cat

Hyphenated Compound

> **Hyphenated compound:** Two or more words connected by a hyphen to convey one meaning.

Examples:
- age-old
- mother-in-law
- force-feed

Solid Compound

> **Solid compound:** Two words that are written as one word.

Examples:
- keyboard
- typewriter

Compound Word Classifications

Permanent Compound

> **Permanent compound:** A compound fixed by common usage; can usually be found in the dictionary.

Permanent compounds usually begin as hyphenated compounds that are temporarily joined; a compound become permanent when usage of the hyphenated compound becomes so widespread that it becomes a solid compound.

Temporary Compound

> **Temporary compound:** A compound of two or more words joined by a hyphen as needed, usually to modify another word or to avoid ambiguity.

Remember that a root word + prefix and/or suffix is not usually considered to be a compound word

Compound phrase: **A phrase that requires all descriptor words to convey a single meaning; it can result in a solid or temporary compound.**

The following general rules apply to forming compounds.

To check whether a compound noun is two words, one word, or hyphenated, you may need to look it up in the dictionary. If you can't find the word in the dictionary, treat the noun as separate words.

Examples:
- eyewitness
- eye shadow
- eye-opener

Indefinite Pronouns as Compounds
The meaning of word combinations determines whether it is considered a compound or not. Some compounds may change in form depending on how they are used.

Examples:
- Anyone may go *vs.* Any one of these will do
- Everyone is here *vs.* Every one of these is good

Compounds with Scientific Compounds
Scientific compounds are usually not hyphenated.

Examples:
- carbon monoxide poisoning
- hydrochloric acid

Compounds with Phrase as a Modifier
Phrases used as modifiers are normally hyphenated, including prepositional phrases.

Examples:
- a now-you-see it-now-you-don't outlook
- a happy-go-lucky person
- a mother-in-law
- top-of-the-line products

Compounds with a Foreign Phrase Modifier
A compound made of a foreign phrase as a modifier is not hyphenated.

Example:
- a bona fide offer
- a per diem allowance

Compound Phrase from Adjective + Noun
When an adjective plus a noun convey a single description/idea the compound is usually hyphenated when the compound is *before* the noun it is describing.

Examples:
- We hosted a fine-wine tasting. **vs.** We hosted a tasting of fine wines.
- I need an up-to-date calendar. **vs.** Keep my calendar up to date.

Others:
- minimum-wage worker • rare-book store • real-life experiences

The hyphen is omitted if using one is awkward and there will be no confusion.

Examples:
- electrical engineering program • bubonic plague outbreak

Compound Phrase with Verb, Noun, and Adjective Forms

A compound phrase used as a verb should appear as an open compound.

Examples:
- **Break + down:** The engine will eventually break down.
- **Clean + up:** I expect you to clean up your room now.

A compound phrase used as a noun or adjective appears as a solid compound.

Examples:
- **Break + down:** There is a breakdown in our teamwork. (noun)
- **Clean + up:** This project needs a special cleanup process. (adjective)

Compound Verbs

Compound verbs are either hyphenated or appear as one word.

If you do not find the verb in the dictionary, hyphenate it.

Examples:
- To air-condition the house will be costly.

We were notified that management will downsize the organization next year.

Compound Nouns with Proper Nouns

Compound modifiers formed of capitalized words should not be hyphenated.

Examples:
- Old English poetry
- New World plants
- Iron Age manufacture

A hyphen is used to combine single-word proper nouns such as place names.

Examples:
- the London-Paris flight
- Saint Lambert-Montreal route
- New York-London route

To join words that are already hyphenated, use an *en dash* in printed material for clarity.

Compound Nouns of Two Equal-Value Nouns

Two nouns of equal value are hyphenated when the person or thing is considered to have the characteristics of both nouns.

Examples:

- secretary-treasurer
- city-state
- time-motion

Compound Nouns Designating Ethnic Groups

When compounds are made with proper names designating ethnic groups, usually such terms used as nouns or adjectives should not be hyphenated.

Examples:

- a group of African Americans
- many Native Americans
- French Canadians in Boston
- a Jewish American organization
- an Italian American neighborhood
- Latin American countries

Currently many of these compounds are hyphenated.

Examples:

- African-Americans
- Asian-American families
- French-Canadian music
- Native-American myths

Open Compound Noun + Adjective

When an adjective is added *before* an open noun compound, the compound is usually hyphenated.

Open Noun Compounds

- wine cellar
- broom closet
- house cat

Adjective + Open Noun Compounds

- dark wine-cellar
- messy broom-closet
- gray house-cat

Compound Adjectives

Generally, hyphenate between two or more adjectives when they come *before* a noun and act as a *single idea*.

Compound adjective in front of noun: friendly looking man [he may not be friendly and is not a "looking man" so it requires both adjectives together to express the desired meaning]

Not a compound adjective: friendly little girl [she is a little girl and a friendly girl so each conveys a separate idea and it is not a compound]

Compound Adjectives with -d or -ed

When a compound adjective is formed with an adjective and a noun to which -*d* or -*ed* has been added, use a hyphen.

Examples:
- yellow-eyed cat • fine-grained wood • many-tiered cake

Many of these compounds have become permanently hyphenated or solid compounds: middle-aged, old-fashioned, lightheaded, kindhearted.

Adverb-Adjective Compounds

A compound adjective formed using an adverb plus an adjective or a participle is generally hyphenated when occurring *before* the modified noun.

Examples:
- He is a well-known actor.
- The book is an anthology of best-loved poems.

Many of these compounds have become permanent and are always hyphenated regardless of placement before or after the modified noun.

Examples: well-worn   tongue-tied

When a compound adjective phrase occurs *after* the modified noun, it is usually not hyphenated.

Examples:
- The actor is well known. [well is an adverb describing an adjective known; combined, they form one idea in front of the noun.]

Adverb-Adjective Compound with -ly Adverb
In an adverb-adjective compound, if the adverb ends in -ly, do not use a hyphen.

Example: a finely tuned piano

Adverb-Adjective Compound with Adverb Not Ending in –ly
In an adverb-adjective compound, if the adverb does *not* end in –ly, use a hyphen.

Example: a long-anticipated decision

Compound Adjectives with high– or low–

Compound adjectives formed with high- or low- are generally hyphenated.

Examples:
- high-quality programming   • low-budget films
- the space shuttles are built with low-bid components.

Compound Adjectives Formed with a Participle
Compound adjectives formed with a noun, adjective, or adverb plus a present participle are generally hyphenated if placed before the noun it modifies.

Examples:
- ever-lasting love • good-looking women

Some of these compound adjectives are permanent solid compounds.
Examples:
- earsplitting   • farseeing

Some of these compound adjectives are permanent and always hyphenated.
Examples:
- far-reaching consequences **or** consequences that are far-reaching

Compound Nouns Formed with Noun + Gerund
A compound formed with a noun and a gerund is usually open.
Examples: • fly fishing   • house hunting

Some of these compound nouns have become permanent solid compounds through common usage.
- –housecleaning   • housekeeping

Compounds with Color
Compound color adjectives are hyphenated.
Examples: a red-gold sunset   a cherry-red sweater

Color compounds whose first element ends in -ish are hyphenated when they precede the noun but should not be hyphenated when they follow the noun.
Examples:
- A darkish-blue color   • A reddish-gold sunset
- The sky is reddish gold

Compounds with Numbers
Spelled-out numbers used with *-fold* are not hyphenated.
Example: tenfold

Figures + *-fold* are hyphenated.
Example: 20-fold

Compounds created with a number and *-odd* are hyphenated.
Examples: four-odd   60-odd

Compounds that combine a number and a possessive noun are not hyphenated.
Examples: one week's pay   hours' work

When a fraction is spelled out, a hyphen is used.
Example: a two-thirds majority

Remember to use a comma, not a hyphen, between two adjectives when you could have used **and** between them (not conveying a single meaning).

Examples:
- I have important, classified documents.
- Jennifer received a lovely, fragrant bouquet on Valentine's Day.

Hyphen

> **Hyphen:** A punctuation mark used to (1) break a word at the end of a typographical line; or (2) to join elements of a compound word or phrase; approximate 1/4 the width of M.

A hyphen is the mark (-) English uses to break a multisyllable word at the end of a typographical line or to link the parts of some compound words. See "Compound Words" for in-depth information about when to use or not use a hyphen.

(Very) General Rule For Compounds and Hyphens

When two or more words together form a single idea as a modifier, they are hyphenated when they appear *before* the noun being modified; if they are *after* the noun, a hyphen is not used.

Example: I keep an up-to-date calendar *vs.*My calendar is up to date.

This is a compound because all three words are required to create the idea of the description being presented; the calendar is not an "up calendar" or a "to calendar" or a "date calendar" so it is not just multiple modifiers.

Hyphens with Short Verb + Preposition

Nouns or adjectives made with a short verb plus a preposition are either hyphenated or written solid depending on current usage.

When the short verb plus preposition are used as a verb, they are written separately.

Examples:
- a breakup *vs.* break up a fight
- a bang-up job *vs.* bang up the car

Hyphen in Homographs

> **Homographs:** Words that are spelled alike but with different meanings and sometimes with different pronunciations.

Certain homographs require a hyphen to prevent mistakes in pronunciation and meaning.

Examples:
- recreation (enjoyment)
- release (to let go)
- recover (get better)

- vs. re-creation (new creation)
- vs. re-lease (to rent again)
- vs. re-cover (cover again)

Compound Numbers

Hyphenate all compound numbers from twenty-one through ninety-nine.

Examples:

- The teacher had 32 children in her classroom.
- Only 21of the children were bilingual.

Hyphen to Break a Word At the End of the Line

In printed text, a hyphen is also used to divide a word at the end of a line due to lack of space. The hyphen should break the word between syllables.

When a word is already hyphenated, do your best to avoid hyphenating either of the compound elements.

Use a good dictionary to show the syllables in a word; syllables are usually shown with a dot or a space between them. If there are more than two syllables, it is preferable to break them after the stressed syllable if possible.

Parentheses

Parentheses: **Punctuation marks used to insert extra information that is not essential to the main idea; may clarify or add interest; the singular form is parenthesis.**

Within the syntax of a sentence, parentheses offer additional information without emphasis. Parentheses are one of three levels of emphasis in which additional information can be inserted. The least emphasis is given by enclosing the information with commas; more emphasis is given with the information is placed within a pair of parentheses and the strongest emphasis is given when information is presented between paired dashes.

Example: Plea bargaining (see Section 3.4) was developed to speed court verdicts.

Parentheses to Set Off Numbers

Parentheses are often used to restate numerals for clarification after being written out.

Example: Each contest will be limited to the first two hundred (200) entrants.

Parentheses to Introduce Abbreviations or Acronyms

After using the full text of an item, parentheses are used to identify the abbreviation or acronym that will be used through the following body of work.

Example: The Department of Human Services (DHS) is directed to protect children.

Parentheses to Give Alternatives

Enclose alternative possibility within parentheses.

Example: Provide the name(s) of school(s) attended.

Parentheses—Conventions of Use

Parenthetical information given *within a sentence*: material inside parentheses does not require punctuation or capitalization, even when the material may be a complete sentence. Punctuation such as a question mark may be included, if appropriate.

Punctuation always follows the parentheses, not before.

Example: He replied to the questions (courteously), but he didn't take them seriously.

Parenthetical information *outside a sentence* structure: Information given inside parentheses but *not* within a sentence structure, should follow standard capitalization and punctuation conventions.

Example: He gave his reply to the questions. (The information was given grudgingly.)

Do not use parentheses inside a set of parenthesis—use [brackets] to set off information inside parenthetical information; if needed, information within brackets would be enclosed by {braces}.   Sequence: ([{ }])

Periods

> *Period:* Punctuation mark used to indicate the end of a sentence; used at the end of abbreviations or initials; used in numbers to indicate decimals.

Period to End a Sentence

Use a period to end a sentence; a period brings a full stop to the thought.

In American English, the period always comes inside "quotation marks."

Period in Abbreviations and Titles

Periods are used (sometimes) with abbreviations and titles.

Periods are not used with acronyms or numeral abbreviations.

Examples:
- Dr. Jones
- NFL
- Mrs. Smith
- NASA
- 12th

Period as a Decimal Point

Periods function as decimal points.
    Example: 43.85%

Period as an Identifier

A period is used to identify levels in outlines
    Example: outline levels: I. / A. / i. / a. / I) / A) / i) / a)
                     Legal outline levels: 1. / 1.1 / 1.1.1 / 1.1.1.1.

In some stylebooks, periods are specified as the punctuation in act, scene, and line references
    Example: II.iii.45–48

Question Mark

Question mark: punctuation mark (?) appearing at the end of a sentence that asks a question.

Question Mark in Direct Quotes

In direct quotations, the question mark must be placed inside the final quotation mark.
    Example: "Where?" she asked.

Question Mark in Indirect Quotes

No question mark is used when an indirect quotation is made.
    Example: She asked where he had been. (a statement telling what the question was)

Question Mark to Point Out an Uncertain Fact

When unsure of a fact or an opinion, a question mark can be used to identify the uncertainty.
    Example: We got word from friends that he died on August 6?, 2006.

Quotation Marks

Quotation marks: Punctuation marks that set off dialogue, quoted material, titles of short works, and definitions.

Quotation marks come in two forms, double and single. In common American English use, the single quotation marks are used when a direct quote is included within dialogue.

Quotation Marks for Spoken Dialogue

Use quotation marks for a direct quotation.

Quotation Marks in Dialogue
- Commas and periods go inside the closing quotation mark.
- Semicolons and colons go outside the closing quotation mark.
- Question marks, exclamation marks, and other punctuation marks belong inside the closing quotation mark if it belongs to the quotation and outside the closing quotation mark if the punctuation mark belongs to the context of the entire sentence.

Examples:
- Please," he requested, "give me that letter."
- Mary looked at Tom and said, "What do you want?"
- Did you hear Tom say, "I want a piece of cake"?
- If a quotation is long (multiple paragraphs), there are two common methods:
  - Do not use quotation marks; indent the entire quotation.
  - Use an opening quotation mark at the beginning of each paragraph but only include the closing quotation mark at the end of the entire quote.

If you are preparing print materials, check to find the style that is preferred; whichever style you select, *be consistent*.

Quotation Marks for Printed Quotation

Use quotation marks for material copied word for word from a source.

Example: According to the *New York Times,* "Employers cut 17,000 jobs in January, the first decline in the work force in more than four years."

Quotation Marks for Special Use of Specific Word(s)

Use quotation marks to indicate that the word(s) being used are slang, jargon or used in a nonstandard meaning.

Examples:
- The media people tried to put a positive "spin" on the oil spill.
- The minutes of the meeting stated that there was a "firm discussion"—some would have called it a screaming match.

Take great care in using quotation marks for emphasis—overuse can result in weakening the emphasis you are meaning to convey, as well as weakening any actual quotes within your document.

Quotation Marks for Short Works

Use quotation marks to enclose the title of short stories, poems, essays, songs and other short musical compositions, chapters in books, articles in magazine and newspapers, radio or television programs and the names of plays.

In printed materials, you italicize the titles of things that can stand by themselves (novels and journals); the titles of shorter pieces should be enclosed in quotation marks.

Examples:
- "The Sopranos"
- Neil Diamond wrote "Daydream Believer."
- I just read the chapter "The Four-Ring Circus Debates" in Hurst's *The 46th Star.*

Semicolon

> **Semicolon:** A punctuation mark (;) used to join two related independent clauses without a coordinating conjunction; used to separate a series of items that include commas within the items.

Semicolon to Join Independent Clauses

A semicolon is used to join two independent clauses that are related and of equal strength without a coordinating conjunction.

Example: I ran to the door; no one was there.

When two independent clauses are joined with a conjunctive adverb, a semicolon is placed before the conjunctive adverb and a comma is placed after it.

Example: I had worked hard; therefore, I expected results.

Semicolon in a Series Containing Commas

When series of items includes commas, the items are separated by a semicolon for clarity.

Example: The children's costumes included a shriveled, ugly hag; a one-legged pirate; a tall, black Darth Vader; and a sparkling, pink princess.

Virgule

> **Virgule:** A diagonal punctuation mark (also called a slash, slash mark, or diagonal) (/) used to separate alternatives; to write fractions; used in continuous lines of printed verse.

Virgule (Slash) to Present Alternatives

A virgule is a slanted line (/) used between two words to suggest that they are alternatives.

    Examples: and/or   he/she

Virgule (Slash) to Write a Fraction

A virgule is used between the parts of a fraction.

    Examples: 1/2   2/3   1/100

Virgule (Slash) in Printing Verse

When lines of verse are printed in a continuous line, a virgule is used to indicate line endings.

    Example: Old King Cole/Was a merry old soul.

Virgule (Slash) Representing "per"

A virgule is used to replace per.

    Examples: miles/hour   miles/gallon   feet/second

Glossary

Action verbs: Verbs that tell what the subject is doing and when the subject does that action.

Adjective: Word that modifies nouns or pronouns; typically shows which one, what kind, or how many.

Adverb conjunction: A conjunction that links items to add an idea, to contrast, to show results, or to show an alternative.

Adverbs: Words that modify verbs, adjectives, or other adverbs; typically show how, when, where, why, how often, to what degree or under what conditions.

Affix: A word element, such as a prefix or suffix, that can only occur attached to a base form.

Antecedent: A word(s) replaced by a pronoun later in a piece of writing.

Apostrophe: A punctuation mark used to form a possessive; used to replace letters in a contraction.

Appositive phrase: A phrase that gives more information or renames the subject.

Articles: Words used to identify nouns.

Brackets: Punctuation marks ([ ]), also called square brackets, used within quotations; used within parentheses; used in mathematical equations.

Clause: A clause that has a subject and a verb; can have a complete thought; can be a complete sentence.

Collective noun: A noun that names a group of people or things.

Colon: Punctuation mark (:) used before a list; used before an explanation that is preceded by an independent clause.

Comma: Punctuation mark used to represent a slight pause in a sentence; separate items in a series.

Comma splice: Two or more independent clauses that are run together with only a comma.

Complete predicate: The verb and all of its modifiers.

Complete subject: The noun or pronoun that is the subject of the sentence and all of its modifiers.

Complex sentence: A sentence composed of one dependent clause and one independent clause and a subordinating conjunction (subordination).

Compound phrase: A phrase that requires all descriptor words to convey a single meaning; it can result in a solid or temporary compound.

Compound sentence: A sentence that uses coordination (two independent clauses with coordination).

Compound word: A word made up of two or more words that together express a single idea.

Compound-complex sentence: A sentence with at least two independent clauses and one dependent clause.

Conjunction: A word that joins or connects words, phrases, or clauses.

Contraction: The result of compressing a word or phrase by omitting certain sounds (or letters) and closing up the string that is left.

Coordinating conjunction: A conjunction that links items of equal weight.

Coordination: A combination of two or more independent clauses that are related and contain ideas of equal importance; the result is a compound sentence.

Correlative conjunctions: A conjunction that links items when there is an inseparable relationship between them.

Dangling modifier: A modifier without a word, phrase, or clause that the modifier can describe.

Dash: Punctuation mark used to interrupt the main idea of a sentence; used in informal writing; an em dash.

Declarative sentence: Sentence used to make a statement.

Demonstrative pronouns: A pronoun specifying or singling out the person or thing referred to.

Dependent clause: Clause presenting the less important idea; cannot stand alone as a complete sentence.

Direct address: A noun that is the name or title of the person to whom a statement is directed.

Direct object: What the verb is acting on.

Em dash: Punctuation mark, usually referred to as a "dash," used to interrupt the main idea of a sentence; the width of a letter M.

En dash: Punctuation mark used to separate compound words (e.g., Paris–London flight; 5–7 pages); width of the letter N, about 1/2 to 2/3 the width of M.

Exclamation mark: Punctuation mark (!) used to show emphasis or surprise.

Exclamatory sentence: Sentence used to make exclamations.

Fused run-on sentence: Two or more independent clauses that are run together without any intervening punctuation.

Gerund phrase: The present form of a verb ending in "–ing" and any other words necessary to complete the phrase that functions as a noun.

Gerund: A verb ending in "-ing" when used as a noun.

Helping verbs: Auxiliary verb that cannot stand alone, but is always used just before the main verb.

Homographs: Words spelled alike but with different meanings and sometimes with different pronunciations.

Hyphen: Punctuation mark used to (1) break a word at the end of a typographical line; or (2) to join elements of a compound word or phrase; approximately 1/4 width of letter M.

Hyphenated compound: Two or more words connected by a hyphen to convey one meaning.

Imperative sentence: Sentence used to issue requests or commands (subject *you* is understood).

Indefinite pronoun: A pronoun that does not specify the identity of its object.

Independent clause: Clause that presents the more important idea; can stand alone as a simple sentence.

Indirect object: The receiver of the direct object.

Infinitive phrase: "To" plus the base form of the verb and any other words necessary to complete the phrase.

Inflection: A change in a word that expresses a grammatical relationship (case, gender, number, person, tense, or mood); the word form or element that is involved in this change—most inflections are affixes, such as –s (plural), or –ed (past tense); some inflections change the base form of the word (irregular verbs).

Intensive/reflexive pronouns: A pronoun that ends in *-self* or *-selves*.

Interjection: A word that expresses a strong feeling and is not connected grammatically to any other part of the sentence; sometimes followed by an exclamation mark when written.

Interrogative sentence: Sentence used to ask a question

Intransitive verb: Designates a verb or verb construction that does not require or cannot take a direct object; may take an adverb descriptor.

Irregular verbs: Verbs that form their past tense and past participle usually by changing the base word.

Latin rule for plurals: Latin words ending in "-um" change to "-a" to form the plural.

Linking verbs: Verbs that show state of being; link subject to the other parts of the sentence.

Misplaced modifier: A modifier that has been placed in a wrong, awkward, or ambiguous position in a sentence.

Modifiers: Words or groups of words in a sentence that function as adjectives or adverbs.

Nonrestrictive clause: A relative clause is said to be a nonrestrictive clause if it is not essential to the meaning of the sentence.

Noun phrase: A noun plus its modifiers.

Noun: A word that names persons, places, things, or ideas.

Open compound: Two or more words written separately that together convey one meaning.

Parentheses: Punctuation marks used to insert extra information that is not essential to the main idea; may clarify or add interest; the singular form is parenthesis.

Participial phrase: A form of verb phrase that functions as an adjective in a sentence.

Participle: A form of a verb that can function independently as an adjective.

Period: Punctuation mark used to indicate the end of a sentence; used at the end of abbreviations or initials; used in numbers to indicate decimals.

Permanent compound: A compound fixed by common usage; usually be found in the dictionary.

Personal pronoun: A pronoun designating the person speaking (I, me, we, us), the person spoken to (you), or the person or thing spoken about (he, she, it, they, him, her, them).

Phrase: A group of words belonging together but lacking one or more of the three elements necessary for a sentence: a subject, a predicate, or a complete thought.

Prefix: An affix put before a word to alter its meaning.

Preposition: A word used to relate a noun or pronoun to some other word in the sentence.

Prepositional phrase: A preposition plus its object and modifiers.

Pronoun case: Refers to the way some pronouns change their form depending on how they are used in a sentence.

Pronoun: A word that takes the place of the noun.

Question mark: Punctuation mark (?) appearing at the end of a sentence that asks a question.

Quotation marks: Punctuation marks that set off dialogue, quoted material, titles of short works, and definitions.

Regular verbs: Verbs that form their past tenses and past participles by "–d" or "–ed".

Relative pronoun: A pronoun that introduces a relative clause and has reference to an antecedent.

Restrictive relative clause: A relative clause is said to be a restrictive clause if it is essential to the meaning of the sentence.

Run-on sentences: Independent clauses that have been combined incorrectly.

Semicolon: Punctuation mark (;) used to join two related independent clauses without a coordinating conjunction; used to separate a series of items that include commas within the items.

Sentence fragment: An incomplete sentence.

Simple sentence: Subject + verb (one independent clause).

Solid compound: Two words that are written as one word.

Subject: The noun or pronoun that is the subject of the sentence.

Subordinating conjunction: A conjunction that links items of unequal weight.

Subordination: The method of combining two clauses that contain ideas not equally important.

Suffix: An affix put at the end of a word to alter its meaning (new word) or to serve as an inflectional ending.

Temporary compound: A compound of two or more words joined by a hyphen as needed, usually to modify another word or to avoid ambiguity.

Transitive verb: Verbs that take direct objects to complete meaning.

Verb phrase: The main verb plus its helping verbs.

Verbs: Words that show action or express being; can also change form in order to show the time (past, present, or future) of that action or being.

Virgule: Diagonal punctuation mark (also called a slash, slash mark or diagonal) (/) used to separate alternatives; used to write fractions; used in continuous lines of printed verse.

References

Adams, M. J. (1990). *Beginning to Read: Thinking and Learning about Print.* Urbana-Champaign, IL: University of Illinois, Reading Research and Education Center. (0262011123, Dallas SIL Library 372.4 A215)

Allen, M. (2003). Eight Questions on Teacher Preparation: What Does the Research Say? A Summary of the Findings. *Education Commission of the States.* Retrieved July 10, 2006, from http://www.ecs.org/tpreport

Allen, N. L., Donoghue, J. R., & Schoeps, T. L. (2001). The NAEP 1998 Technical report. Retreieved from http://nces.ed.gov/nationsreportcard/pdf/main1998/2001509.pdf

Anderson, R. C., & Nagy, W. (1991). Word meanings. In R. Barr, M. Kamil, P. Mosenthal, & P. D. Pearson (Eds.), *The Handbook of Reading Research* (Vol. 2, pp. 690–724). Mahwah, NJ: Erlbaum.

Anstrom, K. (2000). *Step Two in the CALLA Model Presentation: The What, When, Why, and How of Learning Strategies Instruction.* Washington, DC: National Capital Language Resource Center.

Aranti, L. (2006, July 13). Upper Grades, Lower Reading Skills. *Washington Post.* Retrieved July 20, 2006, from http://www.Washingtonpost.com

Ariail, M., & Albright, L. K. (2006, Winter). A Survey of Teachers' Read-Aloud Practices in Middle Schools. *Reading Research and Instruction, 45*(2), 69–89.

Asselin, M. (2002, Fall). Vocabulary Instruction. *Teacher Librarian, 29*, 57–69.

August, D., & Shanahan. T. (2006). *Developing Literacy in Second-Language Learners: Report of the National Literacy Panel on Language-Minority Children and Youth.* Mahwah, NJ: Erlbaum.

Azar, B. (September, 2007). Grammar-Based Teaching: A Practitioner's Perspective. *Teaching English as a Second or Foreign Language Journal, 11*(2), 1–12.

Bailey, A. (2000). Language Analysis of Standardized Achievement Tests: Considerations in the Assessment of English Language Learners. In J. Abedi, A. Bailey, F. Butler, M. Castellon-Wellington, S. Leon, & J. Mirocha (Eds.), *The Validity of Administering Large-Scale Content Assessments to English Language Learners: An Investigation from Three Perspectives* (pp. 79–100). Los Angeles: University of California, National Center for Research on Evaluation, Standards, and Student Testing (CRESST).

Bailey, A. L., Butler, F. A., LaFramenta, C., & Ong, C. (2001). *Toward the Characterization of Academic Language in Upper Elementary Science Classrooms.* Los Angeles: University of California, National Center for Research on Evaluation, Standards and Student Testing (CRESST).

Baker, S., Simmons, D., & Kame'enui, E. (1995). *Vocabulary Acquisition: Synthesis of the research.*

Retrieved August 14, 2006, from http://idea.uroegon.edu/~ncite/documents/techrep/tech13. html

Bakken, J. P., Mastropieri, M. A., & Scruggs, T. E. (1997). Reading Comprehension of Expository Science Material and Children with Learning Disabilities: A Comparison of Strategies. *The Journal of Special Education, 31*(3), 300–324.

Baumann, J. E., Edwards, C., Font, G., Kameenui, C. A., & Olejnik, S. (2002). Teaching Morphemic and Contextual Analysis to fifth grade students. *Reading Research Quarterly, 37*, 150-176.

Baumann, J., & Kame'enui, E. (1991). Research on Vocabulary Instruction: Ode to Voltaire. In J. Flood, D. Lapp, & J. Squire (Eds.), *Handbook of Research on Teaching the English Language Arts* (pp. 604–622). Toronto, ON: Macmillan.

Beck, I. L., & McKeown M. G. (1991). Conditions of Vocabulary Acquisition. In R. Barr, M. L. Kamil, P. Mosenthal, & P. D. Pearson (Eds.), *Handbook of Reading Research* (Vol. 2, pp. 789–814). White Plains, NY: Longman.

Beck, I. L., & McKeown, M. G. (2001). Text Talk Capturing the Benefits of Read-Aloud Experiences for Young Children. *The Reading Teacher, 55*, 10–20.

Beck I. L., McKeown M. G., & Kucan, L. (2002). *Bringing Words to Life: Robust Vocabulary Instruction.* New York: Guilford Press.

Becker, W. C. (1977). Teaching Reading and Language to the Disadvantaged: What We Have Learned From Field Research. *Harvard Educational Review, 47*, 518–543.

Berber-Jiminez, J., Hernandez, A., & Montelongo, J. (2006, Fall). Teaching Expository Text Structures. *The Science Teacher, 73*(2), 38–31.

Biemiller, A., & Slonim, N. (2001, Fall). Estimating Root Word Vocabulary Growth in Normative and Advantaged Populations: Evidence for a Common Sequence of Vocabulary Acquisition. *Journal of Educational Psychology, 93*, 498–520.

Blachowicz, C. L. Z., & Fisher, P. (2000). Vocabulary Instruction. In M. L. Kamil, P. B. Mosenthal, P. D. Pearson, & R. Barr (Eds.), *Handbook of Reading Research* (Vol. 3, pp. 503–523). Mahwah, NJ: Erlbaum.

Blasingame, J., & Bushman, J. (2005). *Teaching Writing in Middle and Secondary Schools.* Boston: Pearson Educational.

Bloom, B., & Rathswohl, D., & Committee of College and University Examiners (1956). *Taxonomy of Educational Objectives. The Classification of Educational Goals: Handbook 1. Cognitive Domain.* New York: Longman.

Brewster, C., & Fager, J. (2000). Increasing Student Engagement and Motivation: From Time-On-Task to Homework. *Northwest Regional Laboratory.* Retrieved July 24, 2006, from http://www. nwrel.org/request/oct00/testonly.htm#1motivate

Brice, R. (2004, September). Connecting Oral and Written Language through Applied Written Strategies. *Intervention in School and Clinic, 1*, 38–47.

Brinton, D., Goodwin, J., & Ranks L. (1994). Helping Language Minority Students Read and Write Analytically: The Journey Into, Through, and Beyond. In F. Peitzman & G. Gadda (Eds.), *With Different Eyes: Insights into Teaching Language Minority Students across the Disciplines.* (pp. 75–110). New York: Longman.

Brynelson, N., Farnan, N., Fleming, D., Grady, K., Guston-Parks, C., Hollingsworth, S., et al. (2004). *Principles and Resources: Enhancing CSU Single Subject Reading Courses.* California State University Office of the Chancellor, Long Beach, Single Subject Reading Task Force, Center for the Advancement of Reading. Retrieved from http://www.nationalreadingpanel.org/ Publications/subgroups.htm

Canale. M. (1983). From Communicative Competence to Communicative Language Pedagogy. In J. Richards & R Schmidt (Eds.), *Language and Communication* (pp. 2–27). New York: Longman.

Carrier, K. (2005). Supporting Science Learning through Science Literacy Objectives for English Language Learners. *Science Activities, 42*(2), 5–11.

Chall, J. (1983). *Stages of Reading Development.* New York: McGraw-Hill.

Chall, J. (1996). *Learning to Read: The Great Debate* (3rd ed.) New York: McGraw-Hill.

Chamot, A., & O'Malley, J. (1994). *The CALLA Handbook, Implementing the Cognitive Academic Language Learning Approach.* Reading, MA: Addison-Wesley.

Chandler-Olcott, K., & Mahar, D. (2003). Adolescents' Anime-Inspired Fan Fictions: An Exploration of Multiliteracies. *Journal of Adolescent & Adult Literacy, 46,* 556–566.

Chomsky, N. (1959). Review of *Verbal Behavior,* by B. F. Skinner. *Language, 35,* 26–57.

Ciborowski, J. (1995). Using Textbooks with Students Who Cannot Read Them. *Remedial and Special Education, 16*(2), 90–101.

Clark, K., & Graves, M. (2005, March). Scaffolding Student Comprehension of Text. *The Reading Teacher, 58*(6), 510–519.

Cook, L. K. (1983). *Instructional Effects of Text Structure-Based Reading Strategies on the Comprehension of Scientific Prose.* Unpublished doctoral dissertation, University of California, Santa Barbara.

Cummins, J. (1980). The Construct of Language Proficiency in Bilingual Education. In J. E. Alatis (Ed.), *Georgetown University Roundtable on Languages and Linguistics* (pp. 76–93). Washington, DC: Georgetown University Press.

Cummins, J. (2000a). Language, Power, and Pedagogy: Bilingual Children in the Crossfire. Clevedon, England: Multilingual Matters.

Cummins, J. (2000b). Academic Language Learning, Transformative Pedagogy, and Information Technology: Towards a Critical Balance. *TESOL Quarterly, 34*(3), 537–548.

Cummins, J. (2001a, Spring,). Interview with Jim Cummins by Carol Jago. *California Reader.* Retrieved July 22, 2006, from: http://www.iteachilearn.com/cummins/calreadinterview01.htm

Cummins, J. (2001b, April 20) *The Academic and Political Discourse of Minority Language Education: Claims and Counter-Claims about Reading, Academic Language, Pedagogy and Assessment as They Relate to Bilingual Children's Educational Development.* Summary of paper presented at the International Conference on Bilingualism, Bristol, England. Retrieved July 12, 2006, from http://www.iteachilearn.com/cummins/

Cunningham, A. E., & Stanovich, K. E. (1998a). The Impact of Print Exposure on Word Recognition. In J. Metsala & L. Ehri (Eds.), *Word Recognition in Beginning Literacy* (pp. 235–262). Mahwah, NJ: Erlbaum.

Cunningham, A. E., & Stanovich, K. E. (1998b, Spring/Summer). What reading does for the mind. *American Educator,* 1–8.

Daggett, W., & Blaise, R. (2006). Achieving rigor and relevance. Retrieved from http//www.pltw.org

Dewey, J. (1944). *Democracy in Education.* New York, Macmillan.

Diaz-Rico, L., & Weed, K. (1995). *The Cross-Cultural Language and Academic Development Handbook.* Boston: Allyn & Bacon.

Dickey, K., Hirabayashi, J., Murray, A., St. John, M., & Stokes, L., with Senauke, L. (2005, December). *The National Writing Project Client Satisfaction and Program Impact: Results From a Satisfaction Survey and Follow Up Survey of Participants at 2004 Invitational Institutes.* Inverness, CA: Inverness Research Associates.

Dougherty Stahl, K. A. (2005, October). Improving the Asphalt of Reading Instruction: A Tribute to the Work of Steven A. Stahl. *The Reading Teacher, 59*(2), 184–192.

Dutro, S., & Moran, C. (2002). *Rethinking English Language and Instruction: An Architectural Approach.* Newark, DE: International Reading Association.

Echevarria, E., & Graves, A. (2003*). Sheltered Content Instruction: Teaching English- Language Learners with Diverse Abilities* (2nd ed.). Boston: Pearson Educational.

Echevarria, J., Short, D., & Powers, K. (2006). School reform and standards-based education: An instructional model for English language learners. *Journal of Educational Research, 99*(4), 95–211.

Echevarria, J., Vogt, M., & Short, D. (2004*) Making Content Comprehensible for English Learners, The SIOP Model.* Boston: Pearson & Longman.

English Language Learners: Boosting Academic Achievement. (2004, Winter). *Research Points. 2*, 1–4. Retrieved from http://www.aera.net/uploadedFiles/Journals_and_Publications/Research_Points/RP_Winter04.pdf

Farber, P. (1999, July/August). Johnny Still Can't Read? *2000-2006 Harvard Education Letter.* Retrieved July 7, 2006, from http://www.hepg@harvard.edu

Firth, J. R. (1957). Modes of Meaning. In J. R. Firth (Ed.), *Papers in Linguistics* (pp. 190–215). New York: Oxford University Press. (Original work published 1951)

Forster, E. M. (1927). *Aspects of the Novel.* New York: Harcourt Brace Jovanovich.

Fountas, I. C., & Pinnell, G. S. (2001). *Guiding Readers and Writers Grades 3–6: Teaching Comprehension, Genre and Content Literacy.* Portsmouth, NH: Heinemann.

Fry, E., Kress, J., & Fountoukidis, D. (2000) *The Reading Teacher's Book of Lists* (4th ed.). San Francisco: Jossey-Bass.

Garza, H., & Mata, S. (2008, January). *CALLI Project Preliminary Findings.* Paper presented at the Hawaii International Conference on Education.

Gleason, H. A. (1967). *An Introduction to Descriptive Linguistics.* New York: Holt, Rinehart & Winston.

Goulden, R., Nation, P., &. Reed, J. (1990). How Large Can Receptive Vocabulary Be? *Applied Linguistics, 11,* 341–363.

Greenwood, S. (2002, May–June). Making Words Matter: Vocabulary Study in the Content Areas. *Clearing House, 75,*(5), 258–263. (ERIC #EJ651926)

Griswold, P. C. (1987, December). Does a Production Deficiency Hypothesis Account for Vocabulary Learning among Adolescents with Learning Disabilities? *Journal of Learning Disabilities, 20*(10), 620–626.

Halliday, M. (1973). *Explorations in the Functions of Language.* London: Arnold.

Halliday, M. (1975). *Learning How to Mean: Explorations in the Development of Language.* London: Arnold.

Halliday, M. A. K. (1966). Lexis as a Linguistic Level. In C. E. Bazell, J. C. Catford, M. A. K. Halliday, & R. H. Robins (Eds.), *In Memory of F. R. Firth* (pp. 148–162). New York: Longman.

Halliday, M. A. K. (1985a). *Spoken and Written Language.* Oxford, England: Oxford University Press.

Halliday, M. A. K. (1985b). *An Introduction to Functional Grammar.* London: Arnold.

Hirsch, E. D. Jr. (2003, Spring). Reading Comprehension Requires Knowledge of Words and the World. *American Educator,* 10–29.

Hymes, D. (1972). Introduction . In C. B. Cazden, V. P. John, & D. Hymes (Eds.), *Functions of Language in the Classroom* (pp. i–vii). New York: Teachers College Press.

Ivey, G., & Broddus, K. (2001). Just Plain Reading. *Reading Research Quarterly, 34,* 12–27.

Johnson, D., & Johnson, R. (1975). *Learning Together and Alone: Cooperation, Competition and Individualization.* Englewood Cliffs, NJ: Prentice-Hall.

Kame'enui, E. J., Dixon, R. C., & Carine, D. W. (1987). Issues in the Design of Vocabulary Instruction. In M. G. McKeown & M. E. Curtis (Eds.), *The Nature of Vocabulary Acquisition* (pp. 129–145). Hillsdale, NJ: Erlbaum.

Kinsella, K., & Feldman K. (2005). *The Book: Read, Write, Reflect. Explicit Whole Group and Small Group Instructional Curricula for Read 180.* New York: Scholastic.

Krajcik, J., Czernak, C., & Berger, C. (2000). *Teaching Science in Elementary and Middle School Classrooms: A Project-Based Approach.* New York: McGraw-Hill.

Krashen, S. (1982). *Principles and Practices in Second Language Acquisition.* Oxford, England: Pergamon Press.

Krashen, S. (1984). *Research, Theory and Applications.* Beverly Hills, CA: Laredo.

Krashen, S. (1993). *The Power of Reading Insights from the Research.* Portsmouth, NH: Heinemann.

Krashen, S. (2004). *The Power of Reading Insights from the Research* (2nd ed.). Portsmouth, NH: Heinemann.

Krashen, S., & Brown C. L. (2007). What is Academic Language Proficiency? Singapore Tertiary English Teachers Society (STETS). *Language and Communication Review, 6*(1), 1–4.

Krashen, S., & Terrell, T. (1983). *The Natural Approach, Language Acquisition in the Classroom.* Hayward, CA: Alemany Press.

LaBerge, D., & Samuels, J. (1974). Toward a Theory of Automatic Information Processing in Reading. *Cognitive Psychology, 6,* 293–323.

Lewis, M. (2000). *Teaching Collocation: Further Developments in the Lexical Approach.* Hove, England: Language Teaching.

Lumsden, L. (1994, June). *Student Motivation to Learn.* (Eric Digest 92). Retrieved April 14, 2006, from http://eric.uoregon.edu/publications/digests/digest092.html

Macrorie, K. (1988). *The I-Search Paper: Revised edition of Searching Writing* Portsmouth, NH: Boynton/Cook.

MacSwan, J., & Rolstad, K., (2003). Linguistic Diversity, Schooling and Social Class: Rethinking Our Conception of Language Proficiency in Language Minority Education. In C. B. Paulston & R. Tucker (Eds.), *Sociolinguistics: The Essential Readings* (pp. 329–340). Oxford, England: Blackwell.

Manzo, A.V., Manzo, U., & Albee, J. J. (2004). *Reading Assessment for Diagnostic-Prescriptive Teaching* (2nd ed.). Belmont, CA: Thomson/Wadsworth.

Manzo, A.V., Manzo, U., & Thomas, M. (2005). *Content Area Literacy: Interactive Teaching for Active Learning* (4th ed.). New York: Wiley.

Marzano, R., Marzano J., & Pickering, D. (2003). *Classroom Management that Works: Research-Based Strategies for Every Teacher.* Alexandria: VA: Association for supervision and Curriculum Development.

Marzano, R., Pickering, D., & Pollock J. (2001). *Classroom Instruction that Works: Research-Based Strategies for Increasing Student Achievement.* Alexandria, VA: Association for Supervision and Curriculum Development.

May, F. B., & Rizzardi, L. (2002). *Reading as Communication.* Upper Saddle River, NJ: Prentice-Hall.

McKenna, M. C., & Robinson R. D. (1990). Content Literacy: A Definition and Implications. *Journal of Reading, 34,* 184–186.

McKeown, M. (1993). Creating Definitions For Young Word Learners. *Reading Research Quarterly, 20,* 482–496.

Meltzer, J., & Hamann F. (2006, April). Literacy for English Learners and Regular Students, Too. *Education Digest, 71*(8), 32–40.

Miller, G., & Gildea, P. (1987). How Children Learn Words. *Scientific American, 257*(3), 94–99.

Nagy, W. E., & Anderson, R. C. (1995). *Metalinguistic Awareness and Literacy Acquisition in Different Languages.* Urbana, IL: Center for the Study of Reading. (ERIC Document Reproduction Service No. ED391147)

Nagy W. E., & Scott, J. A. (2000). Processes. In M. L. Kamil, P. Mosenthal, P. E. Pearson, & R. Barr (Eds.), *Handbook of Reading Research* (Vol. 3, pp 269–284). Mahwah, NJ: Erlbaum.

National Assessment of Educational Progress. (2005). Data from 2002. Retrieved October 1, 2003, from http://natscalescore.asp://nces.ed.gov/nationsreportcard/reading/results

National Center for Education Statistics (NCES). (2002). *Youth Indicators, Indicator 1* (2005). Washington, DC: US Government Printing Office. Retrieved July 7, 2006, from http://nces.ed.gov/programs/youthindicators/Indicators.asp?PubPageNumber=1&ShowTablePage=TablesHTML/1.asp

National Center for Education Statistics (NCES). (2005–2006). *Reading and Math* Washington, DC: US Government Printing Office. Retrieved July 19, 2006, from http://nces.ed.gov/nationsreportcard/ltt/results2004/nat-reading-scalescore.asp

National Institute of Child Health and Human Development, National Reading Panel. (2000). *Teaching Children to Read: An Evidence-Based Assessment of the Scientific Research Literature on Reading and Its Implications for Reading Instruction* (NIH Publication No.00-4769). Washington, DC: U.S. Government Printing Office.

The National Writing Project, Whyte, A., Lazarte, A., Thompson, I., Ellis, N., Muse, A., et al. (2007,

Summer). Teachers' Writing Lives, and Student Achievement in Writing. *Action Teach Education, 29*(2). Retrieved from http://www.siu.edu/departments/coe/ate

Neill, S. B. (1982). *Teaching Writing: Problems and Solutions.* Sacramento, CA: Education News Service.

Neufeld, P. (December, 2005–January 2006). Comprehension Instruction in Content Area Classes. *The Reading Teacher, 59*(4), 302–312.

No Child Left Behind Act of 2001. Public law 107-110 107th United States Congress. Education Intergovernmental relations 20 USC 6301.

O'Conner, R. E., White, A.. S. & Lee, H. (2007, Fall).Repeated Reading v. Continuous Reading: Influences on Reading Fluency and Comprehension. *Exceptional Children, 74*(1) 31–46.

Oglan, G. R. (2003). *Write, Right, Rite!* Boston, MA: Pearson Educational.

Olson, C. (2007*). The Reading/Writing Connection: Strategies for Teaching and Learning in the Secondary Classroom.* Boston: Pearson Education.

Ornstein, A, Lasley, T., & Mindes, G. (2005). *Secondary and Middle School Methods.* Boston: Pearson Education.

Palinscar, A. S., & Brown, A. L. (1984). Reciprocal teaching of comprehension-fostering and comprehension-monitoring activities. *Cognition and Instruction, 1*(2), 117–175.

Pearson, P. D., Barr, R., Kamil, M. L., & Mosenthal, P. (1984). *Handbook of Reading Research.* New York: Longman.

Peregoy, S., & Boyle, O. (2004). *Reading, Writing and Learning in ESL: A Resource Book for K-12 Teachers* (3rd ed.). Boston: Allyn & Bacon/Pearson.

Phelps, T. (1992). Research or Three-Search? *English Journal, 81*(2), 76–77.

Piaget, J. (1959). *Language and Thought of the Child.* London: Routledge & Kegan.

Pressley, M. (2006, April 29). *What the Future of Reading Research Could Be.* Paper presented at the International Reading Association's Reading Research, Chicago.

Pressley, M., Levin, J. R., & MacDaniel, M. A. (1987). Remembering versus Inferring What a Word Means: Mnemonic and Contextual Approaches. In RAND Study Group. (2002). *Reading for Understanding: Toward an R & D Program in Reading Comprehension.* Santa Monica, CA: RAND.

Richardson, J., Morgan, R., & Fleener, C. (2006). *Reading to Learn in the Content Areas* (6th ed.). Belmont, CA: Thomson Wadsworth.

Roseman, J. E., Kulm, G., & Shuttleworth, S. (2001). Putting Textbooks to the Test. *ENC Focus, 8*(3), 56–59. http://www.project2061.org/research/articles/enc.htm

Ruddell, M. R., & Shearer, B. A. (2002). Avid Word Learners with the Vocabulary Self-Selection Strategy (VSS). *Journal of Adolescent & Adult Literacy, 45,* 352–356.

Rupley, W. H., Logan, J. W., & Nichols, W. D. (1998–1999). Vocabulary Instruction in a Balanced Reading Program. *The Reading Teacher, 52,* 336–346.

Sager, D., Ramsey, R., Phillips, C., & Watenpauch, C. (2002). *Modern Earth Science.* New York: Holt, Rinehart, & Winston.

Scarcella, R. (2003). *Accelerating Academic English: A Focus on the English Learner.* Oakland: Regents of the University of California.

Schleppegrell, M. (2004) *The Language of Schooling, A Functional Linguistics Perspective.* Mahwah, NJ: Erlbaum.

Schleppegrell, M. (2005). *Helping Content Area Teachers Work with Academic Language: Promoting English Language Learners' Literacy in History.* Final report to the UC Linguistic Minority Research Institute. (Individual Grant Award #03-03CY-061G-D) (Unpublished manuscript)

Short, D. J. (1993). Integrating Language and Culture in Middle School American History Classes. *Educational Practice Report, 8,* 1–33. (ERIC document reproduction service No. ED 367 163)

Short, K. G., & Burke, C. (1991). *Creating Curriculum: Teachers and Students as a Community of Learners.* Portsmouth, NH: Heinemann.

Smith, M. W., & Wilhelm, J. D. (2002). *Reading Don't Fix No Chevys: Literacy in the Lives of Young Men*. Portsmouth, NH: Heinemann.

Snow, C. E. (1992). Perspectives on Second-Language Development: Implications for Bilingual Education. *Educational Researcher, 21*(2), 16–19.

Snow, C. E. (2002). *Research Described in the Rand Study Report*. Washington, DC: Office of Educational Research and Improvement (OERI), U.S. Department of Education.

Solomon, J., & Rhodes, N. (1995). *Conceptualizing Academic Language* (Research Report No. 15). Santa Cruz: University of California, National Center for Research on Cultural Diversity and Second Language Learning.

Stahl, S. A. (1999). *Vocabulary Development*. Brookline, MA: Brookline Books.

Stahl, S. A., & Nagy W. E. (2006). *Teaching Word Meanings* (Literacy Teaching Series). Mahwah, NJ: Erlbaum.

Stauffer, R. G. (1969). *Directing Reading Maturity as a Cognitive Process*. New York: Harper & Row.

Stevens, R. A., Butler, F. A., & Castellon-Wellington, M. (2000). *Academic Language and Content Assessment: Measuring the Progress of ELL's*. Los Angeles: University of California, National Center for Research on Evaluation, Standards, and Student Testing (CRESST). (Final Deliverable to OERI, Contract No. R305B60002)

Stipek, D (2002). *Motivation to Learn, Integrating Theory and Practice*. Boston: Allyn & Bacon.

Strangman, N., & Hall, T. (2004). Background Knowledge. Wakefield, MA: National Center on Accessing the General Curriculum. Retrieved September 2007, from http://www.cast.org/publications/ncac/ncac_backknowledge.html

Tomlinson, C. (2003). *Fulfilling the Promise of the Differentiated Classroom: Strategies and Tools for Responsive Teaching*. Alexandria, VA: Association for Supervision and Curriculum Development.

Trelease, J. (2001). *The Read Aloud Handbook*. New York: Penguin.

Turner, J. (1993). Situated Motivation and Literacy Instruction. *Reading Research Quarterly, 28*(4), 288–290.

Unrau, N. (2004). *Content Area Reading and Writing*. Upper Saddle River, NJ: Pearson/Merrill.

Unrau, N. (2008). *Content Area Reading and Writing: Fostering Literacies in Middle and High School Cultures* (2nd ed.). Upper Saddle River, NJ: Pearson.

Vygotsky, L. (1978). *Mind in Society: The Development of Higher Psychological Processes*. Cambridge, MA: Harvard University Press.

Vygotsky, L. (1987). *Thought and Language*. Cambridge, MA: Harvard University Press.

Wallace, C. (2004, August 28). *Framing New Research in Science Literacy and Language Use: Authenticity, Multiple Discourses, and the "Third Space."* Retrieved http://www.interscience.wiley.com

Weaver, C. (1996). *Teaching Grammar in Context*. Portsmouth, NH: Boynton/Cook.

Webster's New Third International Dictionary. (1964). (2nd College ed.). Cincinnati, OH: World.

Wong Fillmore, L. (2004). *The Role of Language in Academic Development*. Santa Rosa, CA: Sonoma County Office of Education.

Wong Fillmore, L., & Snow, C. E. (2000). What Teachers Need to Know About Language. Special Report, ERIC Clearinghouse on Language and Linguistics. http://www.cal.org/ericcll/teachers/teachers.pdf

Wong Fillmore L., & Snow, C. (2001). *What Educators—Especially Instructors—Need to Know About Language. The Bare Minimum*. Unpublished paper. Retrieved from http://www.cal.org.rericcll

Wormeli, R. (2005). *Summarization in Any Subject: 50 Techniques to Improve Student Learning*. Alexandria, VA: Association for Supervision and Curriculum Development.

Wright, D. W., & Mitchell, S. B. (1998). *Mendeleyev Periodic Table Simulator*. Burlington, NC: Carolina Biological Supply.

Zang, Z. (2006). The Language Demands of Science Reading In Middle School. *International Journal of Science Education, 5*(28), 491–520.

Index

Page numbers in italic refer to Figures or Tables.